Energy Medicine in CFQ Healing

Energy Medicine in CFQ Healing

✦

Healing the Body, Transforming Consciousness

Master Yap Soon-Yeong

and Chok C. Hiew, Ph.D.

Writers Club Press
San Jose New York Lincoln Shanghai

Energy Medicine in CFQ Healing
Healing the Body, Transforming Consciousness

All Rights Reserved © 2002 by Yap Soon Yeong and Chok C. Hiew

No part of this book may be reproduced or transmitted in any form or by any means, graphic, electronic, or mechanical, including photocopying, recording, taping, or by any information storage retrieval system, without the permission in writing from the publisher.

Writers Club Press
an imprint of iUniverse, Inc.

For information address:
iUniverse, Inc.
5220 S. 16th St., Suite 200
Lincoln, NE 68512
www.iuniverse.com

Legal disclaimers: The authors and the publishers of this book make no representation and give no warranty of diagnosis, prescription, treatment, or cure from following the method presented in this book. Nor shall they be held liable for any harm alleged to result from following this method

ISBN: 0-595-21939-X

Printed in the United States of America

May this book bring
deeper understanding of and liberation
from human suffering and pain.

May all be free at last
May Peace & Boundless Light be revealed to all!

Contents

List of Illustrations

Foreword

Chok C. Hiew. Ph.D.

Over the past decade doing field research on traumatized children I have seen the need for an alternative approach to promoting healing, resilience and recovery in both adults and children. While exploring my own roots in South East Asia, I met a remarkable traditional Qigong healer, Master Yap of Penang Island. Thus began my exposure to CFQ (Cosmic Freedom or *Chaoyi Fanhuan Qigong*), an energy healing method that is proving effective in trauma cleansing, health promotion, and providing cures for otherwise insoluble health problems, and even for terminally ill patients. Since then I have presented workshops and seminars on CFQ as an innovative therapeutic tool for training health professionals in self-healing and healing others. It is evident that CFQ training has produced hope and health benefits for those who have embraced it. To read this book is to understand how to realize one's capacity for an inherent gift of healing. Healing itself is simple, but genuine recovery requires more than treating the person as body parts or as mere physical matter. Healing is complete as the body becomes relaxed free from its energy burden, with the mind's conflicts replaced by peace and together with an energy flow that produces a harmonious consciousness.

CFQ is a meridian based system (of energy channels in the body as postulated in TCM or traditional oriental medicine) and utilizes wisdom inherent in energy-consciousness psychology. Therapeutic benefits have been observed by participants in healing workshops within reasonably short periods of practicing CFQ. Essentially, practitioners learn how to switch off stress responses, release energy blockages and unburden themselves of mental and emotional reactions that traumatize mind and body. For those who persevere in CFQ practice, homeostasis and equilibrium of energy flow are restored, eliminating disease symptoms and achieving complete healing. The purpose of this book is to share with interested readers how they can activate their inner resilience to overcome life's problems and actualize their own full potential.

Energy Medicine in CFQ Healing: Healing Body, Tansforming Consciousness focused on spiritual healing powers as revealed by an experiential study of Eastern medicine, traditional Qigong healing and Buddhist meditation practices. This work contains insights of the founder of CFQ (the primary author), integrated with a current understanding of Western psychological and medical science (the co-author).

The book is a personal narrative by Master Yap Soon Yeong of the CFQ energy healing system from conception to its present level of development. This system makes a breakthrough in the field of alternative medicine by focusing on Qi (energy) healing. This book explains how it works with a clarity and simplicity staying clear of the mystery and complexity that shrouds the ancient Eastern energy healing.

It seizes upon the principles of energy healing that were once guarded in secrecy by the masters and their trusted successors. It attempts to clarify myths and common beliefs, as well as correct misconceptions. It throws fresh light on the energetic origins of disease and provides guidance for overcoming them, even those given up by conventional medicine. Master Yap presents his teachings on healing in a direct style to cultivate CFQ as a safe and effective technique for self care, health maintenance and disease prevention. He details how CFQ treatment protocols can be applied in self healing and healing others. For people with chronic illness this book offers a way to eliminate their suffering. For those in despair, it offers hope and a way to resolve their problems.

Holistic CFQ healing leads to a transformation of the body and a freeing of the spirit involving all levels of being a human. These levels are bioenergetically connected by consciousness which flows from the five senses, the mind (or brain) and the spirit. Such energy forces are acquired, formed, absorbed and stored within, compiling our life experiences and actions. Among these forces is a primordial energy reflex, much like the stress response, which draws in and traps energy forces that traumatize the body and mind. Disease problems and undesirable events are the consequences of past experiences stored as energy forces (which we call memories). These can burden our entire being. The solution lies in fundamentally "letting-go," or "undoing" such burdens. By such "undoing," the burdens are shed along with conflicts and disharmonies. The mind-body is purified and the impurities are replaced by a peace consciousness, which is our greatest healing resource.

Part One of *Energy Medicine in CFQ Healing* begins with the childhood influences and the early life of Master Yap, which drew him to the calling of a professional healer. His experiences as a traditional healer and a series of unique meditative revelations inspired him to create an amazing approach to healing.

Part Two connects the reader with the roots of *Chao-yi Fan-huan Qigong* (CFQ), which lie in the traditions of Eastern medicine and Buddhist teachings and meditation. These wisdom theories and principles have provided a conceptual framework for powerful methods of healing. Next, the CFQ training instructions in healing protocols are clinically detailed with a view to enabling the readers to develop healing skills and to experience for themselves how subtle energy affects the physical body, brain and mind. CFQ procedures are radiant energy-consciousness methods of healing as seen by our contemporary understanding of the psychology of the mind-body unit. These methods are practical, easy to follow. Noticeable results may occur in a matter of days. The spirit behind this book is:

To be well is a basic birth-right. To lay claim to wellness, simply move into action.

Part Three and Part Four of the book describe the healing applications—how readers can be their own healer and, in addition, radiate cosmic healing for the benefit of others. The problems explored include past trauma, stress disorders, injuries, auto-immune diseases, chronic infections and illnesses. The chapters span childhood, aging-related and life-threatening diseases. CFQ healing affects the physical body and is meant not only for persons who are suffering from disease but also for their spouses, parents, children, friends, relatives and care-givers. Rather than ineffectual worrying, helpless inaction, and over-dependence on experts, this book shows how to contribute directly to healing themselves and healing others. The body's self-repair ability is restored and utilized. Resilience is activated to enable complete recovery and in achieving a true sense of well-being free from the burden of disease.

The final message relates to the spiritual approach to realize the consciousness-energy connection with nature and enabling harmony with it. It is a way to claim humankind's birth right to live peaceful, propitious and long lives. Going beyond, it illuminates a journey of self discovery to reveal a full intimacy with the cosmic self.

Acknowledgements

I am forever grateful to the eternal Wisdom for guiding me in my quest for truth, providing me with a energy healing system of cultivation to help my clients and students, and in making the publication of this book possible. I am also thankful to Chok C. Hiew and many Western friends for their generous assistance in the writing and publication of the book.

Prologue

Master Yap Soon-Yeong

I have been a provider of alternative, indigenous medicine for the past twelve years. I do not use herbs, exotic remedies, nutrients, acupuncture, suction cups, moxibustion, massage, bone-setting, laying on of hands, chanting, prayer, finger-pointing, hand-shining, magnetic therapy, peculiar instruments and equipment and shamanic practices. Someone who comes to me for treatment simply lies down comfortably (often falling asleep) for a half hour while I sit quietly at a distance of three feet from their head. Then I teach that client and my students a kind of slow dance-like exercise which, as contrasted with common exercises, does not require any strength. Students also do a kind of moving meditation while absorbed in their own vigorous dance.

Ever since I became a full time alternative energy practitioner in early 1989, I have treated, at my Energy Healing Center, 8000 people with various illnesses and health problems. My work is becoming increasingly more known. My friend of nine years, Dr. Chok Hiew, a psychology professor at a Canadian University has taken an exceptional interest in my healing. Chok, who has had a life-long interest in meditation, eastern healing arts, and various states of consciousness found it so promising that he learned my CFQ and has been promoting this approach to healing and spiritual transformation at numerous training workshops and conferences in the USA, Canada and South East Asia. The participants in these groups are mostly therapists, health-care professionals, and clinicians. Chok also authored two books about it: "*Energy Meditation: Healing the Body, Freeing the Spirit—In Conversa-*

1

tion with Master Yap Soon Yeong," and, *"Tao of Healing: The Incredible Golden Light."*

My system makes a break from Western medicine, Oriental medicine, supplements and herbal remedies, Shamanism and Qigong. For the Chinese community, there are medicinal halls or stores run by traditional Chinese physicians that are stocked with imported and local herbs, roots, insects, reptile and animal parts, and packaged ready-to-use herbal remedies. The ingredients are sometimes brewed in a clay pot of water for several hours. The taste is frequently awful. It appears, however, that the number of these medicinal halls is dwindling. Vitamins, supplements, and herbal remedies became popular in the 1980's and 90's, often claimed to have been prepared from ancient secret formulae, promising cure and prevention of all diseases. However, interest in these seem to have faded in the last few years. Shamanism too has also been very much an indigenous part of Asian culture. Consulting and seeking divine intervention is commonplace. The ethnic Malay community may seek help from *"bomohs"* or medicine men reputed to possess supernatural powers and acknowledged as healers; the Chinese seek out temple mediums who go into a trance and offer advice and remedies; the Indians have their Hindu temples where advice on treating disease is available. Shamans ranging from temple mediums (using Taoist beliefs), monks (trained in Theravada Buddhism), Malay *bomohs*, Taoist exorcists and religious consultants, to name a few, are all available.

Meditative systems of exercise called Qigong became popular in the late 70's and early 80's whereunder the practitioner developed the ability to cure diseases with supernatural powers acquired through such practices. Many forms of Qigong issued from Taiwan and mainland China. Between 1985 and 1995, large groups of people were seen practicing energy exercise in the parks every morning and there was an upsurge of claims of the Qigong masters. In the past three years or so interest in Qigong had declined, probably because too much was promised and too little delivered. The recent crackdowns in mainland China contributed to the awareness of its ineffectiveness.

My system does not employ any of the above methods. I started my energy healing without claiming any lineage from China and so my worth as a healer was, at first, in question. However, my CFQ healing system has steadily gained acceptance and is getting known far and wide. In writing this book, I make no attempts to cite other books. The healing strategies reported are all derived from the insights of *"instinctual knowledge"* gained in meditative states of wisdom. Prior to learning deep meditation for finding solutions to healing issues, I read several hundred books in a hope for developing better skills. But, since 1993, I have found treating disease through meditation more effective so that I have now become totally reliant on this method. Reading draws in information that blocks me from picking up intuitive wisdom.

This book narrates an experiential account of my involvement with CFQ, its development, training methods for promoting self-healing and healing others, and discoveries related to treating untreatable and incurable illnesses. I wish to present this book in a direct, clear, and reader-friendly style. I have entrust Dr. Hiew with this task. The theme of this book is to relax, be at peace, and allow your vast human resilience spirit sort out your problems. The techniques presented here are for you to care for yourself. You can learn to be self reliant in overcoming all health problems. Our primordial human birthright is to live a healthy and long life. This book is offered to help you learn how to lay claim to that privilege.

A Case Example: *The dying woman was gasping for breath with jerky tremors down her legs. Her eyelids were wide opened, the eyes dull and completely rolled up showing the whites. Her mouth was gaping with a protruding, folded tongue that was dessicate. She had been this way since lapsing into coma after a massive stroke several days earlier. After being hospitalized for five days she was released and the family made arrangements for the funeral. It was obvious that she would be gone at any* *moment. I told the family that although no one could do anything for her, I could give it a try. They agreed.*

After a few minutes tapping and stroking down on her abdomen and body, I went into a twenty-minute meditation. Nothing obvious happened other than that her breathing appeared to deepen and her kicking motions were reduced. I told the family that I would return in two days if needed. Against all expectations, she continued to survive. On my next visit, I noticed that her eyes were opened slightly, moving normally and blinking frequently. Her tongue had receded and was moist with normal saliva. Fluid had returned to her body, an important sign of recovery in TCM (Traditional Oriental Medicine). Her body was supple and she could breathe easily. There was a whitish membrane over her eyes and tongue. Blisters were evident all over her mouth (which took two weeks more to clear). She was coming out of her coma.

I continued with twice-weekly treatments. After seven weeks, I reduced it to once a week. By the fifth session, even though she was unable to talk or move, her expression showed recognition of visitors. She was attentive and tears were evident during conversations. Ten sessions later she could move her neck, sit up to watch TV and show visible reactions. Her rigid limbs were gradually relaxing and moving. Throughout this period she was fed with liquid food, without any medication.

By the twentieth session her consciousness, awareness and memory seemed largely to have returned. Her expressions showed understanding and she could respond to questions about what she liked and disliked. She tried to speak by making sounds. She could move all four limbs slowly, albeit with limited mobility. The amazing part was that her paralyzed side did not lag very much behind in recovery except for some visible wasting of muscles. She could by now be seated in a car and be driven around.

PART I

Background and Basics of Energy Healing

1

Early Intimations

I will start my story from a point in my life which had a significant influence on my interest in meditation and healing. When I was barely six, my mother took my older brothers (aged nine and twelve) and me to the edge of the jungle to gather materials to build a shelter for the family. We carried wood and branches for the house frame. We halved and flattened palm trunks with machetes for walls and wove the roof of palm leaves. Soon the whole house, built from indigenous materials and held together with wires and nails, was usable. It was good enough for our family of eight for the next five years. It was 1962, a period of destitution for us.

A few years earlier the family fortune had seemed bright. My father had inherited from my grandfather a large piece of plantation land in Balik Pulau, in a remote corner of Penang Island. From that property, it was an hour's walk uphill to the nearest village. The Communist insurgence broke out soon after Malaysia had become a sovereign country. The declared war against the Communist guerillas badly affected the livelihood of many, especially in remote areas located close to where the rebels had camped. Many areas were put under curfew during the emergency war. My father's land was located in a curfew area and it was impossible to work the land. He was forced to sell it well below its value and with that money he and my uncle bought a smaller lot. My father's share was six acres, which would be insufficient to live on even in good times.

The place was a former plantation with rubber trees that had degenerated into the jungle and my father's land could not produce any immediate income. We lived in extreme poverty for seven years. The government gave subsidy for replanting four acres with rubber but that did not leave any money for food. My mother found partial employment with a neighbor tapping rubber while my father did odd jobs on construction sites, peddling his bicycle for a long distance. He did not have the appropriate skills for the unfamiliar construction work and brought home little.

The situation improved in 1969 when the family decided to terrace the steep hill on our property for vegetable farming. That brought in some steady income. By then the replanted land had rubber trees that were matured enough for tapping. From my birth and until this time, we lived in despair and constant hunger, often running out of such basics as rice.

I soon discovered a way of overcoming my sense of hopelessness. I found a flat rock in the middle of a mountain stream. Sitting there quietly, I held my knees to my chest and listened to the sounds of running water, opening my eyes to the panoramic view of the valley, the greenery, and, in the distance, the sea against the skyline. The sense of peace I discovered helped me to forget the hunger pangs, the quarrels with siblings, the loneliness, and the burden of clearing the land. Unknown to me then, I had spontaneously drifted into a state of meditative transcendence. I soon developed this into a habit and spent most of my leisure time in this manner. I continued coming to this spot as an adult until my parents sold the land in 1990.

My meditative activity helped me in two ways. It made me adept at catching cobras and made me excel in examinations. The jungle area was infested with poisonous snakes especially cobras. The cobras often came into our house especially during the cold and rainy seasons. They would sneak inside and doze under the bed and even slipped into blankets in the middle of the night. Huge pythons, measuring three to five meters, visited our chicken coop and swallowed the chickens whole one after another. When I was six years old, I saw a cobra in the stream holding a catfish in its mouth. I grabbed a stick and began clubbing it. My father arrived, pulled me away, and scolded me severely for not retreating. After that I learned to handle cobras efficiently. I learned how to use the right kind of branch and where to strike to immobilize the snake with one blow. I found that to finish the cobra, its skull must be crushed completely as otherwise it would be able to survive and become even more dangerous. I became the "snake exterminator kid." When village people spotted a snake they would call me for the job. I often removed cobras up to six feet long. I soon became sensitive to the presence of snakes. I knew where it hid. I could also sense and predict a cobra's visit to the house or a python's raid on the chicken coop.

The second way in which meditative activity helped me was to excel in the examinations. After completing elementary school, I did not want to continue with secondary school. We were still very poor and could not afford school. I wore old, tattered, and ill-fitting hand-me-down clothes. I had no pocket money and often ate nothing in school. I was the tiniest in class, and the bullies picked on me. Moreover, my school performance was mediocre at best. Even though I was average in Mandarin Chinese, I was totally hopeless in English as well as the Malay language. I ended six years primary school without learning how to read the English alphabet. However, my father forced me to continue with the secondary school. In the first year of secondary school, a small miracle happened. Instead of the anticipated failure something suddenly opened up and I began to understand. By the end of the school year, I was at the top of class and excelled in all subjects. Of course, I must thank my teachers but I believe an unexplained mystery opened me up. Study became completely effortless. This easy comprehension of whatever I need to study continued. As a young adult, I successfully took the professional examinations set by the association of Certified Public Accountants while working as an articled clerk with an accounting firm. I seem to spend much less time in study compared to my peers preparing for the tough examinations. The failure rate was high and many who studied with all-out effort nevertheless failed. I was one of the few who passed. I concluded that my experience on the rock in the middle of the mountain stream where I sat quietly had helped me. In fact whenever I had a problem with study, at work, or in any challenging circumstance, I would spiritually put myself on the rock, and the sound of the running water would carry the problem away.

Childhood Healing

I remember falling sick, probably with typhoid, when I was seven years old. I had a high fever, vomiting and felt utterly weak, unable to get up or walk. My parents were too poor to send me to a doctor. I laid in bed and in despair for a week. At night under the flickering kerosene lamp, I hallucinated. Finally, an indigenous village healer came. She had a red cloth wrapped around her hair. Her folk medicine technique involved using the edge of a bowl to scrap my back until the skin became reddish black. She also pinched me on my chest and stomach until the skin also turned reddish black. She comforted me and praised me for enduring the pain and being tough. Well, I didn't feel tough! I was so sick in body.

After what she did I felt much better. She gave my mother some herbs to boil in water for me to drink, and I recovered completely. The old healer turned out to be an expert in folk medicine and was affectionately called, "red-headed granny" because she always had her head wrapped in a red cloth. Her traditional treatment method was somewhat bizarre and painful—the pinching and scraping is called, "releasing the sand," and her herbal concoctions included pigeon droppings. But they worked often enough. Her reputation had attracted local clients and her healing powers drew patients from neighboring countries.

My family soon learned her scrapping and pinching techniques which became a home remedy for us. A sick person has a skin texture with a coarseness that feels like sand (*sar* in Chinese) when scrapped or pinched. It suggests the release of disharmony or diseased energy and

when removed by scraping produces immediate relief. To make healing more effective, internal cleansing by herbs was necessary. My
mother became quite well-versed with herbs which she picked from the
wild. Sometimes I was assigned to do the picking. Our family practically did away with seeing physicians. The only time I needed one was
when I became sick with a severe headache when I was nine years old.
The doctor gave me an injection which instantly cleared the headache.
That amused me greatly. My curiosity and profound interest in healing
were nurtured by these experiences.

Mysticism, Martial Arts & Qigong

I remember vividly my maternal grandfather who was a Taoist priest.
As a child, I was fascinated by his colorful costume and the way he
chanted as he held sword and sweeper while performing rituals. He was
famous for cleansing houses of evil spirits and healing people by exorcism. When he stayed over in our house, he often dream-talked. When
asked, he said he was talking to wandering spirits. He once told my
mother that I would grow up to be a spiritual healer. Grandfather was
often an amusing character but unfortunately he died before I was old
enough to remember more about him or learn from him.

I grew up at the mercy of the wilderness in a family harboring many
supernatural beliefs and folk practices. Rituals, cleansing activities, and
consultation of temple mediums were quite frequent. From childhood
I was taught many rules—not to pee on an ant hill, not to turn my head
or answer when someone called from behind, not to wander around on
inauspicious days or month, etc. When my siblings appeared listless or
unwell, my mother would light joss-sticks outside the house in the late
afternoon. She called out the sick child's name and to come home
while waving his shirt. That seemed to make them feel better.

All of this led me to become keenly interested in supernatural phenomenon. I read widely on occultism and tried many of the suggested
techniques. I made friends with temple mediums and observed them
carefully. I tried shifting into trance states and interacted with medi-

ums while in trance. Once I asked some tricky questions that shocked a medium out of his trance. I soon had doubts, not about the genuineness of the trance, but rather about the actual presence of the spirit deity claimed to be there when a medium was in trance.

In grade school, in reaction to being an easy target for bullies, I vowed to be big and strong. Reading martial arts pulp stories of famous heroes stirred my imagination and I became deeply inspired. I wanted to be heroic and to possess superhuman powers. I learned Japanese karate, earning a third degree black belt. I met my first mentor in 1972, the year when famed superstar Bruce Lee died. Sifu Cheah taught me kung fu and Northern Shaolin Qigong for several years and introduced me to Grand Master Wang Kam-Hoong. He made me an instructor in his Praying Mantis Kung-fu Association.

Those were the naive days when a village youth, like me, fantasized being trained in lethal martial arts and aspire to be a super hero of legends. I soon joined a training group. During weekends and school holidays, we had sparring sessions at the beach and nearby quarry. We staged hand-to-hand combats and mock battles dashing from beach to sea, or from cliff-top to ravines. I also took up weight-lifting in an attempt to look more like a muscle-bound fighting machine. I was too hard on myself and the injuries that often occurred took their toll. Both my knees were badly injured in separate incidents. They never healed completely and recurring pain continued.

By this time (1980) I had also learned Vipassana meditation, microcosmic Qigong, hatha yoga, acupressure massage, and touch healing. In fact, I enthusiastically offered touch healing to my friends and sparring partners. It worked very well on their injuries and various other problems. When the massage healing by many kung-fu masters was not effective on my knees, I decided to work on them myself. They got better but never regained their original flexibility and swiftness. My hero's dream was shattered.

I looked to Qigong as my next interest. By 1980s, many Qigong masters from Mainland China and Taiwan had come to Malaysia. The former Cultural Revolution had banned any activity considered as "superstitious and from cultures of the old society." This provoked a yearning for traditional practices. Ample opportunity for the contemporary development of Qigong thus opened, with many masters suddenly emerging and claiming direct lineage from famous ancient masters. Many also claimed that the methods they used would develop supernatural powers.

I was not too impressed by these alleged masters since they did not look impressive. They were too junior and inexperienced compared to myself, who had been practicing Qigong for ten years. I sought out "secret masters" not in the limelight and managed to meet a few. I frequented book stores seeking books on Qigong and on techniques to develop psychic abilities. I diligently tried whatever methods were recommended. By age 32 after wide and extensive experiences, I began to think I was well-equipped to be a healer. The therapeutic touch healing that I was using was working well. I had a continuous flow of friends and their relatives seeking help from me which I provided without charge.

From Accountant to Healer

Becoming an accountant was not really my career choice. I was fascinated by the martial arts and the paranormal but was sane enough to know that these would remain only hobbies. I knew I should study in a profession that would earn me a living. I would have preferred to study botany, biology or medicine. But the tiny rural school I attended did not teach scientific subjects even though I had passed the qualifying examinations. The majors available were in arts or business. I did well enough to be accepted in the top state university but I could not raise the money for a university education. My older brother, by then a successful accountant, encouraged me to apply for a work-study program in a public accounting company. That meant, besides a salary and sponsorship for night study, I would have one month's paid study leave during exam periods. Fortunately, I was successful and became an articled clerk in a large company with international affiliation. I was given on the job training in auditing and accountancy.

In the 1970's, there were few strict rules that segregated the duties of auditors from those of accountants. The problem of incomplete records and unbalanced accounts occurred frequently, at which point company clients would wait for the auditors to come in to sort out the accounts, a most unpleasant job for auditing staff. I soon earned a reputation for this kind of job. Actually, I relied on instinct and on intuition. Sometimes just by flipping a few pages I would zero in upon the source of the problems, especially after my colleagues failed to locate the trouble spots after days and weeks of work. This talent compensated for my lack of communication skills.

Examinations, modeled after the chartered accountancy (CA) system from UK, were tough so that few could pass exams and eventually qualify as accountants. The course required self-discipline and initiative in a self-study program. My peers studied hard in the evenings and weekends, with little time for leisure activities or social life. For me, those thick volumes of textbooks on company law, commercial and tax laws were simply too boring and sophisticated. So, I spent my evenings and weekends in the kung fu and karate classes. During the month-long study leave, I used past exam questions as a guide to read only the relevant chapters. I fudged the rest. It turned out that I passed all three major sections comprised of fourteen papers and eighteen subjects given over six years (the minimum required time was four years and the maximum twelve years). This was a mysterious achievement that still baffles me.

After graduation and a short stint working for others, I wanting to be my own boss. I applied and obtained approval for an audit license from the Ministry of Finance, hired a few people, and started a small public accounting firm. That was the recession year of 1984 but I gave personal attention to my small number of clients who operated small businesses. That enabled my business to survive and expand. I kept abreast of changes in income tax and company laws. But soon, I

became bored with trying to sort out seemingly endless auditing problems, submitting tax returns, adjusting to company resolutions, and so
forth.

Within me was a deep calling to do healing. The success of voluntary healing with some severe cases was encouraging. I was getting two
or three requests for healing almost everyday. I thought it worthwhile
to do this full time. The challenge was to take on some of the problems
baffling conventional medical treatments. Soon, I no longer saw myself
wasting away sitting in my office and I dreamed of saving humanity. So
on March, 1989, I wound up my accounting practice and put up a
shingle for my Healing Center, offering a new service in Penang that I
called "Qigong Therapy." People came for treatment. Satisfied, they
referred their friends and relatives. Within three months, my schedule
were full. Before long, I was able to put aside some income and used it,
along with previous savings, as a down payment for a house with a
large backyard. That would be my residence, healing center, and place
to conduct Qigong healing classes.

Shortly after, I realized my inadequacy. Most of my patients had
multiple chronic problems and had sought medical and other treatment for years without satisfactory effect. Some had life threatening illnesses, including cancer. My treatment worked at some level even in
the first few sessions. However, after initial improvements, progress
then slowed down or stagnated. Many patients with terminal cases suc-
cumbed as expected by their physicians. I was disappointed and disillu-
sioned. That was not my idea of what healing should be. The fault
obviously was that I wanted to play God. Still, I continued to train
myself hard and hope for a significant breakthrough.

One year later, personal troubles began. By then, my appointments
numbered 25—30 patients a day and filled my time from 7.30 a.m. to
11.00 p.m. I felt congestion in my chest, shortness of breath, faster
heartbeat, and a mild throbbing pain in my head. I tried training
harder but that did not help. I began making excuses to reduce the

number of appointments but that did not slow down my rapid deterioration. A real crisis was brewing.

The Crisis, The Savior

At the turn of 1991, my problems were full blown. I had intolerable pain in the head and neck. My hair was falling fast until the top was almost bald. My body was consistently stiff. My chest was so congested that I had to pull in hard in order to breathe. My heartbeat was fast and irregular. I felt constantly tired. I became constipated and my appetite dropped. I could not sleep as well. Then I discovered that my feet would swell up in the evening until I could not wear my sandals. To make matters worse, relationship with my wife became strained. She felt (with good reason) that I was neglecting her and devoting all my time to work. She thought healing and Qigong should be a hobby rather than a career. She found fault with my efforts and was unhelpful in her manner toward my clients.

Despite the obvious failing of my body, my Qigong sensitivities seemed to surge to an amazing proportion. I saw auric colors, lights, and shapes within and around my patients. I felt electricity surging all over my body, particularly, my arms and back. I could hear the static noise it made and caught sight of electrical sparks. My body's energy field felt like a giant magnet that disrupted and damaged watches, clocks, fans and TVs close to me. Chairs and small items seemed to fall as I walked by without contact. My odor was strong (like barbequed pork). My clothes turned yellow and smelled as if heated over an oven. I felt embarrassed, thinking that my patients detected these peculiar odors.

Instead, they thought that I had become super-powerful. I received even more requests for appointments. I greatly disappointed many people by turning down their requests. Many resorted to pleading and begging to see me. But I, using all my reserves of energy, could only manage ten appointments daily.

I felt desperate and despair. My bodily systems seemed to be rapidly deteriorating and I feared that I might drop dead at any moment. I knew that no medicine, East or West, would solve my problem. I could not turn to any of my mentors for help especially those whose claim of super-human powers turned out to be lies.

There were only two who did genuine healing. One would heal only occasionally and dealt only with standard chronic problems. He took a long time to recharge himself after treatment and his fee was exorbitant–almost equivalent to the average yearly income of a working person. The other mentor specialized in treating aches and pains. Nobody thought that healing could be done the way I did it. I had no one to talk to. My wife was too disgusted with me and, moreover she was also pregnant with our first child. I could not relate my troubles to my clients. I still had to continue to work to make a living since I, at this point, had no savings. Many of my clients were quite poor and paid only a token sum for my treatment.

I felt that I was dying–my body felt disconnected and held only a bit of consciousness to keep me alive. I worried about how my wife and expected child would survive. I feared that I would not even live to see my child. If I died, I would be a great laughing stock to people who had been condemning me and my work.

Night of the Hexagram

Late February in 1991, on a Sunday, I finished work at 6.30 p.m. and drove my wife to pick up something for dinner. I parked at the side of the road and waited for her. Suddenly, I saw a whirlwind circling in a swirl of leaves and debris in front of me. My heartbeat quickened. I began shivering. I held on and said nothing to my wife as we drove home. Once home, I could not hold on any longer. I went into strange compulsive movements, though my mind was fully alert. Fortunately, my wife went into the bedroom and stayed there after taking dinner.

As if controlled by some unseen force, I lighted some joss or incense sticks and started to dot and mark my body with the unburnt ends. At the same time, I started walking. I broke into dancing in a ritualistic manner. When the joss sticks burned out, I held my palms together and faced the doorway. At that point, my body went into a sequence of strange movements. At the end of it, I laid on the floor and held my body down. I got up and again faced the doorway, palms together as if sending off an unseen force, then seemingly inviting another force in with a different sequence of movements. Each action was completed by marking the ground in a different pattern and direction. These actions were repeated exactly 64 times. By now, I knew that I had marked the design of a hexagram all over my body, together with a visible huge hexagram drawn right in the center of the hall.

I felt strangely strong, and even invincible. I punched my body with my fists which felt like rubber. I banged my head against the wall and could hear a loud thud but did not feel any pain. The whole process continued until 3 a.m.. For the next three days, I felt strangely fresh, almost out of this world. When I did healing, I felt that I need not act wilfully, since my hands would move automatically.

A strong manifestation of powerful healing occurred on the third day after this hexagram incident. The family of an old lady, who lived close to the Center, asked me to treat their mother. She had fallen during the morning and sprained her arthritic knee. By afternoon her pain was so severe she could not walk at all. As I walked to her house, the thought came that I could receive assistance to help me to heal her. Immediately, the impression of a *Shaolin* martial arts monk flashed across my mind and my body felt as strong as a warrior. I worked on the elderly woman standing fifteen feet away instead of the usual three or four feet. I pointed my index finger at different parts of her body and felt a beam of energy emit from my finger, propel through the air, and be drawn into her. Within ten minutes, I commanded her to stand up and walk. She did! She was instantly and completely cured of her injury. Until today, her sons and daughters who witness this miraculous healing often laugh in disbelief and wonder. I was regarded with respect and some fear. I was equally puzzled by this healing experience.

A hexagram is a sacred symbol of ancient origin from the "*I Ching*," the Book of the Laws of Changes. A few years earlier, I had met a elderly caretaker of a temple. During his younger days, he was a renowned fortune teller. When I asked him about meditation and healing, he looked at my palms. Pointing to a hexagonal sign on the center of my left hand, he proclaimed that I would become a rare healer. He handed me a sheet of rice paper on which he had written some verses invoking the power of the hexagram to lead "*an army of heavenly soldiers.*" He promised that I would have this power if I chanted the verses at 5.00 a.m. for 49 days. I did not follow this procedure as I could not wake up in time each morning but I chanted the verses occasionally for a few years.

Ever since the night of the hexagram, my condition improved tremendously though some problems remained. My work became easier as I felt like an observer during healing and my hands did what was necessary. My training became easier. All I had to do was put in time allowing my body to do what was necessary. But I still did not understand healing and I still yearned to improve the results of my work.

Transparent Gold-Body Light Initiation

I was bent on finding out more about healing and mysticism. Since I felt that I had exhausted every known avenue, I returned to my childhood habit which I had practiced for thirty years. I sat and imagined myself on my rock in the mountain stream, my heaven since childhood days. I imagined hearing the sound of running water and looking at the panoramic view of the lush green valley, the sea, and the sky. I did this everyday after the time of the spontaneous movements.

Over two years later, one night in September, 1993, I felt a very strange sensation. Something was crawling, shifting, and moving in front of my chest area. Then boom! A beam of golden light shot out from my solar plexus from deep within the core of my consciousness. I felt that I was no longer in my body but, instead, I had become the light, which was everywhere and filling up every space. I saw white luminous words engraved on the golden light which had turned into a solid mass. I heard a voice, too, but could not tell where it came from. I was the light, the words, and the voice!

The explanations that came from that transcendent state became the basis of what I teach today and write in this book. Answers to the mysteries of life, from birth to death, streamed into consciousness. Wisdom was revealed about impermanence, the demands of life, and the inevitable process of creation. To heal or solve problems is simply the process of undoing, that is, letting go. When I was back in myself before midnight, I started to hear a phrase of three words, "*Zhen Shan Mei.*" It went on and on non-stop, day and night, for the next three days, even when I was working or sleeping. It seemed to come from afar, from all the space around me, from my mind, and even from every cell in my body. I soon owned it and incorporate this as "*the Mantra*" in my daily meditation routine.

A new breakthrough in healing had finally arrived. When doing healing, I just had to repeat the three-worded Mantra silently. I could feel the Mantra going in to dissolve, dilute, and flush out my patients' problems. I stopped teaching other types of Qigong.

In 1995, Dr. Chok Hiew, whom I had met several years ago in Penang when I attended his psychology seminars, invited me to Canada to conduct a workshop, followed by a presentation at the Monroe Institute in Virginia. I thought I should give it a try. Then some patients suggested that I teach them about Qigong. That gave me the idea that I might well start locally in preparation for the North American trip. I wrote down the "Golden Light" healing principles in the form of workshop notes, dated May 1, 1995.

The Canadian and US trips were highly successful and Professor Hiew was deeply impressed. I have, since my return, accepted students to train them in my Qigong system. Then I faced a shortcoming—people who are sick, though physically and mentally weak, are able to be directly treated by me but not able to train as healers. The healing meditation I taught required them to face their problems bravely but few were sufficiently strong or motivated to do so. That meant that my one-to-one treatment would continue to be time consuming and I would not be available to help all in need. Dr Hiew often suggested the need of a healer training approach that emphasizes skills training for those without a meditation orientation. This issue has now been solved. I devised certain healing movements and actions which are suitable for all. CFQ is now complete and as universally useful as possible.

Chaoyi Fanhuan Qigong

> *Chao fan tuo su xu wu yi*
> *Fan pu gui zhen zi xing huan*
> *Wu gua wu ai wu wei fa*
> *Miao zhi miao jue miao zhen ru*
>
> —*Calligraphy of CFQ (Translation Below)*

The title *Chaoyi Fanhuan Qigong* came to me in meditation when I was contemplating going to Canada. The word *"Chaoyi"* means *"above mental, superconscious, or psychic."* It turns out that the practice, to be explained later, enables the practitioner to access directly the transparent purity of the eighth or *alaya*-consciousness. This is inaccessible by normal Qigong or meditation in which the deepest access is at the sixth (or mind) consciousness.

"Fanhuan" means to *"return to the origin or rejuvenated state."* This can only be done by a radiant effect from the innermost transparent state enabling the primordial capacity to let-go of the fabricated burdens brought about by the normal processes of life. Normal qi practices fabricate a state of relaxation and calmness called "qi energy" within the functional ability of the mind when working with the mind consciousness. Such a fabricated effect will not be able to cancel out the disease and tension burdens existing at the karmic cleansing level, the process needed for a profound cure.

These poetic phrases appeared in my meditation on the meaning of CFQ:

> *Beyond the ordinary, shedding the norm*
> *Void and detached*
> *Returning to Origin and Truth*
> *The Self-nature reveals.*

On the goal of CFQ cultivation:

> *No worry, no hindrance, and Unbounded*
> *Excellent wisdom*
> *Excellent realization*
> *Excellent essential Suchness(Truth).*

A Case Example: *The patient discovered a series of lumps along his right neck and the tumor on his armpit had erupted. The next morning, the neck lumps had swollen to the size of a tennis ball and the lump on his armpit had become the size of a teacup. He rushed to see a Western trained doctor and was immediately operated upon. Specimens were sent for biopsies. He awaited the verdict of further treatment.*

At that time he came to see me. Touching his neck and around the collar bone I discovered at least ten lumps. His chin was also hardened by an amalgamation of lumps. I knew the gravity of his condition—his physician would diagnose the condition as fourth stage cancer. I asked him to come for thrice-weekly sessions, without telling him the extreme seriousness of his condition.

On his third visit, the large lumps on his neck and armpit were greatly reduced and his arm could be positioned normally. He perspired profusely during the session. Some rather dramatic phenomena is observed here. From the fifth to the thirtieth session, lumps (size ranging from 0.5 cm—2.0 cm) kept popping out from his neck and behind his collar bone. These tumors (numbering at least 30) gradually melted away. A fist-size lump swelled up from his chin, that gradually reduced in size. After 30 sessions, the patient was visibly much improved. His appetite, sleep and perspiration was normal. His neck had much fewer lumps—the one on his chin had shrunk and the other in his armpit was peanut size. That took ten weeks of energy healing.

I then reduced the sessions to twice weekly. From the very beginning I taught him the "lotus walk." He enjoyed this exercise so much he replaced his daily morning walk with it. After 60 healing sessions, I taught him the "7-Movement" meridian exercise explaining that with daily practice, further healing sessions were optional. He has since been practicing it daily every morning and night. He still comes for healing two or three times monthly.

Throughout the treatment period, he continued with his normal work load without taking a day off. He owns and is the chef of a restaurant, working long hours from early morning to almost midnight. He made the following remark a month ago.

"I feel this remarkable peace and comfort which I have never experienced before, at least not in the past twenty years."

2

Qigong and Energy Medicine

The idea of Qigong, for many who have heard about it, is "The art of breathing and absorbing the essence from air through special visualization techniques, converting its essence into the body's energy system vital for the promotion of health and other purposes." Many books have been written about Qigong, especially in Chinese. Some authors defined it as above while others simply avoided defining it. The fact that the field has been an object of controversy and confusion encourages some writers to avoid becoming a target of attack. Too much precision has proven dangerous. The lack of a definition, however, leads to a most basic problem: practitioners and the public remain largely unclear about the nature of Qigong. A mystery remains, and the public is often uninformed and distrustful. I shall attempt to clarify this controversy.

Causes of the Qigong Controversy

Qigong is an art that has been practiced for over 5,000 years. Originally, people developed it as a means of harmonizing themselves and dealing with threatening life situations. The healing art has survived a transition of thousands of years in which people experienced natural disasters, wars, chaos, changes of rulers from short-lived dynasties, and on. Consequently, it has become exceedingly complex. Different ideas have been introduced by different groups at different times. Over the millennia, local customs, social trends, religions, and beliefs differentiated by status and class and aggravated by the wide geographical distribution of people, have further intensified the complexity.

Some sources estimate that there existed at least 20,000 types of Qigong practices which number appears reasonable in the light of the history mentioned above. In fact, there was no standard name for Qigong in the past. The term itself was used to generally categorize skills and practices that could not be labeled in the mainstream trades and professions. The term was extended to many skills of living, religions, types of medicine, martial arts or local customs. The word was often used by various groups to enhance the development of skill in their own area of expertise.

A further complication comes from the cunning ability of the dynastic rulers to use superstition to protect and enhance their status and power. The emperors called themselves "sons of heavens," meaning they were "heaven sent" to rule the nation or empire. Every action taken was equivalent to those of the gods, and therefore unquestionably justified. The emperors were shrewd enough to use every available avenue to get the message across to the masses. Scholars of each realm were awarded the highest national awards in rank and status to ensure their support of those in power.

This was the major reason why there were frequent dynastic changes—excessive trust in scholars weakened the defense system. Generals and armies in battle were often intercepted with contradictory orders given by emperors who acted on the advice of their scholars. In return for this, scholars preached absolute loyalty to the reigning emperor. The supremacy of the emperors also became a doctrine added to Taoism and Buddhism. Priests and monks needed the support of the monarchy to survive, build temples and to ensure that the commoners trusted them. As monks and monarchy coopted each other, religious teachings were modified. This strategy was so successful that it found its way in every walk of life. The street ballads sung stories of the might and powers of the "sons of heavens." So it is with ancient sources of Qigong where truth became distorted in subservience to power.

Superstition at times has been the most important unifying force in China. Despite a history spanning thousands of years, despite the size of the country, despite frequent wars and the rise and fall of empires, China remained one nation. The impact of superstition greatly influenced dynastic triumphs and failures throughout the ages.

Science may well be a major way to effectively do away with superstition. However, Chinese superstition is unique in its complexity and fantasy, and is deeply rooted in the culture and civilization. It overpowered many innovations and inventions. The four great inventions of ancient China (the compass, paper, printing and gunpowder), which have significantly influenced the modern world, were never used or developed properly. When the Chinese invented gunpowder they used it to make fire-crackers to ward off "evil spirits and monsters." When Westerners learned about gunpowder they made weapons that helped to bring the Manchu dynasty to an end.

Education was never widespread in the ancient world. Masses remained illiterate. Knowledge was passed down by word of mouth and physical actions. Theories and basics were often regarded as unnecessary, "You just have to know how. Don't ask why." In the old simplistic societies, students were neither inquisitive nor sophisticated enough to ask why. There was also a tendency for some teachers to withhold certain vital aspects of knowledge as closely guarded secrets. Some individual temples or individuals might have obtained books or writings but, since such items were largely difficult to come by, they became precious items of worship instead of being sources of knowledge. Often the owners dared not even open up the revered books for fear that the gods of the books would get angry with them.

Today we can easily obtain large quantities of surviving ancient literature on philosophy, scholastic works, Taoism, Buddhism, medicine, etc. But how many ancient books on Qigong can be found? Few indeed. The theories and writings about it often turn out to be the work of contemporary authors rationalizing and providing justification for ancient practices. Among traditional sources, it was customary to name the author after an historical figure. But if one compares the teaching attributed to that person, contradictions abound. There are also those who claim to be taught by historical persons who are legendary. There were also some types of Qigong that are named from a word or two from ancient literature such as the *Tao Te Ching*. But a comparison of basic principles with such literature finds no consistent match. The point is that claimed lineage to famous names does not authenticate a method. If someone claims to have found a Qigong authored by Abraham Lincoln, Abe will not be around to protest. We, however, know that Qigong was not known in America 200 years ago.

The re-emergence of interest in Qigong, after the Cultural Revolution in late 1970's, gave rise to tremendous opportunities to bring back revered traditions. The limitations of modern medicine called for fresh ideas on healthcare. There was also the belief that needed ideas have all along been part of the Chinese culture but have been neglected. One only has to dig them out, integrate and systematize. Then there was a notion that the East could lead a new scientific revolution. Experiments were conducted on selected masters which gave encouraging evidence.

The news was exciting, the promises and potential were great—so were the opportunities. Masters sprang up from all corners of the country. Many claimed lineage through generations going back to ancient masters. No doubt there were many honest and respectable masters who have quietly practiced their art. But the new opportunities opened the way for the unscrupulous to get rich and famous quickly. Many true masters became sidelined. They were not sufficiently educated to write about their teachings or draw large groups of people to study with them. Their methods were old fashioned and tedious. Moreover, they were too conscientious to make grandiose claims and too honest to cloud their art with mystery. In fact, things became so chaotic and confused that even people in authority found it hard to distinguish genuine masters from quacks. Within a short period of time, the Qigong fire has spread throughout China and the overseas Chinese communities.

To capitalize on human curiosity, these methods often became cloaked in mystery. Many opportunists claimed that supernatural powers could be achieved by their techniques. They held public demonstrations with both gimmicks copied from Western magicians and ancient tricks used by peddlers and medical quacks. Some used electricity and a knowledge of physics to manufacture astounding effects.

Thus, from the distant past until today, gullible people regarded Qigong as a mysterious art. That has hampered its scientific study. Qigong is worthy of serious scientific study but with so much fraud present, investigators at times find research frustrating.

Some masters obviously found that they could easily prey on the innocent using superstition, not unlike the emperors and sorcerers of the past. So they claim that they come from heavenly deities or are reincarnated from past historical figures. The repercussions have been unfortunate. People seeking treatment or spiritual enlightenment suffered financial ruin and lost their health when they became Qigong practitioners taught by "masters" making ridiculous claims and using baseless and harmful practices. Many ended up in mental hospitals. Scientific research came to a standstill. The supposed breakthroughs turned out to be baseless. Loyalty to the country was replaced by loyalty to alleged super-beings. The Government was alarmed. It cracked down against Qigong movements since the 1980's. Fortunately the government did not ban Qigong as a whole. After all, there are many genuine methods that had provided health benefits.

We are faced with massive amounts of information about Qigong passed down from the reservoir of our ancient heritage. Few people dispute its beneficial effects. The problem is sorting out the truth, the relevant from the irrelevant, and the desirable from the undesirable. This is difficult, since no one has the authority and knowledge to do so. Methods abound with contradictory principles yet all claim to be equally effective. Clearly, this is a job for experienced researchers who should do it with full conscientiousness and diligence. Meanwhile, genuine Qigong practitioners endure ridicule from the consumer who seeks evidence for its health claims or efficacy.

Qi: Gems or Garbage

It seems that the crucial word in Qigong is "qi" and is commonly taken to mean bioenergy in the physical body system. However, this does not appear to be its original meaning. The ancients used Qigong to harmonize themselves to better deal with life situations, a way to increase resilience. This suggests a system of healing encompassing psychological, philosophical and mental techniques. Qigong, in this light, appears as a form of exercise replete with a well-developed system of healing, unlike the mere exercise form or method of power-enhancement we know today.

In the Chinese language and culture, the energy word is used to describe an emotion, feeling, or situation by compounding it with another word. Anger is called "raising qi" or "angry qi"; depression is called "pent-up qi"; peace is "harmonized qi"; and an atmosphere of happiness is "happy qi." Atmosphere itself is simple qi and the "smell of qi." In the medical context, qi or bioenergy is said to be the parallel of blood. However, the word qi has more prominence than blood and is used as qi-blood. Thus, using the wider meaning of Qigong, it is a system of practical methods dealing with emotions and thoughts or mind. It is the practical rather than the theoretical aspect of the study of philosophy, psychology and spirituality. The definition and meaning of Qigong thus undergoes a significant transformation.

Fundamental Principles of Qigong

The fundamental principles of most Qigong methods are generally agreed to be:

I. Relaxation II. Stillness III. Naturalness

To apply these principles, one has to regulate the body, breathing, and heart or mind. Let us examine the implications of each:

Relaxation. The word for relaxation is clearly understood as meaning "let loose" or to let go and loosen oneself. It literally means "to do away with" or *"undoing something that has been created or fabricated"* or "dropping off one's strength." For example, if you hold a pen to write, your hand is not relaxed. To relax you just have to open your hand out and let the pen drop. From the 1970's to the beginning of 1990's, relaxation and stress management were hot topics promoted in seminars, workshops and self help books. Today, few people seem to be interested. Despite many people believing in the benefits of relaxation, the techniques taught were not potent enough. The mistake lies in the conception of relaxation—it should be about doing away with what is *not* relaxed rather than creating a relaxation state!

Stillness. Stillness occurs at the mental level and, as well, at the consciousness level itself. When the body is truly relaxed, the person has a peaceful consciousness. Feeling peaceful in this way the mind will not be overly disturbed or provoked by external stimulation and perceptions. Only if the consciousness is still can the body settle down into Stillness.

Naturalness. The core of ancient teaching is that humans are part of nature. First, there must be a basic understanding of the laws of Nature to harmonize oneself and live well with Nature. To be natural means that one should not be fabricating disharmony that conflicts with Nature as in the greedy absorption of energy. It simply means to relax, open or loosen oneself, and find peace.

Regulation of Body, Breathing and Heart. Over-emphasis on any single aspect can be dangerously misleading. Emphasizing the body suggests that one should make oneself strong, but strength contradicts looseness. An emphasis on breathing suggests that one must absorb nourishment from the air and that conflicts with Nature. Emphasis on the heart would not lead to peace but to an inclination to overwork the mind with thinking and visualizing. These elements need to be regulated in balance.

The common misconception among both Qigong masters and the lay practitioners seems to be that qi is bioenergy that is necessary for proper physical functioning. This misinterpretation leads to the dangerous conclusion that it ought to be enhanced, strengthened, and increased in order to optimize health. The common speculation is that this essence comes from the air. So the practitioner is advised how to breathe and how to process the essence from air through mental activity. However, as we have pointed out, bioenergy is an important yet relatively minor aspect of pursuing peace and harmony to increase resilience. Simply relying on breathing techniques to enhance relaxation is inadequate. We suggest that the scope of qi in the context of Qigong be expanded beyond the obsolete notions of breathing, essence from air, and visualization.

Sources of Qigong

Though Buddhism was introduced from India much later than the two indigenous religions (Confucianism and Taoism), the Buddhist system has been generally regarded as the most important source of ideas for Qigong. From the Sung Dynasty onward the indigenous practices absorbed many Buddhist philosophical beliefs.

Buddhism teaches about the origins of human suffering and how such suffering can be let go. The fabricating factor in the mind produces effects that obeys the law of fabrication or karma. Since all matter is impermanent, it has no real existence. Qigong practice appears to be a skillful means to gain insight into the Buddha's teaching by going beyond its conceptualization. The practice involves "undoing" all fabricated effects, including conditioned knowledge, in order to arrive at intuitive wisdom.

Lao Tze (6th Century B.C.), the founder of Taoism, wrote about his teachings in the *Tao Te Ching*. This text presented his ideas on the nature of the universe and provides suggestions for leading to a harmonious life. Although Taoism became distorted with superstition, its most valuable teaching for our purposes lies in the importance of harmonizing one's life with Nature.

I find another interesting clue in the legend regarding Lao Tze's ending. After completing the *Tao Te Ching*, he is said to have left in a westward direction riding on a water buffalo. He rode with his back facing the animal's front. He never appeared again. So why did he ride on a water buffalo? The Chinese regard it as a hardworking but largely brainless animal. The allegory is that to understand the Tao or true way of nature, one must be hard in the pursuit of truth and yet must be as mindless as a water buffalo. Understanding the way of nature is not aided by mental activity that in fact distorts the truth. Why did Lao Tze ride backwards? The true Tao is the opposite of conventional norms which focus on acquiring and fabricating.

Some sources believe that Confucius was the mentor of Lao Tze. The "*Eight Letters*"summary of Confucius's teaching began with loyalty and ended with peace. In a period of history marked by multiple conflicts and warring states, Confucius also taught about the way to true peace.

Oriental medicine holds internal emotional or conscious activity as the primary source of disease. External influences are regarded as secondary. Diseases of the heart or mind or consciousness must be cured by the "*medicine of the heart.*" Medicine of the heart is the calming and harmonizing of one's thoughts. Since the medical profession was not as developed as Taoism, Buddhism, and Confucianism in the medicine of the heart, Oriental medicine confined its treatment program. Qigong practices were primarily restricted to helping physicians stay calm and advance their healing skills. A sentence from *Nei Ching*, the most ancient and substantive medical source, advises as follows:

If a person is peaceful, calm and not greedy, his real energy is harmonious. If he guards his spirit against outside disturbances, diseases find no way to attack him.

Qigong was also applied to developing prowess in the martial arts which is beyond the scope of this book.

Goals of Chaoyi Fanhuan Qigong

In the context of CFQ, Qigong is defined as: *Practical methods of dealing with consciousness in order to enhance our inherent resilience and the self-repair response and thus optimize health.*

In brief, health is dependent on our ability to deal with emotions and thoughts, which in turn depends on a positive state of consciousness flowing with peace, calmness, harmony, and tranquility. These achievements are of course commonly suggested by conventional psychology, philosophy, and various religions. In order for such suggestions to be effective, methods involving our active participation are necessary. Mere preaching and conceptual understanding are largely ineffective.

Fundamentally, a smooth flow of bioenergy in the body is necessary in order for the requisite qualities to be developed in a person's consciousness. This does not imply that one should overemphasize building such energy or that increasing and strengthening energy is beneficial to the body. Attempting such strengthening gives rise to absorbing and fabricating, processes which disrupt harmony, create turbulence and disturb peace at the expense of health.

In CFQ, we adhere to the three fundamental principles of relaxation, stillness, and naturalness. While conventional Qigong methods proclaim adherence to these principles, their practices sometimes contradict them. This shows up in an emphasis on acquisition, fabrication, and visualization. My meditations have given me a clue as to why the term "Qigong" or "air," was used. I have on several occasions felt a kind of transparent consciousness filling up every space. The eternal prevails and the physical body seems to have totally disappeared. This consciousness felt like thin air.

A Case Example: *A Canadian boy, aged ten, had Down's Syndrome, a juvenile Type I diabetes which required daily insulin shots, and poor eyesight due to cataracts. Three months prior to energy healing, one cataract (left eye) was removed and the lens replaced. The ophthalmologist scheduled surgery for the other eye a month later.*

After two energy healing sessions with me, 20 minutes each, the child's facial appearance began to change. His posture looked lighter and he moved and walked with improved coordination and balance. A total of five healing sessions were given during my visit to Canada. The following letter received two months later from the patient's mother reads:

"I am writing to you with good news. I took my son "A" to see Dr. "X," the eye specialist, on Tuesday. After examining A's right eye, the doctor told me A does not require surgery. The cataract had dissolved and cleared up. I was so elated! The specialist was pleasantly surprised. We do not have to go back for one year. Isn't that wonderful news?

"Also, with regard to A's diabetes, over the last few days I have not had to give extra insulin. His sugar levels are excellent.... I am eternally grateful to you for your healing sessions with A and for your care and concern."

Observation of the boy over five years indicated that the cataract was gone for good. His overall condition remained stable.

3

Consciousness-Energy Connection

Meditation training exposed me to strange, vivid experiences that occurred not only at the cognitive or consciousness level but also caused powerful sensations and changes in my body. Such experiences happened frequently among my students and patients. I relied on my past experiences and reading of books on Buddhism for explanations. I did not attempt to pursue a further explanation from books since I have ceased to read for healing information. Reading gives rise to conceptual knowledge which I have found to hinder insights from intuitive knowledge arising from meditation.

I discussed my experiences with Mu Soeng, whom I had the honor of meeting during his visit to Penang in 1999. He is a former Zen monk, author of several insightful commentaries on classic Buddhist texts, and Director of the Barre Center for Buddhist Studies near Boston. He later mailed me a clear explanation on consciousness from the ancient Yogachara literature. There were some minor discrepancies with my perception of, for instance, the seventh *mano*-consciousness that I understand as ignorance and confusion whereas he referred to it as the ego. However, Mu Soeng believed that an experiential account is valuable and encouraged me to explore it.

Before explaining the functions of the various levels of consciousness as described in the Buddhist belief system (see Figure 1), I wish to introduce the concept of cosmic energy, from which life draws its force. The universe exists within an infinite space of pure vibrations of infinitely fine frequency from which all matter, including the planets and galaxies, are created. It is the basic building block of all solids, liquids, gases and light which are differentiated only by the velocity of vibrations. Since the vibration of cosmic energy is so subtle, it can be easily influenced and converted into coarser vibrations by a step-down process. The vibration then precipitates in particle form and becomes atomic molecules which is the basis of all matter. However, within space, there exists all kinds of vibrations, such as light and sound, which are not coarse enough to become solid matter.

The five senses, namely, for vision, hearing, smell, taste and touch, are "windows" of the body with specially developed organs and faculties that provide the body feedback related to its existence. These five sense organs are specialized in converting fine cosmic energy into impressions which register in the remaining three levels of consciousness via a resonance effect. The five senses can be considered the life or "spirit" of the hardware body, without which it will have no reason to live. Any force so registered becomes stored in the consciousness as well as condensed and absorbed into the physical body, fabricating tissue wrinkling or leading to folding, and other physical deformations.

The sixth consciousness consists of the hardwired brain which assimilates, processes, and stores information derived from the first five senses. The brain then is a sophisticated organic machine that sorts out and organizes the accumulated information for memory storage. It is capable of continuously retrieving information from memory to interact with new information forming new memories. It is also capable of commanding bodily actions. It continuously absorbs cosmic energy for its functions. Any stored memory becomes permanent and indestructible. It may be forgotten through long periods of disuse in much the same way as old files in a computer become lost under a stack of new files.

The Eight Levels of Consciousness

Energy-Consciousness Connection	Levels	Consciousness
The Body	1st to 5th	**Five Sense Organs:** Vision Hearing Smell Touch Taste
The Mind	6th	**Brain:** Perceptions Thoughts Emotions Images Beliefs Memories
The Spirit (Life Energy-Consciousness)	7th 8th	**Unconscious-Transcendent States:** *Mano (wu-min)* Energy body of dark clouds with deep-seated memories (ego-ignorance and confusion). These energy forces distress, weaken and age the body *Alaya (Storehouse)* *(a) White Clouds* Energy memories or *karma* condensed from lower seven level—Seeds of future events programmed *(b) Eternal Light* Tathagata-Garbha Buddha-seed or Enlightened Consciousness

Figure 1: Energy-Consciousness & the Mind-Body-Spirit
Connection

The seventh and eight arenas of consciousness bear some similarities to states of altered consciousness expressed within such categories as the sub-conscious or the unconscious. Some people might use a label such as "spirit" for these phenomena which might make them beyond the realm of science. For our use here, spirit refers to a form of energy force or vibration arising from one's stored memories.

The seventh or *mano* consciousness is an energy mass, black cloud-like, and irregular-shaped, that emanates from within and, for an average adult, protrudes out beyond the boundary of the physical body to a distance of about three feet. This seemingly homogenous and shifting dark surface, when opened out, is comprised of millions of distinct shapes, lines, folds, and colored lights. However, the opening-out process is complex and usually occurs only with a systematic technique of letting-go like that taught in CFQ. In other words, the nature of this energy force becomes obvious only if "unwound," "moved out," and "released." Otherwise, the normal survival and adaptation functioning of the human organism continues to thicken and compact this energy mass. The lines and folds are the product of tension in the physical body, and can be experienced as stiffness when a person feels unwell. The continuous compacting effect, as a person ages, gives rise to the elderly's skin wrinkles, osteoporosis and deformations of body structure.

Mano-consciousness (called *wu min*), means cloudy or non-transparent. I interpret it as "ignorance." *Mano* comes from energy forces absorbed through activation of the first six levels of consciousness. It is a form of memory with a "dumb" intelligence because it is unable to analyze information in a sophisticated way such as the brain (the sixth consciousness) can. When a person is subjected to excessive emotional disturbance, the energy forces in the *mano* consciousness become stirred up and flow into the mind. The person becomes disoriented and might seem to lose his or her mind temporarily. This phenomenon occurs quite commonly in the average person, but soon the person settles back to normal. When subjected to extreme or prolonged and excessive emotional states such as fear or trauma, however, a thick layer of black cloud shields the first to six consciousness completely and refuses to settle back. The result is that the person suffers psychological problems possibly including a mental breakdown or phobia, or clinical depression.

The *alaya* (eighth) consciousness is composed largely of milky-colored energy with a translucent light appearance. It is an extract of the *mano* consciousness but functions on its own enabling it to attract future events. All the forces here are like seeds that give rise to actual events in life or are carried forward to the next life upon death. The deepest core of the *alaya* consciousness is a kind of luminous transparent light. In the *Hua Yen* Sutra (according to Mu Soeng) this is separated from the *alaya* as the ninth consciousness or *Tathagata garbha*. In CFQ meditation, during the process of initiating students, I connect the cleansing and radiant effect to this transparent light, so that it will continue to radiate, cleansing the first eight levels of consciousness of disease-causing, karmic-forming energies.

Clarification on Consciousness and Memories

Spirit refers to the consciousness or energy aspect of a being.

1. To exist, energetic forces continue to resonate with the first six levels of consciousness through the sensory faculties and mental activity. This stimulation is processed as experience and is stored as memory that serves as the basis of all actions and future events.

2. Memory in the form of debased energy, drawn initially from the pure cosmic source, is stored not only in the brain but throughout the whole person. Memory in the brain is processed, sorted, organized and has mental intelligence. Memory stored elsewhere in the body's faculties, including the cellular level, are unprocessed or mindless forces.

3. All memories are mutually connected and mutually influential. They exist much like a ball of entangled yarn and are connected everywhere with tendencies or inclinations related to how and where each was fabricated.

4. Energy in the form of memory is the basis of physical existence. In other words, every cell in the body is charged with information from all levels of consciousness. Each new generation of cells produced carries more memory or information than the preceding or older generation. The added burden results in a deteriorating condition and a weaker state of health of every successive generation of cells.

5. The law of conservation of energy states that energies are indestructible. Therefore, any debased energy fabricated by one's consciousness can only be consumed through actual realization of events or actions (i.e. suffering as intended by the law of karma). Such realization leads to new sequences of memory condensations from cosmic energy.

6. At death, energy from the seven levels of consciousness is extracted or embraced by the *alaya*-consciousness and leaves the body. The coarser components become solidified in the physical body and decay.

7. Fear of death and the unknown is a common fabrication. It gives rise to attracting forces leading to rebirth. Once energy in the *alaya*-consciousness leaves the body, which usually takes seven days, it takes the next step in its new destiny. Rebirth can be in physical form from human to animal or even as a formless entity.

8. Common speculations about wandering spirits and spirit possession are largely untrue. My experience with such cases shows that ghosts are merely cloud-like forces in and around a person that are thrown out from the *mano* consciousness. Hallucinations, seeing

things including departed spirits are merely pictorial impressions within the cloud of *mano* consciousness. They are largely past imaginations and fabrications that can be strengthened by current beliefs and suggestions. Though unreal objectively, they are real to the patient and must be dealt with carefully. Wrong approaches, beliefs, and suggestions only aggravate the situation. Psychopathological thoughts-emotions from trauma, depression, fatigue, and psychosis belong in this same category.

9. In some cases, when an individual is subjected to severe agony, emotional pain or trauma, the person's disturbed energy is projected into the surroundings and stored in the objects and atmosphere by a kind of resonance. This is the cause of haunted houses, which may disrupt the emotional state of the occupants and provoke hallucinations. The solution is to clear the surroundings and expose the house to sunlight, since the forces of nature will neutralize the disturbed energy.

10. Though the energy of a deceased person may exist in a formless manner without a physical body, it belongs to a plane of existence different from ours, and therefore does not establish and link with us living in the physical earth. The alleged seeing or communication with their spirits are merely figments of human imagination.

Heart, Ego & Cosmic Consciousness

The word "heart"*(xin)* is commonly used in the Orient to refer to intention. Thus, any process involving thinking is written with a word-character that carries the symbol of heart at the side. It is also used to describe emotion. The normal usage in the language points toward the existence of a control beyond thinking and emotion, perhaps consciousness or conscience. The inherent tendency of a living person is to continuously absorb energy from the cosmic source through the faculty of the sixth or mind consciousness. The absorbed energy forces are processed and stored as memory and, in energy form, continue to excite the mind in an effort to increase its strength. This built-in predisposition is, in the first place, the cause of being born or the wanting to be born. This wanting feature is why the faculties are created each with its natural function. Since memories exist and are fabricated by the wanting and absorbing process, they fight to influence the mind in an attempt to dominate and fabricate more power. When the mind becomes excited (it tends to listen to the strongest voice or what is relevant in the light of the situation), it decides to take action. The decision to take action is called intention and what is intended becomes a fabrication or creation.

Since at any one time there are so many forces urging the mind to do something, there is need to have a controlling authority. Otherwise, situations become chaotic and the mind cannot know who (or which memory) to listen to. This controlling authority, called "ego," is the voice of the winner of the fighting forces. So the ego says, "I am...., I want..., I will...," and so forth. In actual fact where and who is that ego? If we open up our consciousness we only find memories of past experiences. There are infinite numbers of energy forces but which one is "I"? All of them yet none of them! This "I" or personality is a fabrication. So the objective of Buddhist cultivation is to go to the state where personal identities no longer exist. That happens only if the gripping force of memory is properly dealt with in a state called nirvana or enlightenment.

Pure Intention

One's intentions can be traced from beyond the mind to the location where the physical heart exists. Try thinking hard, maybe get emotional about your thinking, and see whether your chest becomes congested. Perhaps you may discover a hive of activity, quite physical, in the heart region. We may call this energy as well as a feeling of full intimacy with the cosmic true self the "psychic heart."

A motive is always behind an intention: "I want to do this *because*...." Motives are often self-centered and intended to benefit oneself. Certain thoughts or actions, however, seem to over-ride selfish motives. These originate from a kind of wider scope of good, compassion, virtue or righteousness. In doing such an act one feels really good. The heart region seems to open up with joy. If one feels guilty, the heart area tightens and the person feels bad. There is a higher consciousness in you that in its ultimate form is called pure consciousness. The function of such consciousness is motivated by purity. Purity is the finest vibration of cosmic energy. Any intention, even a noble one, is a form of self-centered memory and cannot do away with its basic debased energy property. The complete purifying process involves the use of a *"pure instinct"* and does not come with a motive, an intention, or a condition. A successful purification process is one that can melt and dilute the debased energy and free it to harmonize with its cosmic source.

How can this be done? The faculties of the first six consciousness should not be involved. The function of the first five is a mechanical absorption process. If you use your vision, hearing, etc., as in many Qigong methods, you will be absorbing and fabricating instead of releasing. If you use your mind, as in many popular therapies, that is intention-based and fabrication. The seventh consciousness is quite mindless and offers no prospect of being put into any useful purpose.

The eighth *alaya*-consciousness is comprised largely of karmic seeds but at the center is a white transparent body, the basis of purity. You use pure intention, which is not one's intention, and is connected to the pure source of the *alaya*. On the basis of the sincere intention to be pure, you allow this process to function.

Sincere intention is no intention, taken *"as such, understood as such,"* and accepting the present *("let it be, so be it")*. In Zen teaching, it is to settle into a state of, *"not thinking and not not-thinking."* In CFQ meditation, I initiate students by identifying and directly transmitting this pure instinct and help to stimulate the process. To ensure this process is effectively carried out, one must ensure that the mind does not come in to interfere. But the mind is very active especially if you try to quiet it down. So you must give a job to the mind so that it does not have a chance to interfere. I find that the best way is to use a mantra.

The purification process brings through the external cosmic energy which is a kind of radiant energy that dissolves, melts, and dilutes the debased energy, allowing it to be freed back into the cosmos. If this takes place effectively, the changes are physical. Since the debased energy memory has been absorbed by the physical body, the melting-off process creates an *opening effect*, causing sensations of tightness, involuntary movements, and so on.

There is an easier way out. Purity and one's conscience is closely connected to universally good human virtues, and the best of these is peace. We can use peace as an effective healing tool. But conceptualizing peace is not good enough and becomes a kind of thought or intention with the tendency to create-fabricate rather then "undo." It is possible to allow smooth bioenergy flow to bring peace in and merge it with the pure instinct of one's consciousness. This can be achieved through CFQ dynamic meridian exercises that have proven effective in the treatment of diseases. The other virtues that can have a positive purifying effect, and facilitate the disease-cleansing process include:

Harmony—Beauty—Truth—Justice—Good—Compassion—Purity

These must be understood in the wider, pure, and selfless context. In the absence of the element of intention, which gives rise to fabrication, these can be slowly incubated in pure consciousness.

The process of true cultivation is slow and tedious with much pain. There should only be one motive according to Buddhist source: *Clear and illuminate your heart to discover your true instinct*. That means enlightenment. According to a Taoist source: *Repair your heart and nurture your true instinct*. The implications are profound and are well beyond the ability of most people to achieve within one lifetime. However, the cultivator has a consolation: even if one has not reached the final destiny, glimpses of it are possible. The energy of purity radiates and fills every space. It is magnificent, it is almighty, it is pure, it is bright, and it is transparent. It's reality makes physical reality unreal and pale by comparison. At the physical level a by-product of cultivation is that one's health improves.

The Three Bodies. In CFQ, we acknowledge the fact that few people will truly embark on the path of cultivation. For most, their involvement in this "energy stuff" is motivated by the need to solve their painful or life threatening health problems. So we designed the *"meridians and organ cleansing exercises,"* described in Chapter 6, which approach their problems directly without the hassle of spiritual growth details. However, CFQ aims to do much more, cleansing each of the three bodies.

a.   *The Physical Body.* Despite it's complexity, it exists in order to enable consciousness to exist. The body is like a toolkit to consciousness or a house to the spirit.

b.   *The Energy Body.* It is the black cloud of the *mano*-consciousness. It arises from within the body and forms an irregular ball with a boundary extending about three feet from the body. It is made of millions of lines, shapes, folds, and colored lights which become apparent only if opened out. CFQ exercises cleanse and re-create this body into a brightly-colored, oval-shaped ball tapering at the top, extending three to five feet at the sides and five to eight feet above the head. Aura photographs or Kirlian cameras can display emotional and thought vibrations but not the energy body.

c.   *The Spirit Body.* In an average person, the spirit body is completely shielded, and does not appear to exist. The spirit body of an advanced cultivator appears as luminescent rainbow-light shining into the eternal. CFQ meditation develops this spirit body.

The Limitations of Science

Conventional science studies the hardware body. While minute details of the anatomy of the body and physiological functions have been explored, many areas remain a puzzle. Where knowledge is missing, theories need to be formulated. In the life sciences, how close the theories come to the truth remains unknown, but new research is constantly revising previous assumptions and revealing new information and evidence. The reliability of the treatment methods and their validity are subject to constant change and re-formulation.

The body's functions are extremely complex and sophisticated, manifesting nature's wondrous creation. At any moment, all the systems are smoothly functioning simultaneously—heart, lungs, blood, breathing, stomach, intestines, liver, kidneys, brain, the nerves, etc. . Nothing stops working even for a moment. Then there must be a constant supply of raw material, air, food and water. Worn out and old cells must be constantly removed and replaced by new ones while waste products must not be allowed to remain in the body but rather ejected effectively. Within the time taken to blink an eye, uncountable events and interchanges take place within this sophisticated human machinery. Assuming scientists have discovered every minute detail of every organ and its function in the body, even then knowing how to correlate and integrate all the functions in the right order for life to exist is an immense puzzle. We see how great Nature is. By comparison any attempt by humans to play God can, at best, be of limited success. Millions of years of evolution have created for us a body that is amazingly suitable for life. Our species is not extinct! The resultant product of this evolutionary process—the complex human body might well be beyond the ability of science to completely understand. I wonder if this area should be best left to the intrinsic wisdom of nature.

I wonder how important it is that nature's creations should be left to evolve naturally. I have another wondering: perhaps the body exists because it is required to do so in order to provide us with some service we hardly appreciate. The life force in the body, motivated by consciousness to exist, tells the body to exist. Should consciousness run into conflict or disharmony, perhaps these disturbances become manifested as diseases of the body. Consciousness informs the body:

"Hey, slow down! You are going too fast. You are being unkind to yourself and me. You need a break. You are doing things I don't like. You are too greedy. You are too violent in pursuing what you want. You cause yourself harm and fellow creatures. Your pursuits fabricate too much conflict and disharmony, disrupting peace. Be fair. You are being offered the privilege of loving your fellow creatures and appreciating Nature. Look around. See what Mother Nature gives you. Beautiful, isn't it? Be realistic, seek out the truth and discard false ideas and yearnings. Clean them out and purify yourself."

The hardware body has its own mind (perhaps an alter ego) reacting to such lofty thoughts:

"Hey, shut up and stop complaining. I'm the boss. Don't you dare tell me what to do. I will pop some pills to make sure you quiet down. If you don't behave, I'd get my doctor to prick you with a needle and shut you up. If you don't get it he will cut something out and throw you away. You'll be history!"

So we have pharmaceuticals to work on the symptoms of pain and discomfort. We have intrusive surgery to removed diseased organs and tissue.

But what if your consciousness says:

"No, you can't threaten me that way. I will fight to make sure that you do things right. I will get you to listen by some other means. If not, if you succeed and I have to leave, you end up dead!"

Scientific endeavour has produced many medical breakthroughs and technological marvels. When considering the life-consciousness aspect of the hardware body, scientific explorations investigate the brain and come up with mind-mapping techniques and EEG (electroencephalo-gram) instrumentation. They measure frequencies of mental vibrations for different mental activities and emotional states. But is science getting any closer to the life-energy aspect of a being? I don't think so. It merely gathers evidence that a brain does function and has an electro-magnetic field. The science of the new millennium seems to be the study of genetics. It holds much hope and great promises for a new era of scientific discoveries and changes to human life. But is it about life itself? In my opinion, it may not have moved a step closer to the living-consciousness aspect of life. Similarly, psychological science studies human behaviour and its impact on health. These are the external manifestation of the internal consciousness but are not about the con-sciousness-energy phenomenon itself.

We have a problem. How do we go about understanding something as intangible as the life consciousness-energy aspect of a person? Perhaps philosophy and spiritual wisdom can shed some light. Got a coin? Let us say heads is the physical aspect and tails the spiritual aspect (we'll use the word "spirit" for life consciousness-energy from now on). To be alive means to live in the physical plane, signified by the coin's head being up on top. Moving the coin means to carry on the function of living. Inevitably, you cause friction and abrasion to the tail beneath and in no time it (the spirit) will be worn out. Eventually the coin will become so thin that even the head (the physical) will not exist. So how do you help the coin last longer? Maybe you should not push so hard (take life easier) so that there is less friction. Maybe you should put some lubricants on the floor (try to inculcate positive virtues). Maybe you should flip the coin so that the tail has a chance to breath or develop (by doing healing Qigong movements).

The problem posed to science: Can the coin's tail be directly observed when the head is on top? In the realm of the spirit, empirical investigation of internal activity is still valid but does not necessarily use the usual scientific technology nor assumptions. But we have a problem, and this originates not from the scientific community but from the general public's attitude towards science. I frequently have the following type of encounter: After putting all my heart and effort to work on a difficult or conventionally untreatable case for several weeks, the patient shows significant improvements. I think I can relax a bit only to be told by the client that s/he will not come back for further treatment. Though admitting that recovery is obvious, the excuse is usually about my traditional healing method which s/he doubts because it was not scientific: "My family says...., "My friends say..., "My neighbour says..., "My brothers and sisters say..., and "Everybody else says...." They use this pretext to deny reality and discredit me since I seem unscientific to them.

Teachings of the Buddha

Buddhism teaches about human suffering and how such suffering can be alleviated. The root of all sufferings (birth, aging, disease, and death) inspired Gautama Buddha in his quest for truth, which led to his realizations and enlightenment. After attaining Nirvana, he spent 45 years teaching about the doctrine of existence called dharma. His teachings were compiled into books called *Sutras*. The core of his teaching is that all matter is by nature empty. It exists because of casual factors, called karma. Living creatures have a definite lifespan, and are subject to the law of impermanence. They eventually return to a radiant Emptiness. Today, quantum physics seems to be talking about the same thing which the Buddha taught 2,500 years ago. The Emptiness he experienced and referred to might well be cosmic energy, the basis of consciousness as used in the Qigong context.

Since all matter is by nature empty, it has no real existence. Existence is an experience brought about by the law of causation. All dharmas are empty, but karma is not empty. Karma is what brought us to be what and where we are. It is the reason why we are here, why our faculties are designed to absorb and fabricate, why we cannot cognitively undo the fabrication of diseases. Eventually when the rule of impermanence takes effect, karma will lead us to rebirth. What is this powerful force of karma? I understand it to mean the debased memory energy fabricated by our consciousness, which attracts specific experiences and events of life. Sufferings therefore are merely experiences attracted by consciousness.

Followers of Buddhism are encouraged to cooperate with precepts that constitute a code of ethics and conduct. These are meant to reduce wrongdoings which in turn give rise to bad karma, and to assist in developing good karmic seeds that will eventually free a person from the entanglement of such karma that leads to suffering. In the Buddhist tradition, lay Buddhists are bound by five precepts, monks or *bikkhus* by over two hundred precepts and *bikkhunis* (nuns) by over three hundred. For those of the Mahayana tradition, who are cultivators of the Bodhisattva path, an additional thirty seven ethical guidelines have to be observed. For the purpose of our discussion, we can compare these precepts to the major virtues mentioned in this chapter.

Buddhism encourages its believers to develop insight into the teachings of Buddha. Mere teachings themselves can at best give rise to conceptual knowledge which is a fabrication. True comprehension comes from developing insight into what Buddha taught. This path involves:

Precepts *leading to* **Stillness** *leading to* **Wisdom.**

Precepts alone are not good enough, they are merely constraints. Needed is the inspiration to be good and the admiration for good. Needed also is the knowledge that life is not hopeless and that one can be self-reliant and be freed from the entanglements of karma. Such knowledge plant seeds of peace into the heart, and one's consciousness begins to open outward. That sense of peace (a pure instinct within the heart) is the beginning of Stillness. As it acquires force, it gradually leads to Stillness of both heart and body. Eventually, one develops insight when all knowledge is transformed into intuitive knowledge or wisdom.

Becoming free from suffering should not be confined only to the mental or psychological aspect of a person. The Buddha taught that the final destiny of liberation, i.e., nirvana, requires tedious cultivation of the path over many lifetimes. Yet he promised that his teachings can do away with all sufferings, including diseases. Of course, for his teaching to become acceptable there must be evidence. The evidence offered is the elimination of diseases. With such evidence, his followers would be inspired to follow his teachings. Otherwise, if the body and mind are weakened by disease, there would hardly be sufficient peace to start cultivation.

Insightful knowledge is quite the opposite of conceptual knowledge acquired through listening to dharma talks or reading. Insight involves going into, exploring, and eventually seeing the truth. Teachings, therefore, become the background and the basis which inspire the quest for truth but must be discarded in the process to make way for insight. It is logical that meditation be introduced as a practical tool for the achievement of insightful knowledge.

When karma loosens its grip, and when the forces from the *mano* consciousness pour out, the cultivator faces problems. Temptations to fabricate and threats from past wrongdoings appear all too real. The cultivator sees a terrifying reality that feels as real as physical reality. The emotional and psychological pains become converted to physical pains as outward dissolving occurs. These become unbearable even to the strongest and most determined cultivator. To reduce the discomfort arising from this problem, to better cope with it, and to ensure that the path of cultivation becomes easier, the ancients incorporated dynamic Qigong exercises in their daily routine.

The Limits of TCM

Traditional medicine claimed that their treatments used were holistic by nature. They work on the whole being and identify the root causes of diseases rather than working on the symptoms. Let us look at the principles of TCM (Traditional Chinese Medicine). Bio-energy, called qi, is the most basic function in life. Qi flow gives rise to blood flow. When there is a blockage to the flow, pain and diseases occur. When the qi is depleted, the person dies. Qi circulates in special channels in the body called meridians, and is found in abundance within the body. It is also found in the outside atmosphere.

The meridians are channels that form into a network within the body. Along the meridians there are more than 360 acupoints which are sensitive to stimulations that influence the flow of qi. The meridians are neither blood vessels nor nerves. The existence of these channels has been confirmed by delicate electrical sensing devices.

There are twelve major meridians which control and govern the functioning of five organs and six cavities. The five organs are heart, liver, spleen, lungs, and kidneys. The six cavities are large intestine, small intestine, gall bladder, stomach, urinary bladder, and triple warmer. The major meridians are further divided into yin and yang functions (a concept in Chinese culture that has universal usage inherited from primitive society) with six meridians governing the five organs classified as yin and six meridians governing the six cavities classified as yang. Yin means internal, passive, descending, front, and cold while yang means external, active, ascending, back, and hot. All twelve major meridians are connected to the hands and feet, with the yin meridians opening out in the five sensory organs, and yang meridians gathering in the head.

In TCM, when diagnosing a disease, little reference is made to the symptom itself. The diagnostic method is dependent on skills developed over many years of practical experience. Much emphasis is placed on the sensitivity of the physicians enabling them to arrive at a conclusion by assessing a patient's condition. The aspects of diagnosis include facial complexion which is divided into five colors; vocal and body odors; a description of symptoms; and sensing pulsations from the artery in the wrist. The sensing of pulsation is the most amazing. An expert physician can tell whether a woman is pregnant and determine the precise week of conception!

The conclusion derived from diagnosis is classified by its nature-yin or yang, hollow or solid. The weak and depressive nature is called hollow while a strong and aggressive nature is called solid. The diagnostic conclusion determines a basis for dealing with the meridians—whether to clear, to add, or to subtract. Sometimes, in addition to the twelve meridians, the eight special meridians are used to complement a treatment. In considering the treatment approach, the concepts of yin-yang and the five elements are used. When the yin is too strong, yang is weakened, and vice versa. The utilization of yin-yang is to achieve a right balance. The five elements are metal, wood, water, fire and earth, divided into five colors and used to represent the five organs. The five elements are both naturally complementary and mutually conflicting. For example, water (kidney) complements wood (liver) but conflicts with fire (heart). The concept of five elements is used to achieve harmony.

Actual treatment involves the use of herbs integrated with direct interventions such as acupuncture, acupressure, and moxibustion. The use of herbs is a complex skill compatible to a game of chess. Herbs are classified according to their properties of yin-yang, the five elements, and the meridians they influence. A combination of more than ten types of herbs is often used. Complementary treatments are also used requiring careful selection of acupoints guided by the goals of balancing and harmonising. Training to be a mediocre physician is easy but to be a true expert requires a whole life of dedicated involvement.

The root causes of diseases are imbalance and disharmony within the bioenergy system. Why do such imbalances and disharmonies occur? A basic medical concept states:

"The seven types of emotions cause diseases by making way for the attack of external evils and six vices."

External evils and six vices are the natural phenomenon of climate, weather and microbes of disease. By reinstituting balance and harmony a person recovers from disease. But what can you do about emotions?

Of course when one recovers using traditional methods emotions become calmer. Still, if the patient's behavior and mental traits are not addressed, a relapse into illness caused by the same flawed attitudes and behaviors can occur again and again. The area of the spirit-consciousness is also involved but TCM limits its spiritual interventions by the notion that "*diseases of the heart must be cured by medicine of the heart.*"

This mostly hands-off attitude is understandable, for the spirit-consciousness apect of a being was traditionally the responsibility of the three religions—Buddhism, Taoism and Confucianism. Chinese medicine was not even considered a trade or profession in the old society. Practitioners were the "flows of outcasts" in society, looked down upon by even petty traders and poor farmers. They were expected to keep their mouths shut even if they knew what was wrong with their high status patients. Imagine what would happen if they said, "you are sick because you have not behaved yourself." They might get beaten and their houses burnt.

They knew, however, that society placed a heavy responsibility on them. They continued to study and experiment even within their limitations. Knowledge was passed down from father to son as a family tradition. Such knowledge proves useful when incorporated into Qigong practices, and most Qigong methods have taken advantage of this fact. An over reliance on TCM gives rise to a problem—such limited healing, at best, would only be as effective as traditional physicians who had the problem of not being able to do anything much about the spirit-consciousness aspect of the disease. To transcend this limit we can expand the concept of bio-energy and meridians to complement our exploration of the spirit-consciousness, thus bringing increased benefit to humanity.

A Case Example: *The young Caucasian patient lived and worked as a musician in an Asian country for two years. He stopped work for six months as he developed chronic fatigue and severe headaches, which came even after playing his musical instrument for five minutes. He took a break by traveling and stopped in Penang. Someone told him about my energy* *healing. Over a month's period he received eight sessions together with initiation into CFQ meditation. He felt so much better that he resumed work. Three months later he wrote:*

"CFQ is definitely helping me recover from my health problems. I'm feeling stronger, my mind is clearer, my emotional state is steadier. I can now do most things that poor health denied me before. Thanks! On a spiritual level, I'm gaining an understanding of the habits, impulses, and flawed thinking which have caused me everyday frustrations in the past. So I am chewing away at the karma..... "

Three months later, he stopped by at my Center. He was on his way back home. He decided to go back to school to pursue a degree.

4

Roots of Disease

Diagnosis, Treatment & Prevention

Conventional medicine tends to investigate and treat the physical aspects of disease and regard the spiritual aspect as inconsequential. Thus if a person suffers mental or emotional disturbances like anxiety or depression (or fatigue, proneness to irritation and tantrums, etc.), the normal approach adopted is to investigate the organic origins and its biochemistry. The physical aspect can be further divided into sensations, functional symptoms and observable components:

1. Sensations: feelings of pain, aching, fever, numbness and lethargy or the lack of normal sensations.

2. Functional symptoms: lack of appetite, vomiting, restricted movements or incapability of movement, problems with bowel movement or urination, weakness, etc.

3. Observable components: appearances (or results of medical tests) of abnormalities on the body including lumps and abscess.

When medical assessments fail to show physiological causes, the case is classified as a psychological problem. In such cases, the patient is given drugs like suppressants or anti-depressants or is referred for psychiatric help. Pharmacological treatment involves the prescription of drugs aimed at managing the problems. For some problems, the physical symptoms disappear when treatment is applied. For chronic problems, the symptoms need to be kept in check by long-term usage of drugs. More drastic measures including surgery may be used. Treatment on the physical aspect of problems sometimes seems to alleviate the emotional aspect too.

We owe gratitude to the men and women of science who came up with vaccines for the control and prevention of diseases that could have caused epidemics and wiped out a whole civilisation as in the past. Continuous research and development aimed at the prevention and control of noxious bacteria, viruses and fungi gives rise to a better understanding, control and management of problems arising from such agents. Many diseases have become preventable and treatable. There is, however, the ever present danger of noxious agents becoming more adaptive and outperforming scientific technology.

The medical profession rightfully is cautious and responsible when it uses the word "relief" rather than "cure". Indeed, any problem big or small, from a minor cut onwards ultimately depends on the body to heal itself. Nature does the healing and treatment is confined to proper problem management. What can be done humanly is provide the necessary stimulation and support enabling nature to better deal with the problem.

Few problems disappear totally after treatment. Some problems recur frequently even after the symptoms are subdued. For major illnesses, even the best available treatments often only reduce the discomfort or slow down the rate of deterioration. Current medical knowledge is inadequate to deal with chronic problems. On top of that many problems are still regarded as incurable. There is also the problem of side-effects from prescription drugs that subdue one symptom but give rise to another problem or series of problems. Of course, medical knowledge is far from exhausting its full potential. Ongoing research reveals a continuous achievement of new understanding and knowledge.

But a lacuna remains in conventional medicine. Current and developing approaches are centered on treating the physical body with little consideration for the mind's role and no appreciation of the spiritual aspects of problems. Can a holistic exploration bring about greater benefit to humanity by providing better solutions to existing problems as well as transcending the limits encountered by conventional science? For instance, longevity has been dramatically extended today but aging and its related health problems pose great challenges to medical science. Human beings still deserve quality care even when inhabiting an aging and vulnerable body and experiencing increasing spiritual concerns. There is often a problem with impending death and the fear and helplessness associated with it. Though everyone has to face it one day, if there were more and better ways to help people approach dying with dignity and fearlessness, that will be a tremendous benefit for humanity.

The increasing popularity of alternative medicine is encouraging. Non-traditional therapeutic venues can often enrich and complement science as presently developed. Unquestionably, some people benefit from traditional therapies, but there is an exciting frontier beyond the constraints of present day medical science.

Tension As The Basis of Diseases

From the very beginning of my clinical trial-and-error healing in 1980, I noticed physical responses and reactions in the patient's body. There were muscle twitches, vibrations, pulsations, muscles inflating, breathing patterns changes, and so on. Some patients developed strange movements which were beyond voluntary control. Some patients yelled out in a release of emotion. I too felt certain binding forces on myself and my muscles, and my own breathing and posture reflected my feelings. Patients told me of sensations of warmth or cold in their bodies. At first I did not investigate what these meant. Rather I felt proud that I had the power to make such things happen.

The incentive to explore the implications of such phenomenon occurred when I started healing on a full time basis. Large numbers of patients and students gave me ample chances to observe and apply my healing skills, while the pressure to improve results kept me hard at my pursuit of more knowledge. I soon noticed that each person had a unique or different posture, a different shape and different physical proportions. I learned that differences in physique and posture were often related to underlying tensions or hidden problems. I noted the hip, its shape and contact on the chair when a person sits; the angle and inclination of the curve on the person's back; the degree of curve on a person's abdomen, sometimes showing a deep horizontal line; the curvature around the solar plexus; the shapes of the shoulder and neck; the tendency to raise the body or slouch; the angle of the head to the neck; the tightness between the brows; the facial expressions; the way the patient stood and the proportions of the limb's length.

Touching and sensing muscle textures provided much information. The overall texture is different from one person to another. Younger people are very different from the older people, and females are different from males. Within the same person, different groups of muscles appear differently. There are knots of various sizes and shapes appearing all over the body. Such noticeable knots, which readily form into lumps and chunks, appear to tie in with the individual's appearance and posture. These are often a cause for concern.

I discovered that there is a relationship between a person's appearance and posture, and the kind of problem presented. With CFQ energetic treatments physical changes are readily observable. The process of treatment itself gives rise to changes in breathing pattern, muscular twitches, pulsations, throbbing and involuntary movements of limbs and body. In most cases, after a successful treatment of once a week over a period of six months to one year, a person's posture and appearance takes on a very different look. I encouraged some of my patients to take photographs of themselves at the commencement of treatment and compare these with those taken after the completion of treatment. Some patients and students could not hide their amazement as they reported dramatic changes: e.g., increases in height, ranging from 1 to 2 cm, and this in adults in their 30's to 50's!

The knots and muscle stiffness together with the posture are an expression of a person's feeling of tension, pains or discomfort. When patients make such remarks as, "I have pains…; "I have indigestion…; "I am short of breath…," and so on, their named symptoms proved coincident with some postural misalignment.

I wish to invite you to explore this yourself in order to give you a better idea of the relationship between observable physique and underlying diseases. Observe the postures of those you know who have health problems and verify, if they allow, links with their postures. Observe and evaluate young children and note the differences. Tune in to their bodies to sense the disharmonies, the pressures within, the discomfort, the emotional states and on. Or, observe unobtrusively how they sit for five minutes. This is a skill that needs gradual development but the outcome can be amazing.

A word of caution: Do not overdo this! You can easily absorb a lot of undesirable forces and energies from other people which can be harmful to you. For those of you who are not intending to practice CFQ, stop after one or two attempts when your curiosity is fulfilled. Any problem or discomfort arising can be easily dissipated through changing to other activities which distract your attention. For those who practice CFQ, do not be over-ambitious. If you absorb too much too fast, your practice may not be able to clear out the unwanted energies.

My healing work and meditation experience encouraged me to explore the formation of such irregularities and blockages in the body. I began to see and vividly feel the hidden implications. The energy formation observed is a composition of countless lines, folds, wrinkles, sheets, and shapes. It is so complex that I could not find beginnings or ends. It also appears as different shades of gray or darkness manifesting different colored lights and formations. The appearance of energy forces can also be compared to a ball of messed up yarn or crumpled piece of paper soaked in a pail of glue and left to dry. They are centered in the solar plexus or heart region with a heavier concentration in the upper section and they extend beyond the physical body. The body's limbs do not have separate formations but appear to be encompassed within this ball of forces.

This ball of forces seems to be the foundation of an individual's appearance and posture. The knots, weaknesses, and diseased areas show as the presence of heavy concentrations of folds and intersections of lines and sheets forming a darker shade of gray. This energy formation affects blood circulation and body functions and traps bodily wastes, as well as heat and cold. With aging this energy formation becomes more compact and darker. It promotes the wasting of muscles. The space where the muscles used to be becomes filled up with body fluid. This together with poor circulation leads to fluid retention and sometimes give rise to overweight problems.

These tension forces appear to be responsive to bio-energy stimulation, thought or emotions. When a CFQ healer sends in his or her energy, the forces become activated causing visible bodily responses. Acupuncture and acupressure produce similar effects. Emotions and thoughts stir up the tension even more. The effect of CFQ meditative healing is similar to soaking a ball of yarn in a pail of water. The hardened tension dissolves and becomes converted back to glue as the threads are slowly freed. The dissolved glue gradually thins and loses its sticky property. This dissolving process can be quite painful for some people as the muscles, organs, and bones revitalize.

There are some basic patterns that exist even at birth. They appear as crisscrossed patterns generally from left-right or front-back which together form into an energy center of activity. One pattern is located in the head with its center between the eyes, another in the neck with its center in the throat behind the Adam's apple, another at mid-body with its center near the physical heart, and another at the hip with its center behind the urinary bladder. I believe that such energy centers and cross patterns are necessary for body stimulation and life support. Since these are crosses, they generate a suction force attracting life's experiences. Over the lifespan they govern physical and mental growth, deterioration, and eventually death.

Even at birth, there seems in each person an established temperament. Individual characteristics are evident in the features of these centers. Such primary characteristics play a major part in shaping an adult's character. Education and life's experiences play a less significant role. These inherent features also have a big say in an individual's course and experience of life, including susceptibility to diseases. The law of karma offers a possible explanation. Karma can include genetics since it describes departed energy forces in the death transition as finding new parents with similar dispositions and inclinations.

Since, among other things, we are born to absorb and create, the reverse of absorbing and fabricating (letting-go) is extremely difficult. All too often, we hear people complaining, "I can't control my thoughts; I know relaxation is good for me but I can't relax." I will now explore how to overcome such obstacles.

The Spiritual-Consciousness Counterpart

Patients who lie down while receiving CFQ treatments often drift into a dream state. Sometimes their consciousness drifts far away. Frequent remarks are, "I was dreamy; my imagination was very strong; my spirit went out of my body." During treatment, the opening out of the folds throws out a high mass of dark cloud that sometimes appear to fill up every space. Within the cloud, there are images of pictures, people, scenery, information, shapes and so on. This energy cloud projects objects and to me it looks like watching a movie. Alternating between dark clouds there are white clouds.

I am touching on the spiritual-consciousness as an aspect of the energy functions of a person. Tension, manifested as folds, is the *mano* consciousness as explained in Chapter 3. As its dark clouds clear out, milky translucent clouds, from the *alaya* consciousness, are evident in the outward releasing process. These turn into the *mano* consciousness. The release process from the eighth *alaya* consciousness, penetrates the first five senses of the body. The manifestations appear physical as do the pains and sensations experienced. The changes produced are physical.

Where does the raw material from this healing process come from? Within the healer pure transparent light from the deep *alaya* consciousness has, through long periods of practice, become a radiant light with no boundary. It is often tinged with a golden hue, and is the base light of compassion which is necessary for a healer to heal. Purification and the radiant effect create an outpouring in the energy-consciousness field leading to an opening and elongating effect on the physical body.

How can consciousness be so physically intimate with the body? In preceding paragraphs I talked about inherent cross-formations and force centers. These can be categorized according to their functions–the head to heart region for thoughts and emotions and the neck to hip region for physical actions. They are connected and mutually influencing through the shared section of the energy system between the neck to the heart region. Emotions and intentions originate from the heart and press upon the mind. The mind says "I want" and calls upon the body to get ready for action. Actions in turn register as memories within the body, heart and mind. This process fabricates millions of memories in the form of energy folds. They are all enfolded as the images, events, information and forms in a way somewhat similar to the pattern in which a video cassette stores a whole movie. They are in fact nothing but debased energy branded with one's personal identity or "I".

Life is tough, with the millions of "I's" all fighting to be heard. They have strength which binds and squeezes the body, organs, and the mind. The ego allows the winner to speak through the mind to effect its "I want." In acting or doing something one fabricates karma with its consequences and that forms another set of folds. If you do nothing, the "I" continues to ask for attention in its bid for power.

Recall the two sections–head to heart and neck to hip, with the overlap of neck to heart. Every thought and activity is sorted and stored in the brain or mind in an organized way but also stored in unsorted form in the torso. Intention originates from the heart and surges upward to be manifested through the mind. The mind institutes action which requires more mental processing. The mind (sixth consciousness) appears to be designed as the most active energy organ and continues to be compressed upward. As a result, muscular shrinkage occurs in the limbs due to the inability of the body to replace old muscle cells. Eliminating the old, destroyed cells and retaining normal functions of internal organs is inhibited by the compressing effect. Observe the elderly. Watch the way they move. Look for the evidence of suspension from the way their feet contact the ground. Look for evidence of shortening in their limbs to the extent that knees and elbows become bent (unfortunately this problem is medically called arthritis). See how the body is deformed by the compressing effect (called osteoporosis). If the lethargy and rigidity is so obvious outside, imagine the suffering of the organs inside.

The onset of disease of any kind causes a surge of energy forces fabricating a suspending effect. This aggravates disharmony, gives rise to mental and emotional disturbances, disrupts physiological functions and inhibits recovery. Thus the Chinese refer to the old, aged, and diseased states as *"solid on top and hollow at the bottom."* Repair requires clearing the energy blockages by a draining down process, described as, *"when the bioenergy sinks down, hundreds of diseases disappear."* This is easier said than done, as the healing process necessarily involves the spiritual aspect that is not attended to adequately. However, there is clear indication that harmony and spiritual well-being are dependant on energy flow. Nevertheless an over-emphasis on bioenergy seems evident.

Frequent negative and undesirable emotions also produce an upsurge of energy. When a person gets angry or depressed, the energy surge activates the *mano* consciousness forming a cloud-like shield in the upper body, especially the head, causing disorientation. The limbs contract and the physiological functions become compressed causing shivers. If the person becomes violent his strength can be enormous. After the tantrum, the release brings on tiredness and weakness of the limbs. Excessive or frequent negative emotions make a person vulnerable to ill-health.

The Failure of Religion

Our discussion so far points toward the spirit-consciousness aspect of a person as the basic source of disease, suggesting that working on this aspect might provide a more complete solution to human problems. This sets me to wondering why priests, clergy, or monks are normally unable to do healing. They are looked up as experts on the human spirit. Why do so many eliminate healing from their job description? The health-care system (despite its present inadequacies), with its professionals and hospitals has every reason to carry on. They have highly trained professionals to deal with, manage, and control people's illnesses and suffering. I do not like to think of where we would be without this medical care.

But temples, monasteries, and churches can play a stronger role in mutual care. After all, the basic teaching in most religions affirms the importance of peace and harmony as an antidote for human suffering. Since diseases are among the most prominent of human sufferings, one would reasonably expect that healing is one of the responsibilities of religious organizations. The healing tools are readily available in all religious systems: peace, harmony, calmness.

The basic human tendency for absorbing, acquiring and fabricating is widespread. The product is disharmony and disturbance. The solution is to let-go, undo, and radiate with a purity achieve by peace. But in the face of the self-centered tendency (I think of it as ignorance or evil), religious wisdom seems to lose out. What religions advocate is often good and contradicts evil, but when humans are engrossed in evil they suffer accordingly. The so called good they do becomes limited to a selfish good.

Admiration for God and devotion to good becomes ritualistic worship aimed at invoking blessings. In fact, believers would do better if encouraged to contribute to the pool of God's blessings rather than to request for blessings. Throughout history, the enormous wealth of kingdoms and civilizations were spent building golden statues and ostentatious places of worship. Corruption manifests itself as different groups accuse each other of idol worshipping. In addition, some elite and some rulers, either through ignorance or selfish motives, capitalize on human weakness by promoting superstition.

The teachings written in sacred books are meant to inspire. Instead people have used scriptures to obtain and maintain power. The proper use of scriptures requires true faith and utmost sincerity so that the positive humanitarian values will not be held captive in the mind but nurture pure consciousness. Faith in spiritual matter is impoverished in our time. But how could it be otherwise when our bodies are so entangled and disharmonised by ignorance? Strong faith can give rise to great miracles that call us beyond rationality. Strong energy forces produced by faith can introduce miraculous changes that literally alter prevailing karmic tendencies.

If the religious minded were to spend hours daily in liberated prayer or meditation in full faith, with a willingness to eliminate egocentricity and human weakness, eventually they would realize their goal of getting close to the greatest Good. They would see *Go*(o)*d* or divinity within, freeing their own imprisoned Buddha-seed. When the power of *Go*(o)*d* or Buddha light shines, it fills every space. It is pure, it is bright, it is transparent, it is boundless, it is magnificent and it is ultimate reality. Their work should shift from merely preaching to sitting or lying down in prayerful repose. Such total looseness facilitates the purest outpouring of spiritual energy for a purified person (though not suitable for a novice who tends to fall asleep). They need not do anything except let the power of *Go(o)d* permeate them. This good willed action allows them to be cleansed of their fabrications and emerge healed.

Say Hello to Your Spirit

Your spirit is not some cold and unapproachable entity that dwells in some remote place. This life force is right in you and has, for long, been waiting for you to be reclaimed. Now sit back on a reclining chair, close your eyes, loosen your body and relax. Try to keep an open mind, be non-judgmental, and detach yourself. Let peace reign. What is happening now? Is there a uniform patch of darkness? No thoughts? Nothing? Actually yes, there will be plenty of things happening! You see colors, flashes of light among the darkness. You see your thoughts, images, and forgotten messages. You see them appearing and disappearing and reappearing. You might see so many changing so rapidly that you can't keep track of them. They fight and quarrel. Check your body or the space beyond that (supposedly not your body). Feel the sensations, the motions and activities, the feelings and impulses. Explore and go beyond. Remember to remain detached and peaceful and not to participate. You may doze off. Even in that dreamy state you are busy.

Healing & Consciousness

What you have experienced is a glimpse into the sixth and seventh realms of impure consciousness, parts of your spirit counterpart. Already you see conflict and disharmony. Maybe you will say, "No, nothing. That is just my imagination." If so, let it be. Recall our innate tendency to draw in energy forces. These energy forces are inward compressing and upward suspending forming folds, blockages and disharmonies. For healing to be effective, it must involve an outward-opening (radiating) and downward-flushing process to undo the folds, clean the blockages, and bring about harmony within and between the body, mind and spirit.

Healing energy is the reverse of debased energy effected by the human tendency to absorb, acquire, and fabricate. The power of energy healing is pure instinct from the depth of the *alaya*-consciousness. The mind should not be involved in the healing process as its fabricating tendency adds tension. Some healing systems use visualization or intention of the mind to produce fast and impressive results. I avoid this temptation.

Purity is vibrant, homogeneous, and uncomplicated. The healing force in operation must therefore be consistent with purity. This process conforms to the sense of stillness and joyousness experienced by the healer. To ensure stillness, simplicity, and to prevent the mind being drawn into fabricating, the healer relies upon the values of truth, compassion, and beauty. These values interact with elemental cosmic energy to become an ocean of healing energy that is radiant and boundless.

To achieve such interactive purity a cultivator must train for a long time with perseverance and dedication. The ocean of healing energy is actually the spirit body (one of the three bodies). It is transparent with a golden tinge, the color of compassion. Compassionate love is a necessary ingredient without which the spirit body cannot cleanse the negative karma of a patient. Cleansing of karma is called *"Metta"* in Buddhist philosophy, meaning the giving of merits. Only after receiving sufficient *Metta* can the negative karma become purified. It is manifested as physical debased energy folds in the body and as a dark cloud of the *mano*-consciousness leaving the patient.

The word cultivator from the Orient means a person journeying on the way to the realization of truth. It is a life-long process involving much hardship and its rewards are unconditional. It requires a strong faith and excludes normal, analytical intelligence. Cultivation develops the intuitive wisdom that reveals the real meaning of truth. The word cultivator is significantly different from the Western phrase "seeker of truth" which includes much cognitive and intellectual activity.

Healing is performed with minimal physical effort. The healer (sitting if convenient) simply enters the meditative state. The patient is asked to sit or lie down to promote relaxation and looseness of the body. The patient is not encouraged to co-operate since such effort would use the mind and that can prevent optimal healing results. Of course, it is not helpful if the patient is busy thinking of something else. So I tell them: "Lie down and take a nap."

The healing energy generated by meditation becomes an ocean that floods the patient whose energy appears to be like a ball of dark colored yarn. Awareness permeates the energy-consciousness reality, which is often more real to the patient than the physical realities of touch and vision. The ball of yarn frequently changes in shape, size and shades of color. It throws up pictures, forms, messages, shapes and images. The patient drifts between deep sleep, dreams, and being wide awake. The dreams are rich in variety and content, often with the patient reporting, "my soul has drifted far away," or "I don't know where I am." Some of them may snore and yet say afterward that they did not sleep at all. Some will suddenly jump out of bed and take a few minutes to find out where they are and what they were doing.

The changes, for the healer, are felt clearly like the melting of glue. They can cause great pain. The changes relate to the physical reactions of the patient and are readily observable: such as changes in the rate and pattern of breathing, stiffness which is released by a physical jerk of the limbs or body, raising or twitching of the chest, rapid eye blinking, and movements of mouth. The head tilts, the body quivers and vibrates, limbs stretch and elongate like a piece of rubber. The patient may not feel or remember much but often describe some physical sensations.

A Holistic Definition of Cure

One way of regarding a person is as the sum total of his or her life experiences and actions from birth, or if the concept of karma is used, from time immemorial. Such life experiences and actions are preserved in the form of energy forces that are the basis of the formation of the physical body. In so far as they are fabricated effects that conflict with the natural design of physiological functions, disharmony is inevitable. Such disharmony gives rise to physical diseases and undesirable emotional experiences. In other words, diseases are part of being alive as we normally know it.

Symptoms of distress are somewhat like the protruding irregular edges of things sticking out of a shopping bag. A minimal cure, as it were, comes from taking out some of the items from the overloaded bag. More often than not, the items with protruding edges can be easily and visually identified from outside the bag and removed by putting your hand into the bag. However, certain items hidden at the bottom of the bag may only be taken out after clearing most of the items at the top. Persons with chronic problems most often need a healer. A person seeking treatment frequently has a few chronic problems, symptomatically less disturbing than the presenting problem. For middle-aged or older ones with deteriorating physical functions, every part of the body is likely to be in varying degrees of decline, with some parts already showing as physical problems. In such cases, even though a patient complains of one chronic problem, it is probable that at least another ten or twenty problems are developing from head to toe, stretching from inside to outside!

The job for the healer is therefore to throw some of the troublesome items out of the bag. As these items are of the energy consciousness type the healer actually need not do anything physically. But not doing anything physically is doing everything energetically. The items with jagged edges are often prominent energetically and therefore can be removed first. However, if they happen to hide at the bottom of the bag, it takes more time to remove them.

Some symptoms, even those that has been there for many years, can be removed within a few treatments. Other symptoms, even manifesting recent problems, may take one or two years of weekly sessions, even though the results may be apparent and impressive earlier.

Now check out the body (what's left in the bag). The patient ends up with a lighter bag after the treatment. Whether the symptoms have disappeared totally is of secondary importance. At least, now the person's bag can carry more things and is less in danger of breaking. But there are also fringe benefits. The other problems (which were not distressful enough for him to command treatment or were seemingly hopeless) are gone.

Thus, the holistic energy consciousness approach here is applied with little concern for symptoms. But there can be problems. A patient, even though experiencing a tremendous overall well-being, may still continue to manifest certain symptoms (even in a much lesser degree). Such patients sometimes complain the treatments were not effective. There are some who demand to know how long it takes to eliminate a certain symptom. A reasonable estimate is possible but not always accurate. The healer may discover much more about the seriousness of the disease in the process of treatment, so estimates must change. Healing often is a tough, messy job. We declare with utmost honesty that we do it with a sincere, truthful heart. Cooperation from the patient and an open attitude with positive expectations will improve the healing process.

Course of Miracles

Healing is not all pains and heartaches. A job well-done is reason enough for great joy and satisfaction. You can see better aligned posture, the smoother complexion that was once all frowns and wrinkles, the glow of health as the face sparkles, and the patient's cheerful mood and jovial attitude. What a contrast with the depression suffered weeks earlier! You can share in the way parents excitingly narrate how their once sickly children are excelling in school after a few short treatment sessions. If the healer stops treatment after the miraculous session, he would have made a worldly wise decision. The news of the miracle and the healer's reputation would spread like wildfire. But the true healer knows that much more needs to be done and treatment should continue. The miracles cease to cause any more excitement as the patients see the human limitations of the healer continuing to struggle to fix their problems.

Good results that come after a long period of hard work can hardly be called miracles. Some changes, however, are amazing miracles that the healer may only dream of at the beginning of treatment. A person whose acute back pain made his body so crooked he was unable to walk did in fact straighten and walk. Or another who had to be carried in, rose up and walked out with a wide grin, after a half hour session without even being touched. Another who said that he could barely eat for months yelled for food in the middle of the session. A patient who had been constipated for years could hardly wait until the session finished to run to the toilet for his big "dump" and thereafter has regular bowel movements. All these (and hundreds more) have quickened and excited relieved patients. But the healer knows that much more must be done. A manifestation that appears miraculous is not all there is to complete healing. Neither can it intentionally happen. Attempting to force results interferes with healing and leads to a poor session.

For a true cure to occur, physical re-alignment of body structures, muscles, and the bone frame must take place. While this is done without physical manoeuvres pain and discomfort still arise from the healing process. In addition, deep internal pains, trapped at a level beyond nerve sensation, must be released. Also, emotional pains may be converted into physical pains in the releasing process. Pains, numbness, fever, etc. also exist in the energy realm and must be fully cleared out. Patients will feel the discomforts in the clearing process. Such pains and discomforts are often quite bearable. However, some of my patients' reactions defy logic. They are willing to endure great pains from conventional medicine as experienced in surgery, physiotherapy, physical massage, daily physical exercises, and the side effects of prescription and herbal remedies. But when pains come from energy healing, they become very anxious and have little tolerance for the discomfort.

There were people who complained that their problems remained unchanged even after ten sessions. One patient said, "The backache is still there." He initially came for treatment for headache but made no mention of the backache. After treatment, not only was the headache completely gone but he was freed of other problems (not presented for treatment) including a stiff neck, frozen shoulder, trigger fingers, indigestion, and chest congestion. His conclusion, "No, the treatment didn't work." Many find the required regular treatment schedule tiresome and search out some conventional or herbal health product for quick relieve.

Perhaps 30 per cent of the highly successful treatment patients remain appreciative and recommend me to their friends and defend my work. This, by the way, is very good since with a 100 per cent support I would soon be exhausted and burn out.

Buddha, a most effective healer, was right! To meditate and let-go from the spiritual-consciousness level is an "*out of the world method.*" To consume, absorb, and fabricate is a readily acceptable and tangible "*method of the world.*" Worldly beings, however, find spiritual reality unbearable and admire the "*flowers in the mirrors*" and the "*moon in the water.*" I must, arguably, have heavy karma to try to introduce this out-of-the-world approach to healing. My enthusiasm for CFQ comes from my seeing it work. My next focus of attention is on healing and karma.

Karma & Disease

If there is an action, there is a reaction. This principle of physical science has its equivalent in human consciousness—what you are today is because of what you and your world used to be, and what you are doing now will influence how you will be in the future. Your mental and physical activities, experiences and knowledge all contribute to what you are. These influence your energy-consciousness making patterns that are perpetuated, giving rise to personal actions, physical health, and life events. Diseases too are consequences of stored causes, actions done or not done. If diseases are consequences originating from past actions, then suffering once completed, should mean that the problems are over. Why do people have to suffer prolonged consequences without getting over their problems? Why is karma so unfair? In the first place, there is much disharmony and restlessness well before the onset of a disease. Suffering disturbs the peace, causes pain, and facilitates ignorance. There is then the stress of wanting to do something to get rid of the pain. Depression, hatred, anxiety, violence are vengeful products that are directed not only within, but also fabricate blame for the people around.

A distressed person may make poor choices, as, for example, by preparing to fight back, attempting to eliminate the suffering. If the patient had, instead, calmed down and introduced positive values such as peace and harmony, disengaging from the suffering, the disease problem might soon be over. But this cannot be expected from a person with little understanding about the spirit. It could be difficult for people who have rarely shown much resilience in the face of past adversity. Therefore, their natural emotional response creates further conflict or karma which encourages the continuation of suffering and deterioration.

Does that mean that evil persons suffer more diseases? No. On the contrary, conscientious people may tend to suffer disease more than the dishonest person. For all humans, to carry on the process of life involves actions, some of which involve little personal choice. We do not know why nor how we have made the choice to be born. Those who are conscientious may refrain from doing certain things but the mind's numerous needs and desires must be met. Being alive requires that a long list of "wants" be satisfied. The "I want" refrain keeps repeating itself causing disturbances. If things are done against one's conscience, one is disturbed. The pent-up disharmony eventually erupts as a disease. Reprehensible types of people, on the other hand, do not suffer this disturbance. They can have an "I want" selfish motive and do it without any qualms. Their actions may, of course, attract revenge and provoke bad consequences. I am not trying to encourage evil actions but merely making the point that putting one's energy into blaming in either case makes more problems. It is best to take full responsibility for the disease problem and utilize it as an opportunity to cleanse the spirit. Moving forward is the best choice. Karma means that every action will be repaid somehow even beyond this lifespan. From this perspective, it is not a bad idea to have conscience.

To solve karmic problems we can again rely on the teachings of Buddha. The past cannot be re-created, and thinking will not change it. Such speculation can only fabricate obstacles for our future. Be wise enough to walk out of the past. The future cannot be fabricated by wilful thinking, so don't waste your energies in such an act. You only fabricate a stumbling block for yourself. Pose the question: *Where are you?* That "you," one minute ago, is gone and the "you" one minute after has yet to become. Want the greatest good for yourself, smile *now*, think and be good.

Preaching, no matter how convincing, remains preaching. It is useless for a person who is deeply entangled in disease. The sick need direct action from a helper with experience in cleansing others' karma. As a person with "bad" karma I can speak with much experience about this, having long struggled to understand the truth to purity. Over the years, I have learned how to deal with the shrewdness of karma. The patient must also do his or her part to cleanse the disease-causing karma and not rely solely on the healer. Healing that is effective for karmic cleansing has not come easily for me. While exposing others' negative karma during treatment, I learned how to neutralize its bad consequences and protect myself against it. It has now become possible for others to learn how to do it for themselves. So for those seeking help, I recommend that they learn how to do this (meridian movements and meditation). Some patients are unable to be students for various reasons, so I accept them for direct healing. There are those who need direct healing together with their own practice. The majority, however, need not receive any direct healing but can get well through their own practice.

Relaxation and Healing

What we have just discussed about healing is in fact about relaxation. The once popular "relaxation movement" which resulted in many stress management workshops and books has lost steam. Relaxation techniques, even if successful, seem not to have lasting effects. Many people have ceased to believe that relaxation works and is a potent antidote to illness. But generally, people appreciate that there is some value in being relaxed.

Well, relaxation does work! The problem is neither the general public nor relaxation gurus appreciate what true relaxation involves. They don't know the benefits that can accrue from it. My caution is, you cannot succeed in being relaxed when major problems have already occurred. It does not work that way. Relaxation must be systematically and diligently practiced well before the onset of problems. If you do that, problems may not even arise. In the end, the relaxation effect depends on actions that are consistent with the out-of-this-world techniques of CFQ.

A Case Example: *The female patient, in her early thirties, was diagnosed with second stage cancer of the cervix. She was scheduled for the complete removal of the reproductive organs, followed by radiation and chemotherapy. While undergoing the medical tests, she became frightened by the sight of the suffering of patients receiving treatment. Her search for an alternative remedy led her to my Center. It is a five-hour drive from her home. She came over two weekends and received four sessions. Her condition improved and she felt better. When her surgical appointment came, she pleaded with the surgeon not to perform a full-scale hysterectomy. The operation was delayed and only a scraping was performed. The biopsy results showed that the cells had reverted to pre-cancer cells*

Three months later she was scheduled for complete surgery. During the waiting period, she came back to the Center for 16 healing sessions. Two weeks prior to the surgery, she went to the hospital for a check up.

Astounded, she was told that she was completely free from cancer. She continued seeing me two or three times yearly. Her annual medical check has shown no cancer for the past four years.

5

Chaoyi Fanhuan Qigong: CFQ

My personal journey led me to develop a system which I believe will be of great interest to you as a possible solution to your own health problems and those of others. The traditional healing conceptual framework from which I approach health issues and the treatment and prevention of diseases is distinctively different from conventional medicine and even from most methods of alternative medicine.

Strictly speaking, in healing work, I do not do treatment. I do not use drugs, herbs or any medical equipment. I do not advertise. People come to me through friends or family member's recommendations and by their own choice. The healing achieved might be labelled as a power-of-the-mind effect. I know from experience, however, that my energy interventions, developed in a state of meditation, produce physical and healing outcomes as intended or requested by the patient.

Many of the illnesses I treat are life-threatening in which recovery eludes most conventional or alternative methods. Some illnesses are medically impossible to treat. My success rate is far more than the 30 per cent success rate evident in the placebo effect. At least 80 per cent of my cases show significant improvements within the first three sessions, and 70 per cent of those cases continuing with the scheduled treatments recover or are cured completely.

Since my first meditation experience on the rock in the middle of a mountain stream some 35 years ago, I have learned many types of Qigong, meditation and healing systems. I have read many books and tried the techniques recommended. My search for truth led me to a series of strange and unpredictable experiences. This book describe how I developed systematic methods of healing that you can effectively use without going through the sufferings that I endured.

CFQ As Alternative Medicine

My healing work based on the principles of CFQ shows that is effective on a wide variety of health problems including:

1. Those that can just be effectively relieved or cured by conventional medicine. CFQ treatment can be used either alone or as a complement. Some health problems may be cured much faster, even instantaneously, by CFQ, while others may take a longer time than with the use of conventional medicine;

2. Chronic problems that can be controlled and managed by conventional medicine. CFQ treatment is administered while the patient is required to continue with the prescribed medications. Many of these people benefit either by being able to eventually dispense with prescription drugs or by using reduced dosage (their physicians are the ones who make these decisions based on the conditions of the patient during periodic checkups). Some who have to continue with the same medication experienced an added sense of physical and mental well-being.

3. Treatment of illnesses that conventional medicine is unable to influence, including, organic or congenital disabilities or paralysis from spinal injury.

4. Life-threatening diseases some of which are in terminal stages of development including cancer, leukaemia, thalassaemia and coma; and

5. Genetic disorders such as Down's Syndrome.

I do not claim an ability to deal with every illness and disease. I am limited in my ability and my level of attainment and I have turned down requests for treatments for problems which are beyond my ability. Also, given that you and I live in different parts of the world and given further the need for time and personal attention to perform satisfactory work, it is unlikely that I can personally help you. I must disclaim any legal responsibility for, or liability arising from what I have written.

At the moment I am the only full time CFQ healer. Some of my students have developed different degrees of healing ability but need time to further nurture their skills and proficiency. Although healing ability is a natural product of CFQ practice, some students lack the confidence or the sensitivity needed to realize that they too can heal. It is up to you to make of CFQ methods what is in your best interests. In the light of such limitations, I take it as my responsibility to develop a system and training methods which you can do on your own to effectively deal with and eradicate your health problems. My greatest reward will be the benefits you garner from your efforts. Having begun my journey of exploration alone, I will be profoundly rewarded if the product of my efforts can be of benefit to you.

I have a secret motive—that you not only solve your own problems but help others to solve theirs. I hope that one day, you may develop such healing abilities as will surpass mine. In that way, with many manifesting such abilities, society at large will have no excuse for failing to use our skills. We will be able to do much good for humanity.

My goal is far-ranging and the time required for the change-over will be long. But knowing the true meaning of our work and the implication that we can really make a difference in the world, is reason enough for great hope. That gives peace and stills our hearts to be unmoved by difficult circumstances or hardships. Possible storms or turbulence will not lift a hair or disturb you. Even if the world crashes, you will continue to be tranquil. Should heaven shake or earth shudder there will scarcely be a tremor stirred in our hearts.

Disclaimer

When there is a health problem, you must first ensure that you receive proper medical treatment and care. CFQ is an alternative healing practice, but for readers it should only be a form of supplementary treatment. Prompt medical attention is necessary to reduce the risks caused by any delay, which may put the life of the patient at stake, or result in unnecessary deterioration and complication. Infections can often be well taken care of by conventional medicine. Self-practice or receiving CFQ treatments together with medication can greatly shorten the time taken for recovery.

Proper care and management are necessary for injuries. In some cases, for example, broken bones, the patient will be completely restrained from any movements. Therefore it will be impossible to practice CFQ until much later. Treatment by a CFQ healer can ensure proper healing and reduce the risk of deformation or permanent damage. Practice CFQ to get rid of any negative residual effect and to regenerate muscles and cells. From my clinical observations backed by hundreds of actual cases, this is a more complete healing method than normal exercises or physiotherapy. Residual effects of say ten years can be easily cleared by practice.

In cases of emergencies, life-sustaining and emergency measures can only be performed by medical professionals. However, the effectiveness of CFQ treatment for coma and amnesia cases may be well beyond what medical professionals think possible. To avoid any complications or risk, the patients must also seek medical treatment.

I am trying my best to enable you to benefit from the practice of CFQ. However, as you come from varied social, cultural and educational backgrounds, the positive conditions under which you practice CFQ may be complex or difficult to follow. I believe that CFQ will be beneficial for you despite the varying conditions unique to each person. We believe that most of you will be able to restore your health through practice. Patience and perseverance are necessary as the duration taken to heal varies in each person. In case of doubt, you would do well to check with your physician to see if you can safely practice CFQ. Some of you may not follow or understand the instructions completely. Some of you may find that your personal unhealthy habits are too strong or that you are overly self-centered and have difficulty reducing such tendencies. This may make your practice less effective.

While I honestly and sincerely believe that CFQ is safe and effective for you, I am unable to completely foresee the kinds of problems you may face when you embark on CFQ practice. They may not have any connection with, but may nevertheless be blamed on, your practice. Therefore, it is fair that I should not be held responsible for unsuccessful practice, damage or injury related to the practice of CFQ. You undertake to follow the practices entirely on your own accord. I, or any persons authorised by me, hereby disclaim any liability or responsibility arising from, or alleged to be arising from your practice of CFQ, either through books, workshops, classes or any other medium.

CFQ Exercises As Preventive Community Health

The life-threatening danger of disease, risk of long-term or permanent disability, and incapacity arising from disease, give rise to the urgent need for preventive measures to reduce the escalating disease rate. CFQ practitioners and persons receiving treatments generally report a better sense of well-being in addition to health improvements. Reduction of recurring illnesses and relapse are readily observable. Many recipients felt that their immune systems improve to the point that they experience themselves less vulnerable to common infections like flu. Injuries and cuts take a much shorter time to heal.

The holistic nature of the CFQ approach means that neither the practitioner nor the healer determines what is to be cleared out. When the energy solvent produced by pure consciousness is introduced, the tension melts and dissolves in its own energy-selective manner. Scientific experts have discovered that a glue-like substance produced by food glycosylation, oxidation and normal metabolism is a cause of cell deterioration and disease. The letting-go with its undoing and unfolding effects gives rise to the experience of vivid sticky sensations that can be physically felt, and readily manifested as involuntary physical movements. The clearing-off results in healing, relaxation, improvement in posture, and overall resilience. Clearly, the debased energy-glue is what causes physical deterioration in body functions, diseases, and aging by hindering, hampering and shutting-off physiological functions. CFQ may be what is necessary for the prevention of diseases since it strengthens the host or practitioner and enhances smooth functioning of biological systems.

Popular beliefs advocate physical exercise and activity as an important measure to ensure good health. Staleness and lethargy resulting from mental activities can normally be cleared through physical exercises. From the CFQ point of view, physical activity works with a balancing effect on mental tension to make a person feel better. A stressed mind fabricates a top-heavy situation causing poor circulation and sluggishness. Exercising restores blood circulation and creates a balance which makes the body feel more comfortable. It is necessary for most people whose daily work involve heavy mental activities, and those who do are physically inactive.

There may, however, be some risk from over-exercising which can be detrimental to health. I believe that some tension in the body is fabricated through exercising itself. This adds on to the accumulated burden a person already carries with the danger of long-term hazardous consequences. Practitioners witness that the de-stressing effect brought about by the CFQ letting-go method is more relaxing and beneficial. Many popular types of exercise build up muscle and stimulate heavier body mass. Although many people tend to enjoy the feeling of thicker, bulky muscles, CFQ suggests that this may be undesirable as it obstructs blood circulation and hinders physiological functions. There is also a problem with age. A person may be forced to reduce certain exercises or give them up completely. The psychological setback can involve lowered self-confidence and a harsh reminder that one is growing old. In contrast, CFQ exercises can be practiced until a ripe old age. Traditional longevity experts suggest that rigorous exercises can *"burn away your own life."*

Nutrition & The Stress of Living

Proper nutrition is vital for good health. Nutritional needs, however, differ from person to person, and are complicated by gender, age, work, and personal health. A highly stressed person requires more nutrition in order to feed his stress. This in turn gives rise to further stress problems. Nutritionists and health care experts differ in their opinions as to what constitutes proper nutrition. The problem is further compounded by on-going research which continues to shed new light on nutritional requirements and discovers errors in previous beliefs. Too much nutrition may cause more harm than a mild deficiency as the body is forced to deal with the excess food consumed.

Traditional wisdom has this to say about food:

"Medicinal (herbal) nourishment is inferior to ordinary food nourishment. Food nourishment is inferior to bio-energy nourishment."

The implication is that the body is able to process and convert simple food for its nutritional needs. Indeed, many of those who are known to live long and healthy lives lead a simple life with simple food consumption without awareness of nutritional requirements. From the spiritual-consciousness point of view, rich food and an over-emphasis on nutrition gives rise to cravings and enhances stressful tendencies which burden the body systems.

In my Center I have often been asked what makes people more vulnerable to diseases. The older generation has a more stoic attitude toward illness. People nowadays are more affluent and can afford to be health conscious. They are also driven into fear by media information about diseases prompting them to pursue treatment even at the slightest sign of disease. "Looking for problems" and excessive suspicious attitudes soon lead to the development of chromic problems. More often than not, people who are overly health conscious become the ones who suffer ill health. Those who are tensed and over-concerned are the ones who are more likely to fall victim compared to those who are relaxed. If chemical poison in food is your concern then you should resort to eating plain simple food, which is normally as nutritious but less chemically processed than rich, complex foods.

I have successfully treated a few cases of mild food poisoning in humans and pets. Poisons manifest as a discrete tension formation which causes failure of the body's systems. Any factor causing an effect on the body, must first act as a kind of binding force on the body. A tensed and easily excitable person can fabricate self-damage by being constantly anxious. With problems like pollution, which are often beyond an individual's ability to control, the best way to deal with them is by reducing mental tension and anxiety.

By far the most important cause of disease is modern living itself. Modern living places demands on the use of the brain, which produce an energy suspending effect that draws in more tension especially if the physical activity of manual work is missing. Cramped living space, traffic jams, and the pursuit of material possessions all increase stress. Obviously a counterbalance to the stress of modern living is to de-stress.

The aging process leads to a deterioration of physiological functions and a long list of age-related diseases. Aging itself can be considered a disease. Modern scientists believe that longevity can be extended much further than previously thought possible. While the natural lifespan of humans is documented to reach 120 years, genetic scientists predict that it may be feasible to stretched it many fold through genetic engineering.

From this perspective, a human lifespan of a 100 years, considered a ripe old age today, is actually a premature death. What has prevented people from living longer? Scientists blame the residual or glue-like waste produced by glycosylation of food, oxidation, and metabolism as

the cause of aging. Anti-oxidants and other suggested anti-aging remedies do not seem to produce satisfactory solution. I discovered from my
meditation that the glue is actually the debased energy of tension
which can be traced to a spirit-consciousness origin. Many of my students and patients show apparent signs of age reversal including the
disappearance of wrinkles and the restoration of a youthful slim and fit
appearance. Post-menopause women regained menstrual periods,
straightening of their body frame, darkening and restoration of hair,
etc. Personally, in many ways, I feel much better than I did twenty
years ago even though I have not regained my lost hair, and the graying
process has not been fully arrested. Perhaps the nature of my work in
dealing with people's problems and the 1991 crisis (see Chapter 1) has
caused too much damage. I hope one day to regain my full head of hair
as clear evidence of the age reversal power of CFQ.

But if dramatic longevity is really possible, we have to examine its
moral implications. Life is meaningful only if it can be used to contribute to the betterment of humanity. I have seen many healthy persons
deteriorate rapidly soon after retirement. Somewhere in us we are created to contribute. But we need to think twice about adding to the
overpopulation of the earth. The old should not deprive younger people of resources and living space. What people are most concerned
about now is to live a long life with few health problems. CFQ with its
self-help and self-reliance approach holds promise in this respect.

The next problem is the life quality for the aged. The aging process
with the squeezing effect of increasing tension gives rise to fear and
anxiety, and a prominent concern is one's own mortality. Watch the
actions of the elderly and listen to their conversations in order to
understand them better. CFQ is able to reveal peace and awareness of
the spirit-consciousness aspect of existence naturally, in addition to
doing away with the physical tension which pressurises the heart with
fear. Freed of tension a person becomes calmer and when their time is
up, they will be able to leave life here more peacefully. This is a great
benefit to humanity with profound karmic implications.

CFQ Bridge to Spiritual Evolution

Despite advancement in sciences, mankind is still greatly threatened by disease. What if medical science is near its full potential in the war against disease? We may ask if life shortening disease is inevitable. If treatment is the process of creating the right conditions for the body to restore its healthy functions, it means that diseases occur only when there is conflict or disharmony. Where does conflict or disharmony come from? Recall the example of the coin mentioned in a previous chapter. Submitting to the demands and pressures of physical existence fabricates friction for the spirit. If the pressure is excessive, the spirit tries to warn its physical counterpart by means of disease symptoms. If the person pays heed and the pressure is subsequently reduced, health is restored. If the person persists with loading on more pressure, their body may no longer be able to sustain life.

Every activity or function leaves an energy reaction imprinted on the energy-consciousness level. Such imprints will be carried forward even if the body is destroyed. The driving force for birth, aging, disease, and death, according to the Buddha, is the law of karma, manifested as lust, hatred, and ignorance. A possible solution at the root level is the *"method out-of-the-world"* involving the letting-go-undoing approach aimed at cleansing the energy-spirit-consciousness.

So we have a choice. Worldly methods tend to encourage us to let someone help us with whatever methods they have developed. But such methods, no matter how sophisticated often work only at the physical level and are equivalent to *"the stars at dawn, the bubbles in the stream, or a flickering lamp"* when viewed by the out-of-the-world method. If you are contented with conventional methods, let it be. Just take it with full trust and sincerity. Let it be such.

Obviously not many people are so contented. Since their dissatisfactions continue, so does the search. There may be many more methods of the world that will be developed to fulfill treatment needs, but the outcome will not change much. If the real need remains unfulfilled, many will continue to be discontented. The fact is that most consumers do not know what they want or need. My experience suggests that the need is to eliminate fear and insecurity which is still very much a part of every person's existence. Now it is time to consider the out-of-the-world method.

Even a spiritual-energy method, however, has its shortcomings when it comes to treating disease. It was never meant for such a purpose. The disappearance of disease is only a by-product of the method, not the objective. Indirectly, healing provides evidence that the meditation method has been properly followed. It guides you beyond the risk of being solely concerned about physical existence. It informs you that your spirit is equally important. However, the roots of human problems will remain with us unless the basic cause of birth, aging, disease and death as we know them is resolved. That is achieved by a liberated, emancipated, pure consciousness which for most people requires many lives of cultivation.

All matter has a limited physical existence before changing its form or state. We study that in science. Even planet Earth is not meant to exist forever. When there is birth, there will be aging, diseases and death. The law of impermanence rules. Even if a person lives to a ripe old age without experiencing the slightest problem of pain and disease, s/he may still experience a lot of fear when death draws near. Even were it possible to live a thousand years the end could well bring discontentment and anxiety. Stretching the end out could add greatly to one's burdens.

So the suffering never ends as the result of human fabrications. It ends only if there is a true understanding of the nature of existence. In the face of pain and suffering from disease, with a true understanding, a person can calmly come to terms with life. What and who is suffering? Not the "I" of my own fabrications. Such an "I" is only a fiction. Suffering is not suffering as this fabricated meaning system does not really exist in real terms. In the face of death, the liberated person knows that s/he is stepping into a new beginning. The person knows the Absolute, God's love, pure consciousness which will gladly take her or him back to heaven. Death can be transcended with a smile. That is a home-coming, a joyous celebration. This, of course, is easy to say, but I hope I will be capable of living it when my death comes.

So what exactly do we really need? No-thing! What we need has always been there. Amazing grace! It has never been lost. We simply have buried it by being too busy. To find it requires calming down. Let the dust fall off and it shines. That is the true peace revealed with spiritual awareness. With true peace comes true courage. All sufferings then cease to be sufferings. All thoughts and actions become peaceful and harmonious. We realize utterly as we come to care for each other that wars and violence are disgraceful and plain silly.

So take your next best step right now: The past cannot be re-created. Smile to it. The future will come and you need not create it. Smile to welcome it. What about the present? Relax and smile. It is already now past. And you have every reason to smile—as all of life's rights, wrongs, successes, and failures flashed by within the blink of an eye. The sun continues to rise and set; nothing ultimate will ever change. Smile now and smile forever.

Conflict: Physical versus Spiritual

We live in this world of physical existence and it is our responsibility to carry on living in the best way we can. But what is the best way? We eat, we work, we care for ourselves and our families. We are concerned for others too, and we need many resources to insure that we are not deprived.

How do we make sure that we do not cross the self-centered border and cause harm and conflict to others and ourselves? A moral code of conduct has not proven sufficient! Even a simple and honest man can get into trouble just minding his own business and earning a living. In a competitive world others are also fighting for their own survival. Further, life is filled with temptations of every kind! So we exercise restraint.

But some small voice in your mind keeps saying "I want something more." That is enough to drag us into trouble.To be alive itself means that nothing seems to be right. But we can take a different attitude. Whatever it is, let it be. Instead of being your mere physical self, spend a bit of time everyday, perhaps an hour or so, letting your spirit breathe. This may be just what is needed to free yourself from all your troubles. That is the only time you can truly say you spend on yourself and simultaneously for everyone else.

Time spent on spiritual resuscitation allows pure consciousness of spirit to shine, illuminating the darkness and sorting out the disharmony fabricated by the fact that you are alive. This is the time when *Metta* radiates loving-kindness to benefit all sentient beings. Let your spirit tell you how to live. Let this heart energy chart out for you what you should do and what you should not do.

What else is possible? Patience! In time to come, perhaps your spirit will reveal and tell you. Right now, you have to contend with the demands of both your physical and spiritual needs and bear with their conflicts. The Buddha taught that the human realm is the only plane of existence whereby a being is able to cultivate and free oneself from the entanglements of karma. Our job is to create the proper conditions whereby we can eventually evolve into another plane that is more conducive to the existence of our Spirit. That means to be free from all pains and suffering. Human existence is truly worthy. But reality can only be known if intimately experienced. Thinking about it is not enough! Smile and *"it is just as it is."* Conflict? No conflict, no war, no violence, no suffering or destruction. Acknowledge the absurdities of our fabrications-the unreality of it all. Smile and be peaceful. Life is a divine game *"Eternal Smile! Eternal Peace!"*

A Case Example: *The ten year old girl fell and injured her left arm playing in school. The school authorities did not realize the seriousness of the injury. Two hours later the arm was swollen and she was crying uncontrollably in pain. In hospital the X-rays indicated that the radial bone on her swollen arm was indeed broken. An immediate operation was required to* reset the bone but no orthopedic surgeon was on duty late that night. The operation was delayed until the following morning. After resetting the bone, her arm was put on a cast. Two months later the cast was removed. She was scheduled for physiotherapy three times weekly for a period of six months. After three sessions, however, her mother was alarmed at her child's condition and brought her to me.

I examined her during the first visit. Her arm was still painful and remained on a sling, her neck and shoulder were stiff and she could hardly hold her head straight. The elbow joint was so stiff that she was unable to straighten her arm more than 120 degrees. There was an obvious curve on her forearm where the bone had broken and the skin appeared red, swollen, and painful to the touch. Her fingers appeared curled, the palms cold and wet and her grip was weak. She was unable to raise her arm above her shoulder and could only manage to move her arm 45 degrees from her arm-pit.

I told her to gently remove the arm sling during the energy healing session. She felt the pain flowing out from her whole arm all the way out through the hand and fingers. The muscles in the arm throbbed and the elbow suddenly loosen in several forceful jerks. At the end of the session, she felt that she no longer needed the sling. She could then straighten her elbow much more (about 20 degrees left) and also lift her arm above the shoulder. The following day she returned to the physiotherapist who immediately noticed the improvement.

On her second visit to my Center most of her physical movements were restored. She continued with her regular physiotherapy. After the third healing session, the physiotherapist told her that her arm had recovered completely and she need not continue therapy. He felt that the speed of recovery was miraculous (a total of five weeks).

PART II
Training in CFQ Healing Methods

6

Dynamic Qigong Cleansing: Meridian-Organ Exercise

A seven movement protocol of bioenergy cleansing is presented here to enhance whole body meridian energy flow, reversing the tension and trauma accumulated in the physical and energy bodies. This practice harmonizes the body's systems and creates an opening effect to replace conflicts with a peaceful consciousness, the all-powerful healing resource. Since it stimulates the body's self repair response, it brings about healing, regeneration and self-regulation. It is helpful for practically every kind of health problem with the following few exceptions:

1. Physically incapable people, unable to practice these exercise, will find it helpful to practice those recommended under "complementary techniques (Chapter 8)."

2. Pregnant women are advised not to begin with this practice, until birth has occurred, as enhanced blood flow to the womb may increase the risk of a miscarriage. Although such a risk is quite remote and no such case has ever been reported, I still prefer to be cautious. Those who become pregnant after commencing the practice, however, are encouraged to continue. They will benefit tremendously, experiencing easier, less painful delivery, a healthier baby, and a reduction in confinement blues.

Concept of Meridians

The body contains network-like series of channels called meridians which together guide the flow of bioenergy (qi). There are twelve major meridians and eight special meridians. The twelve major meridians are:

1. Hand lung meridian *(fei ching)*—*yin*

2. Hand heart meridian *(hsin ching)*—*yin*

3. Hand heart governor meridian *(hsin pao ching)*—*yin*

4. Hand large intestine meridian *(ta ch'ang ching)*—*yang*

5. Hand small intestine *(hsiao ch'ang ching)*—*yang*

6. Hand triple-warmer meridian *(san chao ching)*—*yang*

7. Foot spleen meridian *(p'i ching)*—*yin*

8. Foot kidney meridian *(shen ching)*—*yin*

9. Foot liver meridian *(kan ching)*—*yin*

10. Foot stomach meridian *(wei ching)*—*yang*

11. Foot urinary bladder meridian *(p'ang kuang ching)*—*yang*

12. Foot gall-bladder meridian *(tan ching)*—*yang*

To understand this chapter, you need not learn the details of the meridians. CFQ practices a wide-open method that neither requires nor recommends detailed knowledge about meridians or acupoints (more than 360 in number) on the meridians. Being overly concerned with such knowledge limits the use of radiant energy and restricts the healing effect. The twelve major meridians are therefore summarized and simplified for the purpose of the CFQ exercises to be described.

Each hand's three yin meridians are straight lines that run downward along the inner arms to the fingers. Each foot's three yin meridians are straight lines that run downward along the inner legs to the feet. The hand's three yang meridians are straight lines that run upward along the outer arms from the fingers. The foot's three yang meridians are straight lines that run upward along the outer legs from the feet. In the torso all six yin meridians run downward along the front and all six yang meridians run upward to the head along the back.

Of the eight special meridians, only three of them are used for these exercises. They are:

1. The *jen* meridian that runs along the center line of the front of the torso.

2. The *tu* meridian that runs upward along the center line of the back of the torso to the head, and

3. The belt meridian that runs round the waist below the navel.

As an individual works on these meridians, all other meridians and the entire body's system will be cleansed and regulated. Qi flow enhances blood flow. More qi flow along the twelve major meridians promotes the optimum functioning of all the internal organs, which in turn ensures that the faculties of the six senses are properly regulated and repaired.

Bioenergy (qi) flowing through the meridians is vibrational by nature, that is, it is fluid-like and responds to electrical stimulation. For the harmonious functioning of body systems, the meridians must be cleared of blockages and the yin and yang must be balanced. Such a state is not easily attainable by physical assistance, for example, even with acupuncture or herbs. It is also easily disrupted by changes in moods and emotional states. However, the radiant energy generated by CFQ practices, along with a peaceful non-fabricating letting go mind-set, can readily clear blockages and ensure that the yin and yang are properly balanced.

Guarded Secrets of Healing

In ancient times, it was a tradition for masters of martial and esoteric arts to protect principles and important details of their arts. These were carefully passed on to their sons or to selected disciples who, after having vowed to keep the tradition secret, became successors. This practice led to a situation whereby fewer and fewer people were aware of the important insights and features of a practice. Even if they had read about these secrets somewhere, they were often unsure of how they were implemented. These secrets are incorporated in the CFQ methods.

Without a knowledge of these guarded secrets, any Qigong practice is, at best, mediocre and lacking in potential for progress. I discovered some of these secrets through CFQ meditation. Since I am not bound by any vow to keep this tradition to myself, I am able and willing to share these secrets. They are, in fact, fully incorporated in the exercises which are to be taught in this chapter. But to ensure that you are fully aware of them, I will list and describe them.

1. ***Downward Flushing:*** A TCM saying goes, "*when the bioenergy sinks down, hundreds of diseases disappear.*" A central belief of traditional medicine holds that a basic mechanism contributing to the cure of all diseases is draining energy down. But can this be done? Without thorough knowledge of how to bring the energy down and out of the body the above saying remains a mere theoretical concept. The fact is, few therapists have mastered this skill. Another piece of guidance applicable here states, "*where the mind reaches, bioenergy reaches.*" In the light of this saying, many Qigong therapies use visualization to harness qi flow and bring the qi down. Proper visualization techniques, however, are not easy to master. Insufficient concentration renders these techniques ineffec-

tive while over concentration may lead to qi congestion with negative health consequences. Even if visualization is correctly practiced, the effect may not be lasting as it involves mental fabrications. The cause of blockages and suspensions is tension, which can only be reduced by the release of tension via the letting go process.

The practice of CFQ exercises does not require any visualization at all. What is required is to perform the steps without cognitive activity. The simplicity of the steps ensures that stale tension energy has no room to hide in the body but must flow downward and outward through the limbs. Once it reaches the ends (hands and feet), it can no longer grip the body but is freed into the cosmos. The body naturally replaces stale tension energy with pure cosmic energy.

2. *Speed:* The exercises use slow and smooth movements to produce the best results. The speed of bioenergy flow is almost the same as the speed of breathing. Fast movements do not encourage energy flow but instead hinder it. On the other hand, if the movements are too slow, energy will be constrained and become a form of conserved energy which is not good for health. The time required to perform all the seven movements and the conclusion should be thirteen to fifteen minutes.

3. *Breathing:* Except as instructed in the preparation and conclusion procedures it is best to breathe naturally throughout the exercises. There is no need to bother to ensure that your breathing is coordinated with the movements. If you follow the principles and procedures correctly, your breathing will eventually spontaneously keep pace with the movements. In this way, you can do one thing at a time, i.e., you are free to focus concern on the movements. This secret promotes harmony. Attempts to blend breathing with move-

ments, as in some Qigong forms, may cause chest congestion and heart problems.

It is still a popular belief among Qigong practitioners that bioenergy is derived from air. Such a belief is wrong! Qigong practice is not about learning how to breathe or to absorb the essence of air. The term "breath-work" used by some Western writers to describe Qigong practice is incorrect. Some people practicing breathing techniques may indeed experience relaxation and improvements to health. The way a person breaths, however, and the depth of the breathing is regulated by biological systems dependent on one's physiological condition. Therefore, to change nature by introducing a method of artificial breathing may bring undesirable consequences to some people.

4. *Loose Movements:* Performing the exercises without strain or strength ensures the smooth flow of bioenergy and blood. Strength and forceful muscle action give rise to a contracting effect that binds the body and hinders physiological functions. The prolonged practice of CFQ promotes slimming of the body with an optimal removal of undesirable body fluid, fats and waste products.

Exercising without the use of strength ensures that the tension (a form of strength) melts away. This helps eliminate hardening of the body's muscles and naturally soft tissues. The organization of cells is thus optimized and the space between them also becomes optimal, thus facilitating proper physiological functions, waste removal, cell growth, repair, and replacement.

Loose or strength-less movements are "hollow" or yin behaviors. Alone, therefore, they are unable to bring about maximum health benefits, as they are unable to penetrate deep enough to clear internal blockages. In order to cover this inadequacy, inner strength *(nei jing)* in "solid" or yang movements is used to balance the hollow movements.

It is not easy to maintain looseness in the movements. Most beginners will be using plenty of strength without realizing it. Habitually using strength when moving builds stiffness and tension in the body. With prolonged practice, cultivators gradually understand and appreciate the necessity for effortless movement. In regular practice, rather than be contented to think that you are already doing it right, reduce strength and loosen further whenever you realize you can do so. In this way, your progress is ensured.

5. **Relaxing the Hamstring (song kua):** The words *"song kua"* are commonly used in most forms of martial arts involving soft movements. The same is true in Qigong, but such relaxing is seldom done correctly. *"Kua"* is the region where the hamstring meets the groin at the hip. The most helpful stance for the proper execution of *song kua* is achieved by placing both feet one foot apart and parallel to each other. From the normal relaxed standing position, loosen and bend your knees in order to drop your body weight. If properly done, you should feel: a loosening all over your body, especially around your shoulders and chest, as if some confining force were removed; the contact between your feet and the ground become firmer; the body weight being transferred to under your feet; and a comforting sensation in the groin.

The following guidelines ensure that you are doing the *song kua* correctly. The angle of the bent knee should be about thirty degrees. Bending beyond thirty degrees will render the loosening ineffective. For the elderly, or those with knee pains or other restrictive problems, just loosen with a slight buttocks drop. Increase this gradually as you are able. Make sure that you let go of your strength completely. Especially your neck, shoulders, lower back, thighs, calves, and toes should be free of strength. If you look down, your toes should be visible. Your kneecaps should not protrude beyond your toes. Drop your buttocks as if to sit on a high chair, but make sure that your entire head, hip and torso structure is vertical like a plumb line. Most beginners are too stiff and when they perform the *song kua* they tend to push their hips forward and lean backward. This is an extremely ineffective posture and will not result in any relaxing effect. The simple procedure of *song kua* requires long practice to perfect.

When properly done, the *song kua* move causes a rapid improvement lessening hypertension and relieves chronic ailments. It can even help eliminate the symptoms of such common infections as flu. It is most effective when combined with *"fa jing"* (to be discussed next) and they are performed in a dynamic manner together. Holding *song kua* without moving for a long time is not efficient.

6.   ***Releasing the Inner Strength (fa jing):*** Begin with the body relaxed, the limbs loosened and the arms on the sides. Lift the hands to the upper end of the pelvis with hands hanging loosely by bending your elbows. Press down to straighten your elbows. At the same time, arch the hands so that the palms are horizontal to the ground. Hold for a short while (two to five seconds). This is done together with the *song kua*. When done correctly, you should feel a kind of solidity spread evenly throughout your palms and fingers similar to the firmness you feel under your feet with the *song kua* position. Take care not to focus excessively on your hands, as balance with the *song kua* is important if the bioenergy is to flow downward and outward. Also, take care that strength is not held in any part of the body especially in the joints. This will insure that your internal physical body (including the tendons and the muscles beneath the surface muscles) is optimally extended and can elongate to achieve a more opening effect, thereby facilitating the flow of bioenergy and blood, enhancing the replacement of disharmony with the healing energy of peace.

With the *song kua-fa jing* movement, bioenergy flow along all six yin meridians of the hands and feet is enhanced. Stale inner strength is projected outward to be exchanged with pure cosmic energy, which flows back along the six yang meridians as the loose movements are performed. What I am teaching here is called "gentle *fa jing*" and is very different from "martial *fa jing*" which, traditionally, has been kept as a strictly guarded secret since it is capable of inducing fatal damage in combat without any external trace. Their principles are similar except that the guideline "*swallowing the qi from heaven, borrowing the strength from earth*" is used. Do not try to modify my teaching for martial art purposes, as incorrect practice can induce serious negative repercussions. Moreover, the use of such martial *fa jing* brings severe karmic consequences not consistent with my goal of promoting peace, love and health.

7. **Method of the Heart (xin fa):** In the past, "*xin fa*" was taught only to ordained disciples, and was used to distinguish a true disciple from a common student. With the practice of *xin fa* a beginning cultivator's progress can be accelerated. Today, however, *xin fa* is absent in most disciplines involving meditation, Qigong or the martial arts. Most know that to get a job done efficiently it must be done calmly. But how to achieve calmness? First, we must acquire an "unmoved heart." The unmoved heart comes about when the mind is not attached to any conditions. There are no objectives, no pressures, no thoughts of right or wrong, success, or failure. Calmness cannot be achieved simply by directing your mind, which rebels against such pressure. To demand calm may only provoke more restless thoughts and emotions. Neither can the body be forced to calm down. The end result is to use a lot of strength and will power trying to hold still, which does not lead to calmness but rather to strengthening the ego and increasing the karmic load. The purpose of the CFQ exercises is to enable you to be at peace. You have no motives nor intentions. The practitioner, at least for that period, is not bothered about problems or health,

and is not even inclined to speak of wanting to recover from difficulties. This is the greatest secret of healing: not perturbed by anything, not even the desire to heal yourself!

True cures come from not doing, from trusting that the wisdom of
your body knows best. Some therapies can produce a remedy, but
not bring about complete healing. The greatest healer, with the
capacity for genuine and total cure, is peace. With diligent and
prolonged practice, it is possible to get to see and feel peace. It
appears as a magnificent, pure, luminous mass without a boundary. It is a reality that makes any physical thing seem absurd by
comparison.

The exercises and movements are tools to enable you to achieve
intimacy with peace. They are important as major aids to making
peace pervade your life. Peace might be an idea, a concept, or even
a burden you carry. With these exercises peace can become an intimate partner in your life.

Your mind, in the meantime, can continue to function and think,
even when doing the exercises. You need have no business with it.
Make no attempt to control it, as that gives rise to a futile fight.
Just proceed with the exercises. Thoughts can not infect you, so
long as you ignore them. The thoughts necessarily react as you
implement the dissolving process, activating and diluting them. In
time, they will vanish along with the other unnecessary burdens
you are carrying. My hope for you is that you exercise self-reliance
and persevere, for when you are busy doing the exercises you are
relaxed and restful. If you need to rest and relax but have not been
able to, CFQ can provide a way.

Dancing the Hexagram

*There is yang within yin, yin hidden behind yang, hollow contains
solid, solid motivates hollow. This is the core philosophy of the ancient*

Book of Changes (I-Ching): the yin-yang and 5 elements, mutually complementary and mutually contrasting ways, create all changes. With proper use of the principle, arises the hexagram.

The Set-Up: In the seven-movement meridian exercises to be described, the yang (solid) meridian energy flow is enhanced by the yin (hollow) movements. The yin meridian energy flow is amplified (by ensuring a projection through the hands and feet) through the yang movements.

Thus all matter in the universe comprises "*a thousand changes and ten thousand transitions*" as symbolized by the hexagram. By utilizing this principle in the CFQ exercises, the physiological functions of the body are brought in tune with the universal law of changes. According to ancient beliefs, a human body is equivalent to, and comprises every secret of the universe, thus enabling it to "*flourish and nourish without extinction*" and to "*continue in perpetuity.*"

The Seven-Movement Sequence (as in a "movement" of a symphony):

Measure with your left foot its length from the right big toe. Use this as a guide to spread your feet to a parallel position one foot-length apart. (See Illustration of "Starting Position" overleaf)

Completely loosen your body and let go of controllable strength. Take a deep breath, breath out, and smile.

Note: A breath, in and out, symbolizes a willingness to step out of your past. A smile helps to facilitate peace and self acceptance by generating good energy. Try without strain to remain smiling throughout the exercises. Smile now and forever—in these CFQ movements you are free of problems.

Movement I: Flying Cloud Hands *(fei yun shou)*

1. Raise both hands with arms straight to the front until they reach shoulder level. The hands should hang loosely, with your fingers pointing downward. *(Step 1 of Illustration overleaf)*

2. Bend the elbows and pull the hands back until they reach the sides of the chest below the shoulders. *(Step 2)*

3. Drop the hands straight down, until the arms are straight, at the same time bending the knees to relax the hamstring *(song kua)*. When the arms are straight, the palms should be parallel to the ground *(fa-jing)*. *(Step 3)*

4. Straighten the knees while doing Movement I again.

Repeat ten times

Notes: Step 1 loosens and stimulates the bioenergy flow along the yang meridians of the arms and feet. Step 3 opens out and clears the yin meridians of the hands and feet, and at the same time releases stale energy.

Effects: Movement 1 clears and smooths the energy flow in all of the twelve major meridians, improving general well-being. It is specifically effective for the treatment of frozen shoulders, neck pain (including spondyliasis), fatigue, insomnia, migraine, tinnitis, sinusitis, cataracts, glaucoma, tonsilitis, asthma, heart ailments, menstrual disorders, constipation, anxiety, depression, high blood pressure, diabetes, erectile dysfunction, infertility, and arthritis. With prolonged practice, short and long sightedness may improve. In addition, it helps to lift the depressive mind-set of cancer patients, thus promoting recovery.

Step 1   **Step 2**   **Step 3**

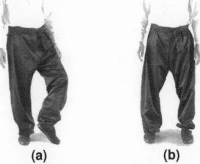

(a)   **(b)**

Starting Position: Position the feet (a) and parallel them (b)

Movement One: Flying Cloud Hands

Movement 2: Touching the Jade Belt *(mo you dai)*

1. Continue from Movement 1. Turn the palms upward and raise the hands to the sides of the hips, at the same time straightening the knees. *(Step 1 of Illustration overleaf)*

2. With palms open and facing up, move the hands straight forward until the arms are straight. *(Step 2)*

   a. Stretch the fingers open, then relax and loosen.

3. Turn the palms downward, allowing the hands to hang loosely. *(Step 3)*

   a. Bring the hands back toward the lower abdomen until two to four inches in front of the navel.

   b. With palms facing the body, move the hands one to the left, the other to the right, horizontally around the abdomen to the sides.

4. Turn the palms downward, move down and at the same time bend the knees (song kua-fa jing). *(Step 4)*

Repeat ten times

Notes: Step 2 clears the hands three-yin meridians. In Step 2a, when stretching your fingers, attend to the firmer contact of your feet on the ground as well. This detail ensures good energy flow to the hands and feet, and as this is built into your practice, it will help free you from all diseases. Steps 3 and 3a ensure a good return flow of bioenergy through the yang meridians. They activate and energize the lower abdomen. Step 3b activates the belt meridian to bring about good energy and blood flow in the lower torso and Step 4 opens out and clears the yin meridians of the hands and feet while at the same time releasing stale energy from within.

Effects: This movement is specifically effective for the treatment of erectile dysfunction, menopause problems, prostate problems, ovarian cysts, fibroids, urinary and kidney disorders, back pain, sciatica, hemorrhoids, constipation, indigestion, post-natal disorders, low sperm count, infertility, obesity, gout, and arthritis.

Step 1   Step 2

Step 3   Step 4

Movement Two: Touching the Jade Belt

Movement 3: Happy Heaven Happy Earth *(huan tian xi di)*

1. With palms facing forward, raise the arms in a large circle up from the sides until both palms touch forward of the top of the head. *(Step 1 of Illustration overleaf)*

2. Stretch the arms upward a little. *(Step 2)*

3. Move the hands down until four inches from the front of the fore-head and turn the palms inward. *(Step 3)*

    a. With the palms facing the body, continue with the downward movement until the hands are in front of the lower abdomen.

4. Continue to move down at the same time bend the knees *(song kua)*. Separate the hands to move until wider than the body, arch the palms *(fa jing)*. *(Step 4)*

5. Return the hands to the outer sides of the body with the palms facing the hip, while at the same time straighten the knees. *(Step 5)*

Repeat 10 times

Notes: Step 1 opens your whole body to facilitate an exchange with pure cosmic energy. It stimulates energy flow along the yang meridians and the *tu* meridian. Step 2: while stretching your arms take note of the contact of your feet on the ground. Make sure you do not use any strength. This step promotes a longitudinal release and an extension of your whole body. Steps 3a and 4 cleanse the body of stale energy, releasing it downward. The release is further enhanced by *song kua-fa jing*. Bioenergy flow in the yin meridians and *jen* meridian at the front of your body is enhanced.

Step 1

Step 2

Step 3

Step 4

Step 5

Movement Three: Happy Heaven, Happy Earth

Effects: This movement enhances the wholeness and harmony of the energy system by integrating what you have done so far. It improves blood circulation, enhances the immune system and at the same time facilitates greater effectiveness in the subsequent Movements 4 and 5, which work on the internal organs. It is specifically effective for treatment of diabetes, migraine headaches, dizziness, fatigue, insomnia, tinnitis, hearing defects, cataracts, glaucoma, sinusitis, tonsillitis, frozen shoulder, heart aliments, tuberculosis, chronic hepatitis, gastric disorders, indigestion, numbness, and arthritis.

Movement 4: Oh My Precious *(xin gan bao bei)*

1. Place the left hand across the neck below the chin with the palm facing downward. Place the right hand in front of the groin, with the palm facing upward. This is called *"holding the energy ball."* *(Step 1 of Illustration overleaf)*

2. Spread the feet so that their inner sides are at shoulder width, with toes pointing slightly outward.

   a. Turn the body toward the left, at the same time bring the hands to the left, and shift the body weight to the left leg, bending it slightly. Straighten the right knee. *(Step 2)*

3. Stop the movement of the lower right hand, but continue to move the upper left hand out, until the arm is straightened. *(Step 3)*

   a. Drop the left hand at the same time arch the palm up *(fa jing)*.

4. Bring back the left hand and switch positions with the right, again assuming the holding the energy ball position. *(Step 4)*

5. Slowly swing the energy ball around the front of the torso.

6. Repeat similarly on the right side.

Repeat ten times: Left-right counted as one.

Notes: Step 1: By focusing bioenergy on the torso, more qi and blood are supplied to the internal organs. Step 2a: when moving your energy ball across the body, the internal organs are activated. When this movement is performed in a relaxed way, and slowly, the movement can be felt internally. Bending the left leg is *song kua* on that side. Steps 3 and 3a release pressure, and clear out stale energy to facilitate an exchange with pure energy. This is enhanced by the *fa jing*.

Effects: This movement improves blood circulation to the internal organs. It is a very relaxing movement that helps the digestive, immune and nervous systems. Specifically, it is good for most kinds of chronic and old-age diseases including Alzheimer's, goitre, anxiety, depression, gall bladder, and kidney stones. It can help to clear chronic infections of viral, bacterial or fungal origins. It promotes recovery from cancer.

Step 1   Step 2

Step 3   Step 4

Movement Four: Oh My Precious

Movement 5: No Strings Attached *(wu qian wu gua)*

Begin in the position of holding of the energy ball in Movement 4.

1. Turn the left hand outward and upward, continuing to move the left hand up until the arm is straightened into a "pushing the sky" position, at the same time turn the right hand downward and straighten the arm into a "pushing the ground," position. *(Step 1 of Illustration overleaf)*

2. Swing the upper left arm across to the left side of the body, bending the arm slightly so that the hand hangs loosely at shoulder level. At the same time, swing the lower right arm across to the right side of the body, bending the arm and letting the hand hang loosely at shoulder level. *(Step 2)*

3. Push outward until both arms are straight in an "open the door" movement. *(Step 3)*

4. Return the arms to the holding the energy ball position, now with the right hand below the chin and left hand in front of the groin.

5. Repeat similarly with sides reversed.

> *Repeat ten times:* Left up right down—open the door; and
> Right up, left down—open the door, counted as one.

Notes: There is a tendency to use strength in performing this movement. Avoid such a tendency. At the completed positions of pushing the sky and ground and open door, bring your awareness to both palms and feet.

Effects: This movement complements the effects of Movement 4 and unfolds areas where weaknesses are hidden. It enhances the health of the internal organs and clears arthritis, rheumatism, joint pains, and numbness.

Step 1

Step 2

Step 3

Movement Five: No Strings Attached

Movement 6: Happiness, Success, Longevity *(fu du sou)*

Begin by dropping the hands to the sides of the body.

1. Open the arms and sweep forward with a hugging action: at the same time, bend the body forward. *(Step 1 of Illustration overleaf)*

2. Sweep the hands over the forehead at the same time leaning backward. Your hands come down over the shoulders and into position at the sides for the next hugging action. *(Step 2)*

3. Repeat, with the hugging action coming in towards the throat. *(Step 3)*

4. Repeat, with the hugging action coming in towards the abdomen. *(Step 4)*

Repeat ten times: Forehead, throat, and lower abdomen counted as one time.

Notes: Use minimum strength but ensure that your feet are firmly grounded to maintain your balance. The yang meridians, together with the *tu*-meridian, are cleared by leaning forward and sweeping up, back and down. The yin meridians, together with the *jen*-meridian, are cleared by the leaning backward. At the same time, the tension knots in your head, your neck, and throat are swept clear, releasing through your arms and hips by releasing through the legs. (For some beginners, the elderly, and those with hypertension, dizziness, and for those who feel generally weak, it would be wise to start with five repetitions instead of ten. Increase gradually as conditions improve).

Effects: This movement enhances flexibility of the whole body and unfolds the weak areas where problems tend to be hidden. Specifically, it is effective for lower back pains, sciatica, spondyliasis, ovarian cysts, fibroid, erectile dysfunction, infertility, obesity, hemorrhoids, gastritis, digestive disorders, hepatitis, gall and kidney stones.

Step 1

Step 2

Step 3

Step 4

Movement Six: Happiness, Prosperity, Longevity

Movement 7: The Universe's Gift of Gold *(tian chi huang jin)*

1. From Movement 6, bring the hands back to the front of the lower abdomen. Interlace the fingers and bend the knees to a "horse-riding" stance. *(Step 1 of Illustration overleaf)*

2. Raise the hands, fingers gently interlaced, to the area below the chin. *(Step 2)*

3. Straighten the knees and continue the upward and now outward movement of the hands while at the same time turning the palms outward. Stop when the arms are straight, with the hands above your forehead level. Turn the head up to look at the hands. *(Step 3)*

4. Bend forward and swing the arms straight down until the palms face the ground. *(Step 4)*

   a. Turn the palms and bring the hands back to the front of the lower abdomen in a scooping action while at the same time bending the knees back to the horse-riding stance.

5. Separate both hands and swing out to the sides up to the level below shoulder height.

6. Sweep the arms back down, holding them straight with the hands arched outward. Return to the interlaced finger position in front of the lower abdomen.

Repeat ten times

Notes: Steps 2 and 3 involve sweeping in the reverse direction of the flow of the yin meridians. Clearing off with Step 4 gives rise to a greater cleansing effect. The horse riding stance ensures that you are properly grounded, to recreate a system whereby your bioenergy sinks down to help free you from *"hundreds of diseases."* For reasons stated in Movement 6 above, some people should start off with only five repetitions instead of ten.

Movement Seven: The Universe's Gift of Gold

Effects: This movement summarizes and connects all the seven movements and highlights the sinking effect.

Wrapping up the Movements
1. Affirmations (to amplify positive effects)

Bring the feet together, toes pointing comfortably out (in ballet, this would be called "third position"), and say the follow affirmations with the hands one over the other holding the lower abdomen. *(See Step 1 of Illustration overleaf on Step 1 of "Resilient Breathing")*

> *My qi and blood are flowing smoothly*
> *I am filled with peace and joy*
> *I am free of pain and illnesses*
> *I am blessed with good fortune.*

Repeat three times

Notes: People in general tend to have too many negative thoughts and emotions, and consequently, they may lack self-confidence. Faith is often weak. People in these circumstances are too frequently controlled by undesirable states such as their past behavioral and emotional patterns (karma). This state of affairs can prevent people from achieving good health and leading better lives. Using the affirmations recommended above can boost important positive aspects of life and health. The best opportunity to achieve good effects is after the exercises, when there is peace and the bioenergy flow has improved. In Chinese, "luck" *(hao yun chi)* means "good energy flow." Saying these affirmations silently, however, is not good enough. They must be spoken, to help radiate their meaning. Vocalizing, even softly, sends an instruction to the energy-consciousness to take action.

2. Conclusion: Resilient Breathing

1. Begin as in position for "Affirmations" *(Step 1 of Illustration over-leaf)*

2. With the hands, one resting on the other, palms facing up, move up along the center line of the body, from the waist to the upper chest, while breathing in through the nose. *(Step 2)*

3. Turn the palms downward, and while breathing out though the mouth, move the hands down until the arms are straight. *(Step 3)*

4. Spread the hands and move out in a sweeping circle with the palms facing down until at shoulder level. *(Step 4)*

5. Bring both hands towards center, bend the elbows and continue to move the hands forward until they are in front of the upper chest, palms down (all this while breathing in). *(Step 5)*

6. Move the hands down while breathing out until the arms are straight.

Repeat three times

Notes: This procedure is a way to formalize the completion of the movements. Anything done properly must have a beginning and a conclusion. Those intending to repeat these movements for a second or third set are still advised to complete every set with the affirmations and conclusion. This will help you to feel the increasing effectiveness of each succeeding set.

Conclusion: Resilient Breathing

Why CFQ Movements?

From the karmic viewpoint, disease arises from past causes which we in the present cannot easily identify. This does not necessarily imply that one is personally responsible for one's illnesses. Any ordinary life seems in the normal course of events to involve challenge and hardship. Further, it is certainly not wrong to be hardworking and ambitious even though these attributes may lead to our stressing our physical bodies to the extent that problems are inevitable. Problems are a price we pay.

In the Buddhist teachings, karma is a force that survives death. That means even an innocent new-born has some future events (diseases included) programmed into his or her life. The causes of such events arise from time beyond memory and are called into being simply by the wish to be born and carry on living. Today, geneticists are finding clear evidence that some diseases are genetically induced. This can be explained by karma. A bundle of karmic forces looking for a human machine (body) to carry on living, selects parents based on matching karmic similarities.

If suffering is the effect of karma, then the problem of disease should be over once the karmic effect is dissipated through suffering. Why doesn't it happen that way? Why does suffering occur over and over again, even becoming chronic? Why does suffering often get worse, and at times lead to death? Why is karma so unfair? Why are conventional methods of treatment ineffective in arresting much suffering and disease? The answers to these questions are attempted below.

Pain and suffering naturally draw our attention. Our faculties are created and trained in such a way that we instinctively act and fabricate. We respond by trying to fight and get rid of pain and suffering. This fighting adds fresh disharmony onto the original disharmony. Our attention to problems and our feelings toward them bring about fresh karmic consequences of more suffering, instead of allowing the suffering to wear out. The original warning system, activated by a problem, becomes a cause for more problems. More attention, more thinking, more treatment, and more doing results in even more problems.

A solution can come from the purity of our innermost consciousness. Most people do not even realize that such purity exists. Even if one has heard about it, skepticism is common. To be able to use our inner purity of consciousness requires long periods of training. We must go well beyond thinking, or believing that we can use it in the right way. The realities here are fraught with uncertainty.

Seeking treatment of various types is a common response to disease. These are the *methods of the world*. If they work, it is your karma. If they do not work, or if they provide an incomplete solution to your problem, it is also your karma. If you are not ready to learn how to use your pure consciousness to solve your own problems, it is O.K. That too is your karma. If you want to try this out, that decision is karma too. I wish to congratulate you and assure you that you will not regret really trying. Further, it is not uncommon if you were to think that all this stuff about karma is absolute nonsense.

I do hope you believe in something cosmic or in what some people call God. You have every reason to believe in something more powerful than yourself. People need to have a spiritual faith, and you are no more than a speck of dust in a huge mansion, considering that you are just one of the six and a half billion people living on earth. And planet Earth is no more than a speck of dust compared to the billions of planets and stars in the heavens. It proves advantageous to trust God. The Omnipotent One does not mind being blamed for every human misfortune, nor does God get angry if you curse and swear. But when you return to a sense of calm, do not forget to put your trust back in the One who will be well pleased.

Since you want to be well, you will need to have a proper system not only to get well when you are sick, but also to make sure you will stay that way. You cannot just think yourself well. Thinking without action does not get results. The habit of over-contemplation without action leads to dreaming and can lead to failure in your career as well as in your larger life opportunities. Positive thoughts about getting well are simply too weak to assist a sick person, when compared to the negative tendencies of the disease forces. Such thoughts serve only to remind you of your problems and lead to more anxiety, fear and anger. Moving from one method of treatment to another is also a poor idea. Most methods have a common shortcoming—they work on life's physical aspects and not on it's spiritual component. Furthermore, getting into the business of seeking treatments and remedies can keep you busy, but fail to achieve positive results.

The CFQ exercises, on the other hand, contain what is needed to get you well. Action is essential. Put your thoughts to work for yourself. Move out of your problems, move out of your thoughts and out of your past, to claim your entitlements for the future. Smile, and let peace fill you. Only when action expresses thoughts of peace can true peace be yours. Merely thinking about peace can give burdens to bear, inviting conflicts promoted by reminders of the troubles and turbulence of so called "real life." Merely thinking about getting well can make you more unwell. Relaxing without doing anything can increase pent up stale energy, making you less relaxed. To enjoy real relaxation, move!

Trust and Time Well Spent

Curing yourself of diseases requires that you disentangle from problems. This can be extremely difficult, as problems originate from complex forms of mental fabrications, actions, thoughts, trauma, experiences and behaviors. The key to avoiding such complexity is peace. Only a simple solution can hold the promise of resolving problems arising from complexity. Sophisticated and complicated solutions tend to make things worse.

Trying to bring about best results by throwing yourself into action is not easy. Obstacles are plentiful. Diseases are dense negative elements, which readily manifest in your thoughts. It therefore would not be fair to yourself if you just did the exercises half-heartedly or just a few times. You owe it to yourself to understand more about CFQ, so you can get the most out of this remarkable approach.

Accordingly, I suggest that you read through this book carefully, perhaps more than once, with an open mind. This can help you see the merits of its message, and come to some understanding of why and how the methods work. This may help overcome any initial distrust, and suspicion of the unfamiliar. Try out the exercises with trust and sincerity, acknowledging that trust does not arise overnight. As time goes by and as you taste some of the benefits, trust can grow. To be fair to yourself, work toward thinking of CFQ as a remedy worthy of the same respect and faith you would have walking into a trusted physician's office.

Eventually, CFQ can become a solution to your health needs. If you choose to trust it, it will do the work. It can even work miracles in hopeless situations. Try it thoroughly now, when weakness and despair are not in control of your life. You stand to lose nothing, and you can develop a system that protects you at all times.

Just wishing to be freed from health problems, to be lucky and successful, to be peaceful, to relax and to be restful is useless. If you sit back and merely think of getting any of these, they will not materialize. Your thinking will excite the negative elements within your consciousness that will draw you further away from your highest goals. The harder you think, the worse off you can become. You need to spring into action. In other words, when you practice CFQ you actualize your best thoughts and move toward achieving your best desires. I assure you that with the right attitude, your practice will be restful, enjoyable and rewarding. This is the time to relax and become intimate with pure consciousness; it is an opportunity for you to spend time for yourself as well as for humanity. All other activities, including sleep, are spent on being a slave to the karma that says "I want...; I need..." and on. They are not for the benefit of your true self, but only strengthens the karmic "I".

Most people, even very busy ones, are reasonably able to spend three-quarters of an hour to an hour daily in CFQ practice. The way a person spends time is often a matter of choice. If the person is convinced that she or he can truly benefit from something, time is found. Even if a person takes one hour out of sleep time, sleeping six hours and practicing CFQ for one hour, the sleep will be more restful than sleeping seven hours would have been.

There is no particularly suitable time; rather, any time is good for this practice. Evenings might be especially helpful when the day's work has been completed. The practice will be least disturbed by the burden of work and also provide a necessary cleansing from the stress of the day. This can pave the way for a wonderful tomorrow. Practicing at any other time is fine, but make sure you do not rush. If you have recently eaten and feel full, you will not be able to relax in an optimal way. If you have an empty stomach, I suggest you take a snack before your practice.

CFQ practice can be broken up into two or three sessions. However, the exercises are most effective if performed more than once consecutively. The first set is more of a warming up. The second or third sets are progressively more effective. For those who have few problems, practicing three sets daily is sufficient to relax yourself and prevent you from getting into serious difficulties. Those with more problems, can reasonably practice one hour or even more. You can even select specific movements which you like or prefer, to practice for a longer time without counting. But do this only after you have done the entire sequence as suggested.

Transcendent State

The practice of the CFQ exercises, performed with diligence, brings about a sense of peace, which often become very joyous. At certain times, the whole atmosphere, including the space within your body, is filled with magnificent energy-light. This light can be of many different colors, and is often blue, which is the base color of peace. This transcendent state can be defined (refer to Chok's *Tao of Healing* book) as "an awareness and perception beyond one's normal ego-self into a universal knowing and awareness." It can be measured by EEG brain frequencies as "a pattern of high-powered and rapidly synchronous beta and gamma frequencies," a state which is different from both the normal waking state and the shifts in the lower frequency alpha, theta and delta states noted during rest or sleep.

This transcendent state is a phenomenon of the whole person including, all physical and energy space. Although we speak neurologically in terms of measurement, if the state were linked only to the brain, then would merely be a state of disorientation; a floating consciousness with suspended energy tension. This would be a state of reverie, dissociated from the real world. Such a limited event might better be conceptualized as a chemically induced "high", such as can be brought about by psychotropic drugs. The transcendence experienced in CFQ is not a "high;" rather, it is a real, free, peaceful, joyous, and boundless state.

A truthful and sincere practice of the CFQ exercises can potentially realize transcendent experiences after, say, six months or so, although initial experiences may be neither lasting or vivid. They come almost as a sensing, feeling, or knowing. When vivid experiences appear, they are clearly more real than any perception of physical reality. They can continue after exercise and last for several days. It is impossible to control or intentionally duplicate such experiences. Rather, they come and go in response to movement of the debased energy. These energy forces within the first seven levels of consciousness (in the body and mind) are organized in bundles. When, following a period of performing the exercises, an individual is freed from a bundle or bundles, prior to the appearance of the next bundle, s/he experiences the transcendent state, with the radiance of peace.

The energy body of an ordinary person appears like a black cloud entangled with lines, folds, and wrinkled, somewhat like a piece of paper crushed into a ball. CFQ movements, performed in order, clear and dissolve the black cloud and re-create the energy body. This takes on the shape of an egg, about three to five feet at the sides of your body and five to eight feet at the tapered end above your head. Initial visions of this energy body may occur as early as one year after practice has been initiated, but they are more likely to occur after three years or more. Complete clearing of the black cloud, however, is not expected. This is a life-long process. Such total clearing exists only in a perfected being, a Buddha.

A Case Example: *The female patient, age 52, had chronic insomnia for twenty years. In addition she suffered from backache, stiff neck, numbness in her fingers, constipation and gastric problems. Medication and herbs were of little help. When she first came for treatment, she had been unable to sleep properly for three months. She was literally floating, moving and responding to my questions "zombie-like." The following day she telephoned to say that she had managed to sleep well the previous night. By the third session, her movements and responses had returned to normal.*

I gradually introduced the meridian exercises over a period of five weeks. Her group practice at the Center was sufficient to maintain a positive mood and overall health. She gave up her ten-year practice of tai-chi. She complained that some symptoms remained but acknowledged that they were less distressing then before. I assured her that this was normal, as problems had to be cleared off one layer at a time. It was most important that she remain calm and peaceful, and not over-react to any new symptoms that might surface. She continued daily practice at home.

Several months later the changeover was complete. She looked healthy and cheerful. Her depression and excessive worries about her children were no longer problems. She no longer searched for herbal remedies, food supplements and treatments.

7

Goal of CFQ Energy Meditation

Meditation, as it is taught in many parts of the world today, can be an occasion of confusion. What exactly is meditation? What is its purpose? What expectations are appropriate for those who meditate? Controversies abound, complicated by principles, source, heritage, and the experiences of teachers and students. To meditate is not merely to relax, or to achieve material possessions for physical comfort. It is meant neither to develop superhuman powers nor to gain advantage over one's fellow humans; it is not for curing diseases, nor for escaping from the pressures of the real world.

It is important, then, that the purpose of meditation first be defined. Otherwise, the meditation endeavor is doomed to failure before it is even started, and the consequences can prove disastrous. Meditation, even at its best, does not help either to prevent or control the natural manifestations arising from one's consciousness, though this is taught in many meditation methods. Sooner or later, one must inevitably come face to face with spiritual reality. It is too powerful to be controlled or suppressed. Confusion about meditation is also compounded by speculations and hearsay about spirit entities. These stories are often accompanied by fantasies aimed at provoking chills and thrills. In addition, there can be negative consequences associated with the practice of meditation, and it is impossible to predict the form these consequences will take or how serious they might be. Meditation-related problems can be a long time coming, and all the while, one may happily be enjoying the apparent benefits of this practice and unknowingly fabricating the karma that inevitably seeds disaster. Additionally, when bad experiences begin to occur, if they do, one might never know that they resulted from poor meditation practice. At worst, one might even lose one's sanity.

During meditation, one shifts away from familiar activities and normal state of consciousness. The shift from normal functions frequently leads to one's coming face to face with another reality, commonly called "the mind." When this occurs, thoughts become more complex and powerful and the meditator is forced to see personal tendencies and weaknesses previously ignored. These are cognitions and emotions that s/he may not normally see or might prefer not to see. As the saying goes, "*one's greatest enemy is one's own self.*"

When a person meditates, in other words, the spirit is encountered and the spirit, as previously discussed, is clouded by debased energy. In the meditative state, debased energy often gives rise to bizarre experiences described by some as the "*battle between good and evil, with creatures, wild beasts, and demons.*" Few people can truly face and overcome such challenges. To have any chance of success at such a battle, they must, somehow, summon their innermost pure consciousness, originating in pure intention, that is, selfless intention, or unconditional intention. Traditionally, the meditation teacher helps students to identify and mobilize this pure consciousness.

Origins of Meditation

Defining the content or purpose of meditation is difficult. Perhaps, then, the most reliable way to begin discussing it, is to trace its source. One authentic source is Buddhism. The Buddha encouraged his followers to develop insight into his teaching. Merely listening, remembering, and trying conceptually to understand his dharma (teachings) is not insight. Insight involves experiencing, seeing, and feeling such knowledge in such a way that it validates itself. One natural way for insight to develop is meditation.

Buddhism was introduced in China almost 2,000 years ago. And one branch that emphasized insightful experience is called Chan or Zen. The founder of Zen Buddhism, *Bodhidharma*, came to China from India during the 4th Century A.D., and the Chinese traditionally acknowledge that Zen Buddhism is the authority on meditation, calling the practice *"sitting Zen or being fixed on Zen."*

The purpose of Zen cultivation is simply to illuminate one's heart to see one's real instinct. One who sees the real instinct becomes a Buddha. How can the heart be so illuminated? It can be done simply by clearing away the delusions, fabricated by defilements *(samsara)* of the world. But defilements have an apparently real existence in a consciousness that is fabricated by thought, knowledge, and experience. This has its foundation in the debased energy, fabricated by the first six levels of consciousness. To clear it one must dilute it with loving-kindness (Metta), generated by pure intention from deep within the alaya or 8th consciousness. It is a straightforward process but one that is complex, tedious, and time-consuming. The black cloud of ego-ignorance (7th consciousness) knows nothing, but clings tightly to the one who is conscious. Even showering ignorance with all loving kindness does not produce appreciation, nor does it placate a seemingly natural desire to fight and struggle. It knows you completely, much more than you know yourself. In Buddhist thought, it is precisely the "I" to which you are accustomed. It knows your weaknesses. It knows how to tempt you and threaten you. Clearing such defilement is normally an extremely long and tedious process that requires patience, perseverance, and diligence.

According to Buddhist belief, final attainment leading to ultimate liberation requires many lifetimes of sincere cultivation. To start off, one must be equipped with sufficient background knowledge. This is best provided by someone who has wide experience with the challenges of meditation. This battle is unlike other battles. You stand there doing nothing and let the fabricated forces within metaphorically punch and kick you left, right, and center. Yet, you continue to be happy and smile until those creations become exhausted and leave. In the first place, your motive must be to *"illuminate your heart to be able to see your real instinct* (true self)." This means that you are prepared to purify your spirit to see the *shunyata* (empty and radiant nature) of all existence. The perfected state, free from any karmic entanglement, is called nirvana or Buddhahood.

Meditating for any other reason is counterproductive. Even the idea of meditating to rid oneself of diseases, or to relax, is not a good idea. Strictly speaking, meditation does not involve any form of doing or fabricating, only letting go. Concentration and visualization fall under the rubric of doing or fabricating; thus, to meditate in order to bring about a cure or a relaxation effect is seen as having the wrong motive and using the mind's fabricating tendencies. With the right motive, that of purifying one's spirit, the healing or relaxation effect comes as a by-product. Meditating under any rubric may bring about some short-term benefit, but it is ultimately self-defeating if the meditator is not clear about the proper outcome. Anything less allows karma to be an insurmountable, all-powerful and invincible force.

Exclusions from Meditation

The high-stress, high-demand, high-indulgence tendencies of modern living in society run counter to the movement toward spiritual pursuits, the most challenging of which is meditation. A high-stressed person feels the need to be "on the go," physically and mentally, at all times. Stilling oneself awakens a great struggle causing many to fail, even on the first attempt. In addition, when a person embarks on meditation, the radiating effect from the loving kindness can incite some people in the surrounding world to turn on the cultivator as a target for bullying and ridicule. The simple society of the past was much more conducive to meditating, since it had fewer temptations for physical comfort and luxury. Spiritual pursuits, which normally led to meditation, used to fulfill the idealistic, heroic, and romantic instincts of the young. Spiritual mastery was the most prestigious accomplishment, commanding high respect from society. Even emperors had to pay homage to spiritual cultivators!

In today's world, however, the need for spiritual openness is truly urgent. People trying to keep up with unprecedented and ever-changing material, luxury, physical, and technological advances, are experiencing overwhelming stresses. A true solution can only be achieved by tipping the scale from physical inclinations to spiritual development. Perhaps, some day in the future, more people will realize this. Today we seem to be at *"the cross-road before the dawn of the spiritual era."* One of the implications of this is that the pioneers risk suffering hardships. But then, those who face great hardships may bring about great accomplishments.

CFQ meditation will now be discussed, in order to describe more completely how I practice and what I teach. But first, I must say that there may be people who are not yet ready to practice meditation. For those who might be motivated by health problems that have proven insoluble by conventional therapies, for example, the recommendations in Chapter 6 are exactly what is needed. These provide a faster, better, and more direct solution to health problems than does meditation. In meditation, health benefits are by-products, not objectives. CFQ meridian exercises are capable of producing a transcendent effect that is in no way inferior to that of meditation. Its advantage is that you work from the bioenergy, physical aspect, and gradually move into the spiritual. It is good for all, and in practice you need not face such difficulties as occur in meditation. In meditation, you dive straight into the spiritual-energy-consciousness arena and come face to face with your karma.

But some people yearn for spiritual insight. There are some who wish to develop spiritual skills to help others recover from diseases. These are the people who should practice CFQ meditation. However, I would discourage the following groups of persons from practicing meditation at present:

1. Children below fifteen years of age. They are both physically and mentally under developed. Introducing meditation at this early age can cause physical and mental changes that could disrupt their development and deflect the stimulation that is required for growth, so that they end up unable to fit into society. The age required for children to be ready for meditation is after fourteen (7 x 2) years. (Seven is the number for any propitious or profound change). Children, however, can safely practice CFQ meridian exercise as described in Chapter 6.

2. Patients who have received major operations and organ transplants. These people normally require long-term medication to stabilize their condition. They also tend to be very cautious and easily panic over slight changes and discomfort. Practicing meditation might bring about such changes and discomfort which, though beneficial in the long run, might not, under the circumstances, be faced calmly.

3. Those with self-confidence or self control problems as in cases of schizophrenia, severe anxiety, depression, insomnia or other psychological illnesses.

4. Those with agonizing and disturbing pain and discomfort. It is more effective to practice the CFQ exercise until their health is improved than going straight into meditation and come face to face with their problems. They are unlikely to succeed, because they have been habitually stricken with fear and worry.

5. Pregnant women, for reasons and conditions mentioned in Chapter Six.

6. Those well above middle age. It is better to introduce spiritual development slowly, starting with CFQ exercises, than to begin with meditation. They have lived beyond "7x7" years, an age which is considered rather late for abrupt changes. Those, however, who are generally fit and healthy may consider meditation after a longer period of practice of CFQ meridian exercises, say six months to one year later.

7. People with life threatening diseases, e.g., cancer. The demonic fabrications of karma are very vicious. A new meditator can be torn asunder spiritually on their very first encounter. If peace is hopelessly lacking, they should practice the CFQ exercises and benefit from the practice.

Sincerity and an open mind are most crucial at the beginning to initiate your spiritual endeavor. Unlike the use of your physical faculties, and the mind, which you have been trained to rely upon since birth, you might be like a brand new infant in this endeavor. If you are not ready and lack proper pre-requisites, do not even bother to try. You will find yourself feeling disappointed at the very least, too ready, perhaps, to explain your experiences away with routine logic. In meditation, the facts are largely non-rational. Other people can condemn, criticize, laugh and scoff at such an idea. You, the novice meditator, simply cannot afford to do so. Cynics with a close-minded attitude think, "Oh, this is mere faith. I don't believe in such rubbish!" Dogma and bias can also distort the profound insights that can be experienced. The responsible adventurer into meditation, will be aware of how the mind works, begin with trusting what is done with full faith, sincerity, and an open mind.

Most religious meditation masters like to draw a rigid line between meditation and Qigong. Qigong masters on the other hand, insist that meditation is an important and advanced component of the discipline, called "quiescent Qigong." Generally speaking, any relaxation technique involving quieting down can broadly be called meditation. Meditation techniques involving intense visualizing, concentrating, directing bioenergy flow, absorbing energy, and creating special effects, as practiced in many Qigong methods, are all too frequently karmic fabricating processes. Thus, religious meditators can scoff at them and say that they involve "*Zen of the wild foxes.*" But those who inform their practice by using ego in order to hold their body still, thus displaying an external appearance of dignity, are no better off. The strengthening of ego is a karmic-fabricating creation. A wild fox is greedy, but in some ways better than a block of dead wood.

Karma is a formidable force that spares nobody. Once created it must be lived out. One never knows how and when its fruits will be born. Meditation should therefore be strictly a karmic-cleansing process through the use of the *Metta* state of consciousness. If the karmic-cleansing process is not effective during meditation, the natural consequence, whether intended or not, is karmic creation. In effective karmic cleansing, you vividly see and feel, often with pain and discomfort, the karma and the combat between purity and impurities. It is a therapeutic process focused on the experience of complete letting go.

CFQ Meditation: Ancient Practice Revealed

CFQ meditation is a karmic cleansing process. Karma is the force that brings about birth and life experiences in a continuous process of creation and fruition, exhibiting the patterns of cause and effect, disease, aging, and death. After death, the karmic seeds, energetically stored, cannot be destroyed but continue their wandering through the various realms of existence, including the human realm.

Karma. Karma is the basic driving force of all creation. From the pure energy source manifesting fine homogenous vibrations called "Emptiness" *(Shunyata)*, the karmic threads lead to the creation of all matter from the tiniest particle to the planets by way of condensation, that is, slowing down the velocity of vibrations. The differentiation in frequencies gives rise to differences of form in matter. Therefore, the

Buddhist saying, *"All dharmas* (methods, laws, ways, reasons, causes) *are empty. But karma is not empty."* Everything comes from *Shunyata.* There is no "why" given, for the "why" question can never be fully answered. It is as it has happened.

The human realm is unique when compared to other realms. Existence in other realms is largely a process of passive consequence, with hardly any prospect of humanly controlled modification. The human realm is blessed with free-will, free-thinking, and free actions, thus offering the possibility of change leading to a final emancipation from karmic entanglements. Only in the final emancipation from all karmic influences does suffering cease. The "no suffering" stage only occurs in the emancipated, enlightened, purified, and perfected person. Suffering, however, is extraneous to Emptiness and has no real existence; rather it exists only as a sensation, a feeling, an emotion, or a thought. Learning about its true nature can greatly reduce the suffering resulting from the struggle against it. Accepting it as it is, further alleviates the problem, since you dis-identify from the suffering. You are not the suffering. Every existence is a passing process. All are ruled by impermanence.

Emancipation, therefore, is dependent upon freeing oneself from the grip of karma through a process of cleansing. Without cleansing, the mechanical process of cause→effect→cause→effect compounds endlessly. Effective cleansing can only occur if you incorporate cleansing into yourself, and that is achieved by meditation. Reading, listening, and reasoning give rise to concepts, which are karma. No doubt, such a karma may eventually lead you to wish to pursue insight for cleansing.

Karma, then, is a natural occurrence in everyday life. The only way to cleanse it is through meditation. Therefore, it is only wise to limit the use of meditation to the purpose of complete karmic-cleansing, leading to complete purification of the spirit-consciousness. It is not a good idea to try to make something happen or request something. In meditation, every thought, motive or desire has amplified karmic effects. If you wish to create karma, it is better to use normal thoughts and physical actions to do it. Do not use meditation. You cannot predict the "how," "what" or "when" of the consequences.

Metta. Karma has a "drawing-in" effect. The frequency of the pure energy source becomes differentiated and debased and become attached to the being. It is debased energy that is charged with events and thoughts. To undo the drawing-in effect requires a kind of radiating. While the drawing-in is fabricated by a kind of "self-centeredness" or egocentricity, it can be reversed when one acts without any motive, thus countering the drawing-in feature. Only then can the absorption be neutralized and return to the cosmic source.

The Metta or loving-kindness that then becomes available is unconditional, wide-open and boundless. It is called "compassion." Loving-kindness is not a narrow love for someone special, nor is it some kind of act, focused on a particular person. That would be karma. Metta is to love and be kind to all, yet to no one in particular. When energetically manifested as light, the base color of Metta is gold.

The Lower Abdomen. Karma exists as a bundle within and around the physical body. As it arises from the "I want" or acquisition tendency, there is an upsurge of energy as well. It is manifested as physical tension in the body, with an *"inward-drawing and upward-suspending"* characteristic. To undo the tension, and thus cleanse the karma, involves the reverse of such a tendency, i.e., radiating and downward-flushing. Simply using Metta to radiate is not good enough, as karma can hide by consolidating into a firm mass that blocks Metta's influence. Even Metta cannot find the source of problems. Therefore you must counter the upsurge tendency with a downward flushing. This movement is facilitated by your bringing awareness to your lower abdomen while doing Metta.

The lower abdomen is the center for insight, while the head is the focal point for conceptualization and karmic fabrication. A traditional meditation method using the lower abdomen is Vipassana meditation, called the *"Zen for Wisdom"* by the Chinese. Wisdom here means insightful wisdom. Many Qigong schools place emphasis on the lower abdomen, but restrict such emphasis to a point called *"dan tian."* Ancient literature describes an area behind the urinary bladder as the *"Palace of Life."* Evidence from my healing work, especially while reviving comatose patients, validates the fact that the healer can put life back into a person by using the *Palace of Life*. This is most important in healing, since curing disease means enhancing the life of a person. The cleansing of karma involves reducing forces detrimental to life. And life, of course, is fundamental. Without it, there can be no cure, cultivation, karmic cleansing, wisdom, enlightenment, or Buddhahood.

In CFQ, we bring awareness to the lower abdomen as a whole, not just to one point. Awareness means knowingly present, not focusing or concentrating. (Concentration, of course, brings about drawing-in, thus fabricating karma, even when CFQ principles are fully understood and followed). Awareness enhances the radiating effect, which fills up every known space. In time, the lower abdomen becomes the center of purification. Its location includes the hip, the pelvis, and the organs within it. Wherever there is impurity, i.e., karma, the lower abdomen is the action center from which purification is accomplished.

Simple awareness of a knowing presence, is not easy to do. Such awareness gets blocked, stopped in the head and chest, prevented from moving down. It seems it can be anywhere, except in the lower abdomen. This is an expected challenge, and informs the meditation practice. Someone who could move the awareness to the abdomen with ease would be perfected (a Buddha), and would not need to cultivate. Do not try hard to bring awareness to your lower abdomen. Rather, continue with knowing that it should be there, and that eventually it will happen.

The Unmoved Heart. Purity is a void, empty, or a "no-thing" when compared with impurities. Karma is a fabricated creation. It seeks to have or possess something. It arises from the "I", and from that which is normally treated as mine. Therefore, purity occurs only from the finest instinct, the innermost consciousness. To get at purity, you must summon your clear intention, which means no-intention (no impurity-focused intention). The pre-requisite for arriving at purity is to stop the normal mental creating and to arrive at Stillness. Stillness must first occur at the innermost intention, called the Heart. It should not be directed at the physical heart region as that can cause serious problems. The Unmoved Heart is most effective if it merges with the awareness of the lower abdomen.

When Stillness is wrongly interpreted, and taken as stillness of the body, it enhances the egocentric center that controls or holds the body still. That is a strong karmic-fabrication process. When karma is cleansed, the body is left in such a state that it cannot be kept still. Even in the advanced stage of meditation, where there are few external movements, there is still a tremendous internal physical struggle. Sitting comfortably still is impossible. Only a perfected being, a Buddha, can sit still in a perfect, cross-legged and harmonious posture.

The Mantra. To keep the Heart still, it must be given a task. Otherwise, it becomes entangled with karma. The most effective way I have discovered to enhance Stillness of the Heart, while at the same time doing Metta, is to use a "mantra." The Mantra I use in my meditation came to me during my unusual experience in 1993 and is a three-word phrase, *"Zhen-Shan-Mei."* The meanings of these words are: *Zhen*–True, Pure; *Shan*–Good, Compassion, Perfection; and *Mei*–Beautiful, Perfection. Together the Mantra, *Zhen Shan Mei*, means, Perfectly True, Pure and Good.

Do not think about the meaning of the Mantra during your meditation. Just recite it silently and mechanically at about 20 repetitions per minute throughout the duration of your meditation. Any form of thinking disrupts Metta, and prevents karmic cleansing. Silent recital is advisable, but some people may not be able to do so initially, in which case they can softly vocalize. Reciting slowly is important to bring peace and relaxation, but doing it too slowly can induce forgetfulness. Reciting too fast does not bring about the desired effect either. Reciting with the lower abdomen melts away body tension and dilutes debased energy in a karmic cleansing process. The act of recital converts pure cosmic energy into radiant energy as defined by the Mantra, and brings peace.

The meditation process can often be interrupted by your karma, which forms a shield to block off the Mantra. Distractions are to be expected. Once you realize what is happening, come back to the Mantra. The Mantra may sometimes become too fast. Slow down to an even speed once you realize this. If it gets blocked from your lower abdomen, realize that it is somewhere else. There is a shield blocking it. There is no need to try hard to bring it to the lower abdomen. Even if you try you may not be able to break the shield. Just carry on with the understanding that it should come from the lower abdomen.

The Postures. Begin your meditation by sitting loosely and relaxing on a stool about the height of your knees (see Illustration overleaf). Spread your feet shoulder wide. Standing in the *song kua* position as described in Chapter 6 is also a recommended posture. During meditation, it will be virtually impossible to sit or stand still. You will tilt, shake, or burst into physical movements. The cross-legged sitting position, frequently used in meditation should not be adopted since the way this position suppresses the legs prevents tension from being released through your limbs. Where there is no relaxation, there will be no karmic cleansing effect. The karma will then form into a shield around you and seduce you into a form of sleep, a blanking out, or dreamy state.

CFQ Meditation and Mantra of Healing

Initiation. Traditionally, meditation was taught by first imparting an initiation called *"passing on the method of the Heart."* I still do an initiation for beginners, that brings about an immediate meditation effect. However, it is highly unlikely that I will be able to do an initiation for you. My initiation is not needed if you meditate with full sincerely and trust. You must also try to understand the principles described in this book. The time required to achieve such understanding and insight can take, say, three months. Three months or 100 days is traditionally considered the time required to lay the foundation. You should practice the CFQ exercises diligently for that period before attempting meditation. I also want you to know that I sincerely hope that you will be able to meditate successfully. CFQ energy is radiant and does not diminish with distance thus non-local or remote initiation is possible. For now, however, you must take the initiative. Initiation introduces the radiant and downward flushing design to you, and at the same time connects the pure transparent consciousness from alaya to the Mantra. Such connections will naturally occur if you truly believe before attempting meditation.

Freeing Off. It is possible that you will feel or see your karma, even on your first attempt at meditation. It appears either as stiff, physical pulling forces, a heavy load or black clouds. Some of you may find it hard to remain awake. Recite your Mantra from your abdomen, be detached, and emotionless. Your body will tilt or shake but do not wilfully participate. Your job is to simply recite the Mantra and let whatever happens occur on its own. If your posture has shifted to a very uncomfortable position, tell yourself to get right out of the meditation, reset your position, and then continue. If you are jammed in a very uncomfortable position, do not use physical strength to pull yourself up before you get out of the meditation. You may find that you are unable to do so, or that you injure yourself in trying to do so.

Some of you may be pulled to the ground by the initial downward flushing effect, as the tension is thick and sticky. Allow your body to gently roll down on the ground. You may be stuck and feel a pulling force seeming to suck you into the ground. You will only be freed when this force wears out. Continue with your Mantra from your lower abdomen. Try to detach yourself and be like an observer of every experience and sensation. If you need to leave the meditation, will yourself out of it. The forces will disappear as you form this intention, so you will be able to stop moving.

Spontaneous movements are the consequence of a clear radiating and downward flushing effect, and will normally occur after an initial period of struggle ranging from 2—3 days to a few weeks. Some few will take 2—3 months. Some people move spontaneously on the first experience; others may develop spontaneous movements by doing the CFQ meridian exercises or merely by reading this book. The bioenergy blockages can dissipate after the meridian exercises or while you rest. Stay calm and do not worry or be attached to the movements. You can easily control them if you are relaxed. It is better, however, to let these movements occur naturally, so that you can benefit from their regulative power. When you have something else to do, the movements will stop.

Spontaneous Movements. Your meditation is a karmic cleansing and releasing process. Such a process can not only be vividly felt but also physically seen. Karma is tension bundled about the physical body and is formed of debased energy. When pure radiant energy is introduced, the melting influence manifests as an unfolding, unwinding, and uncoiling motion. During this time. It is most important that you remember to recite the Mantra continuously. The movements are not the objective or intention. They are not indicative of how smart or how advanced you are. They are not your business; rather your concern must be with the Mantra.

CFQ meditation is made simple, in the sense that you rely totally on the Mantra. The Mantra switches on the meditative state. When you want to switch off you simply stop the Mantra. Keeping the Mantra slow and steady from your lower abdomen is not easy. Most people alternate between forgetting it when obstructed by a shielding effect, and coming back to it when the shield clears off. Often, one finds that the Mantra cannot come from the lower abdomen but from somewhere else. It is clearly obstructed, and even concentrating forcefully cannot get you back to the proper focus. When this happens, just continue, knowing that it will come back naturally, and that it does not matter when. Sometimes, the reciting can get very fast, especially when there are fast physical movements. When aware of it, try to slow it down. Sometimes, you might unknowingly recite the Mantra aloud, as in the case when there is a struggle to release the tension from your head. Quiet down when you realize what is happening. Not doing the Mantra properly happens only when the layer preventing you from doing it right is clearing off, although you might not fully understand the implications in the moment. Being unable to do it right is part of the practice. It is because you are trying to undo what is not right in you. When you can do the Mantra perfectly right, you will be a perfected being.

Spontaneous movements often start with simple swaying, vibrating, shaking, or swinging, and gradually develop into a system of movements. They can become extremely complex and highly imaginative. They can even be quite bizarre. For instance, a craving for food might be highlighted, and you have the urge to eat immediately after meditation. If hidden sexual fantasies surface, you may spontaneously feel the urge to arouse yourself sexually. It is OK for things to happen in these ways. You are fully alert and at no time do you lose your mind. Pure energy knows the rules, and will not do harm to you nor anyone else. Even if shameful acts need to be done in order to clear your pent-up frustrations, it need not cause any embarrassment to you. Such bizarre tendencies will clear off after happening a few times and will not reoccur, but you will notice that your health and emotional well-being improve tremendously. This improvement is proportional to the clearing off of conflicts formed by suppressed tendencies.

Spontaneous movements can generally be classified as follows:

1. Shaking, vibrating, swinging, and stretching to enable physical loosening.

2. Sophisticated ways of releasing your disease problems which involve complex steps that cannot be duplicated by normal consciousness.

3. Changes in respiratory pattern and depth due to internal physiological changes.

4. Sighs and vocalizing of problems, crying and laughing, expressing emotional release.

5. Uncontrollable yawning, belching or gas discharges from improvements in physiological functions. These can also occur during normal times. What happens is that the body's natural physiological functions, which have been obstructed by stiffening as a result of high stress that gives rise to diseases, now become more relaxed, so that the natural physiological functions can be restored. Initial restoration results in the need for your body to "catch up" with its functions causing some inconvenience. The restoration of the natural regulative ability of your body is extremely beneficial for the treatment and prevention of diseases.

6. Kung fu or dance steps due to the materialization of hidden feelings of admiration.

7. Prayers, kneeling postures, chants, manifestations of your religious beliefs. Some people develop "mudras" or religious hand symbols.

8. Holding, clinging or sticking to objects, like trees or plumbing lines. These actions manifest a need to exchange energy or release it to enhance speedy recovery.

9. Spinning movements in a screw-like downward flushing. The beginning manifestations of these movements are often quite uncomfortable. Panic can cause dizziness. Try to flow along and remain grounded with your Mantra as you hold awareness in your lower abdomen. Watch out for corners and sharp edges in the surrounding objects or furniture. If you cannot manage the situation find a place to lie down on the ground and continue your Mantra.

10. Acupressure, self massage, tapping, brushing or clearing actions can occur. Even though you may not know anything about massage, meridians, and acupoints, you may work with expertise and a precision that even experts are unable to achieve. Often the effects are amazing. This development can be a very helpful preparation for work as a healer.

Initiates may face some problem within the first two weeks. Their bodies tend to move or sway after meditation times. Stay calm and do not feel alarmed. Your body is excited with your new ability to relax, and is trying to catch up with its needs. You can easily control the movements by holding on. It can be beneficial, however, for you to calmly allow such movements, say when you finish your work and relax in your own privacy.

Cooling Off. Spontaneous movements are useful for repairing body systems and bringing about healing effects. They evidence the release of karma. They occur throughout one's meditation practice, but with prolonged practice there will be less external movement. A no-movement state with absolute peace and joy, comes when you have cleared off all karma. That is the stage of a perfected being, an enlightened one, a Buddha. A perfected body is immortal. A perfected mind comes from a perfected heart without emotions other than perfect peace and joy. Such a stage requires long cultivation and is not expected in one lifetime. But in true cultivation that does not bother you. You benefit tremendously even though you are not perfected.

Your movements during meditation will be different at different times. There will be spurts of rapid movements, some slower movements, and occasionally, stillness, depending on the karma layer clearing at that time. Try to keep your Mantra going at all times. When there are fast movements check your Mantra to ensure that you go at a slow and even speed. This can normally slow down your movements. Do not use physical force to stop spontaneous movements. You can stop them simply by willing yourself out of meditation. Deep, strong and fast breathing can help when used after fast strong movements have slowed down. When there is an interruption, say when the telephone rings, there is no need to stop. Just answer the phone while continuing your movements.

Non-Physical Movements. When movements slow down or stop, you are likely to feel or see things vividly. There may be heavy burdens that feel physically real. There may be dark clouds or patches of clouds, flashes of light, or swirls of colored lights, images, messages, thoughts, geometric patterns and shapes, muscles throbbing, electrical sensations, things rippling or moving within your body, and so on.

Many people say, "Oh, these are just figments of my imagination." But it is more probable fact that this idea is a way karma plays with you and prevents you from further progress. If you embrace this idea, you will not be able to learn more about your karma, or melt it off. Whatever happens will be regarded as imaginary and considered nonsense. Retreating in this way into your mind helps your karma and interferes with your lower abdomen's radiating and clearing your karma. Give yourself a chance. Be open and remain unbiased. Non-physical movements and sensations exist. Even thoughts are information, messages or pictures that expand beyond the brain. Simply stated, the meditator's challenge here is to learn to accept things as they present themselves, rather than theorize about them.

The movements, images and sensations may happen even in the middle of busy activity and overshadow less vivid events. In advanced meditation, you see and feel the forces as folds, wrinkles, lines, layers and blocks that make up your physical body. The melting off causes physical pain and discomfort. The character of these forces is like glue. Beyond them is the clear and boundless light with a golden tinge, which is Metta or pure energy consciousness.

Threats & Temptations. If you are able to remain open-minded, every sensation, vison and experience will feel real, much more intensely real than physical seeing or feeling. Evil, monster-like creatures that appear to threaten you can provoke fear. If you see God, Buddha, Jesus or any being you love and respect, they all appear more real than when seen in a movie. They are holographic, or three dimensional and you can feel them. They are able to interact and may offer you fantastic promises.

Such visions are energetically and karmically real but have no eternal existence. They come from things you have seen or imagined that have become patterns in your karma. You benefit and improve only if they are diluted and cleared off. Do not take anything for real and believe in it. In other words, citing the Diamond Sutra:

"Do not be excited when seeing the forms. You shall be unconditional with your motivation."

Thus seeing a Buddha is not seeing a real Buddha. Regard it as a demon of your heart. If you are unmoved, you will observe these appearances changing form. God turns into the devil, creatures become deities, and eventually upon further dilution, they change into black clouds and dissipate. You will realize that they are simply images representing your personal challenges.

Qigong practice, unsupported by proper teaching about visions, can give rise to the risk of illusions and deviations. Such risks become much higher and even inevitable if mentors teach superstition or idol-worship (especially of themselves). Using CFQ, trust the Mantra and you will be completely safe. It may also be entertaining to go through such visionary experiences.

Conclusion. Daily meditation practices of between half an hour to two hours is recommended, preferably at fixed times and for fixed durations. Do not be over-ambitious at the beginning. Increase the time of meditation gradually. Coming out from meditation is achieved by stopping the recital of the Mantra. Most people, however, especially beginners, need sure and convincing actions to prevent a lingering effect that may cause disorientation and confusion.

Instructions:

1. Tell yourself you are coming out of meditation and give it fifteen to thirty seconds to "tail off." Do not attempt to conclude in the middle of strong sensations or movements, but wait until they weaken.

2. Open your eyes and breath deeply and heavily three to five times.

3. Stand up and put your feet together. Do the deep breathing concluding exercise of the hexagram dance (in Chapter 6). Repeat five to ten times and finally,

4. Open your feet to shoulder width and slap your body in a downward and outward direction to awaken it and to clear away uneven tensions stuck there. Do this, starting from your upper chest down along the front of your body, inner sides of your legs, down to your feet, lower back, and hind side of the legs to the ankles. Next, the inner side of left arm to palm; outer side of left arm to fingers; inner side of right arm to palm; and outer side of right arm to fingers. Finally, slap both sides of the body from the sides of the chest, and outer sides of your legs down to the feet.

CFQ Meditation and Healing

The CFQ approach to healing is different from most other treatment methods, in that it undoes every problem. Other approaches control, suppress, and hide symptoms. In addition, CFQ also clears the karma, the most basic cause of problems. Karma includes every pain and discomfort arising from diseases, and normally stored energetically in the consciousness, even when the symptoms no longer exist. It also goes deep within to take out the emotional pain of normal life experiences that manifests as physical body pain in the outward clearing process.

Whether or not disease is cleared will be obvious, in that discomfort flows out and can be felt dissipating. Even when debased energy leaves the body before being properly diluted, you can feel a packet of pain or discomfort in an energetic region that is not normally regarded as your body. Pain can also be converted into sensations of heat, cold, numbness, electricity, magnetism, itch and so on. Disease symptoms are cleared step by step in this manner, and from deep within. The deep-seated pain and discomfort will spread to a large shallow area in its outward movement. Some discomfort will be converted to pain. The truth is, deep inside, there are no nerves for pain. However, deep seated problems without apparent pain may be dangerous. By the time they move out and manifest as pain, they fortunately have been reduced in magnitude and danger.

Some old scars left by injuries and operations, may in the course of healing appear infected and ooze pus and other fluid discharges. When they are free of infection, the scar becomes smoother and fades in color. Keloid formations in old scars will be cleared in this way. Sometimes old injuries manifest as blue-black marks before becoming fully healed. There is truth in the saying *"No pain, no gain."* If you can relax and watch calmly, you will be able to see the true nature of pain as a clearing effect. The intensity of the pain is also greatly reduced by calm. Panic aggravates pain by not allowing it to flow out smoothly. Fear also exaggerates the degree of suffering. Many people are used to pain in the daily flow of life, including physical exercising, being massaged, or receiving physiotherapy, but are quite frightened by the pain of "undoing".

The CFQ exercises recommended in Chapter 6 have similar effects, but the intensity is much less when compared to the sensations to be experienced in meditation. At times even though you are totally healthy and usually without pain, you might still feel pain and discomfort during CFQ meditation and exercises. Take it calmly. It is evidence that your practice is effective.

Poltergeist & Unusual Phenomena. Sudden and strong releases of pent-up emotional conflicts and disharmonies may bring about damage to small electrical appliances. During certain periods your watch, clocks, TV sets, cars and electrical switches may break down for no apparent reason. In extreme cases, there have been reports of flying pans or small objects and strange noises around the practitioner's house. Meditators are likely to feel the departing forces that bring about such occurrences.

Such occurrences, when they appear, normally happen a few times over a few weeks to one or two months, and will end once the strong pent up energy is reduced. There should be no rush to repair appliances, as after a while they typically return to working order. Accept such problems when they come. After all, the cleansing of karma resulting in a cure of disease and improvement of life is no small matter!

The Transformation. In the advanced stages, normally after at least three years of practice, you will discover the folds and wrinkles within the karmic clouds. The unfolding process involves physical tearing off that can be seen, by an observer, as muscle movements, blowing up and popping off. Much stiffness and pain will be experienced during the struggle for release.

And all of this experience is necessary. The normal inward-drawing and upward suspending of the physiological body must be reversed in order to bring about changes that will not support disease. Disease can be manifested as deformations of the body. The clearing of disease involves overhauling, repairing, and improving physiological patterns. By the time this happens, most likely you will be medically certified as healthy. But good health is not an end point. Life is a continuous process of encountering disease-fabricating factors. Even though now, you can deal with your life to minimize the disease fabricating process, you should continue the CFQ process to effect thorough changes. Remember your motivation for meditation is to illuminate your heart and discover your true self, not just curing disease.

The tearing off process and the melting of the "glue" takes place in turn in every muscle, bone and organ in turn. It covers every aspect of our physical, mental and emotional lives. It is brought about by spiritual purification. The opening-out brought about by the radiating effect of meditation, and the elongation brought about by the downward flushing are physically and painfully felt. Ancient literature describe such a stage as *"shedding from the ordinary womb and transforming into the immortal bones."*

Beyond our physical boundaries exists boundless, transparent light, often tinted with gold. That is the spiritual body. Even though it appears as light, you feel your consciousness in it. This is cosmic consciousness, described as *"heaven and human merged as one."* Cosmic consciousness, however, cannot be felt at all times. It often gets shielded off by dissolving karmic forces. I suspect in the perfected state, there will be total clarity and transparency dominated by rainbow colored lights, without a tinge of obstruction.

A Case Example: *The subject, in his fifties, is a bikkhu (monk), devoted to daily meditation and religious studies for over 20 years. He had multiple health problems including tinnitis(ringing noise in the ears), chronic fatigue syndrome and poor digestion.*

He came to Penang to seek treatment for his problems and was brought to my Center. I gave him direct healing together with teaching him the 7-Movements exercise. He received a total of six treatment sessions during this period. He also asked to be initiated into CFQ meditation. At first the moving meditation made him spin uncontrollably. He collapsed and vomited, but he was undeterred and continued with the practice. At the end of two weeks, he remarked, "Sifu you have definitely made an important discovery for dealing with karma."

He had not enjoyed the first week of practice as he was used to concentration, discipline and vigorous forms of Qigong and kung fu. Soon he learned to relax from the meridian energy exercising. By month's end, tinnitis no longer bothered him. His stomach upset was reduced, and he felt more energetic. Most significantly, he ceased to be antagonized by loud noises. Now traffic noise, barking dogs and even the loud hammering noises from a nearby construction site did not bother him.

8

Complementary Techniques: Sit, Walk, Heal

Meridian Standing: Freedom Hands *(xiao yao shou)*

This single energy exercise provides a loosening, relaxing and freshening effect within a short time of three to five minutes. It also helps to check whether you are adequately slow and relaxed when performing the movements. Strength will be trapped in the joints causing pain if the movements are too fast and strenuous. It is a useful warm-up step before CFQ exercise or meditation to prepare the body for more effective practice. It is very beneficial if performed during short breaks from work.

Instructions:

1. Spread the feet one foot apart and relax the whole body.

2. Lift the right arm straight up to the front until slightly below the shoulder level, with the right hand hanging loosely, and bend the right knee at the same time.

3. Bend the right arm pulling the hand back to the side of your right chest.

4. Straighten the right arm downward with the palm facing the ground.

5. When doing this movement lift the left arm straight up to the front until slightly below the shoulder level, with the left hand hanging loosely and bend the left knee at the same time. Continue as with the right hand.

6. Alternate between the left and right with a continuous movement.

This exercise is similar to the "flying cloud hands" (Movement 1) recommended in the CFQ exercises (Chapter 6) except that the *song kua-fa jing* is performed on each side alternatively. Take care not to exert any strength at all. Find the correct rhythm and move comfortably at a speed of about 50 repetitions per minute (left-right movements counted as one). Perform this movement for up to 15 minutes.

Meridian Energizers

Meridian Energizers: Freedom Hands and Freedom Walk

Meridian Stepping: Freedom Walk *(xiao yao bu)*

Similar to the above technique. This gives a better sense of freedom if done by walking in a wide open space. However, as the way you walk may look strange to passers-by, some may feel shy about walking this way in public. This technique helps to improve your sense of balance and enhances the grounding effect, bringing about faster recovery from disease. It increases flexibility and strength in the lower limbs. Do not use strength in your legs or hands.

Instructions:

1. Move the hands similarly to the "Freedom Hands" technique except that when you lift a hand to the front, you step forward using the alternate leg. The right arm is raised forward with the right hand hanging loosely together with the left leg stepping forward.

2. Without moving the legs, float the right hand back to the side of the chest. Move the right hand down with the palm facing the ground. Raise the left arm and at the same time step forward with the right foot.

3. Continue to walk in a similar manner. Take care not to exert strength during the exercise.

Meridian Walking: Lotus Walk *(lian hua bu)*

The Lotus Walk is about "not doing." Do nothing, just walking and be peaceful. Peace and joy reveal themselves when a person has or wants nothing (no-thing). A normal person has too much of everything. To help you to be emptied, bring your awareness under your feet. Walk easily and be aware of the sensation under each foot as it contacts the ground. Take care not to exert strength or try to increase the firmness of contact by pushing your feet down. Unwinding tension may lead to strange walking movements. You might appear clumsy or un-coordinated.

Instructions:

1. Walk easily and be aware of the sensation under each foot when contacting the ground. Take care not to exert any strength. Do not try to increase the firmness of your contact with the ground by pushing your feet down.

2. Walk easily without the exertion of normal walking. This way, the whole body is relaxed.

3. Do not purposefully swing your arms but let them move naturally.

4. The whole body should be loose and move easily at the speed of a slow stroll. Maintain a peaceful composure.

5. Your walk may turn into spontaneous movements of arms and the whole body. Unload strength, tension, stiffness, or whatever flows down and out naturally.

Note: The point of this walking is to be relaxed and easy. Just walk. Without walking, it is difficult to become relaxed and easy. Eventually, what is left is the contact of the feet on the ground. When nothing else exists, there is true peace and joy. Remember: Peace is God consciousness. It is healing. Bear in mind that it is simplicity that will work and heal. Complexity causes problems.

Origins & Implications. Many Buddhist temples have paintings or statutes of Buddhas or bodhisatttvas sitting or standing on lotus flowers. The lotus is symbolic of the attainment of enlightenment. There is no intention of encouraging people to destroy a flower. If the ancient saints had such an intention, they would be committing a bad action and cease to be enlightened. The East uses the lotus flower as a symbol of purity, described as *"originating from the mud but never tainted by the* *slightest trace of it."* The pointed appearance of the petals is the symbol of radiating wisdom. Purity equals wisdom, which comes out from within, and radiates and illuminates every non-transparency (or act of ignorance).

Complementary Meridian Exercises

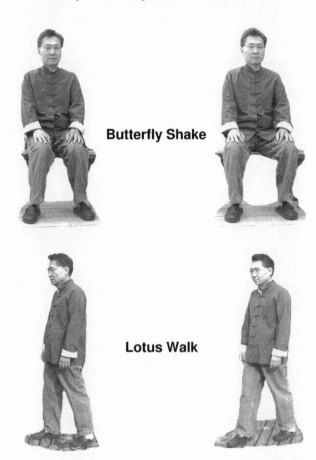

Complementary Meridian Exercises: Butterfly Shake and Lotus Walk

The cultivation process involves the letting go of karma, ego, and non-transparency (the debased energy of tension). Letting go is a downward process, as advocated by TCM. This is a crucial process for curing disease. It is the opposite of the suspending effect fabricated by the mind (the center of conditioned knowledge, thoughts, concepts, delusions, and the works of karma). Through systematic and diligent cultivation, the attaching karma is completely cleared off. What is left is pure consciousness with perfect transparency. At this point, the enlightened being does not have any thoughts or emotions. He or she has absolute peace and joy. The sense of physical existence is confined to the contact of his or her feet on the ground.

True teachings talk about harmony, non-acquiring, non-doing, non-creating, non-visualizing, non-intending with the mind, and gentle forms or methods so as to be truly with the Tao (being "*one with the way of nature*"). This is also an important verification of Taoist teaching which says, "*The qi (bioenergy) of a true being originates from his heel.*" A "true being" is one who has realized the Tao or the supreme way of truth thereby lives harmoniously with nature and is able to perform miracles. Such a being is called "*sien*" or demi-god and enjoys great calmness and peace. Sage-hood involves not being disturbed or influenced by the problems of life. Breathing becomes so calm that it appears to ordinary people that there is no breath. Consciousness has completely settled down so all that is felt is the contact of the feet on the ground. When breathing, the expansion and contraction of heels against the ground is also felt.

Effects and Problems. The lotus walk offers not only an additional means of cultivation but also an excellent way of ridding oneself of disease. With prolonged practice and as one's health improves, the practitioner feels the contact of his or her feet on the ground becoming light and bouncy, similar to the stepping on a cushioned carpet. She or he will be able to feel a variety of strange but comfortable sensations, including an explosion of a ball of light with each step walking into the transcendent state. Meditating in this manner is more effective than conventional walking meditation, which is too slow for most modern people to follow, as it requires concentration. The normal but slow lotus walk enhances relaxation. It is recommended for all who are simply able simply to walk, and does not have the restrictions of CFQ meditation as recommended in Chapter 7. The act of walking itself ensures that at all times practitioners are in touch with physical reality instead of throwing themselves completely into the spiritual-consciousness side of themselves.

The lotus walk should not be used merely for the sake of walking. The peace-consciousness aspect is much more important. To facilitate this, parks with scenic greenery are preferred to barren asphalt roads surrounded by concrete buildings. Parks naturally enhance a feeling of freedom. Take care not to indulge in active thinking as this will fabricate a suspension effect that obstructs letting go. However, the dissolution of tension in the process brings about thoughts which should be allowed to manifest naturally without control. You should realize that you are the walking and not the thinking.

Best results are achieved by doing away with any tendency to hold back. When there is a pain or discomfort in the joints or any part of the body, simply allow the pain and discomfort to flow down and out, without visualizing to bring about such an effect. The act of visualizing is a natural tendency, but doing it may prevent the desirable effect from occurring. Such an act may only serve to give the practitioner satisfaction because of your mistaken belief that s/he has cleverly fought to overcome problems.

Note: If the contact of your feet on the ground is not balanced, as in the case of someone with a limp, do not try to force a balance. Pains, discomforts, and numbness occur due to the outward releasing process. At this point, the demonic voice of karma may say, "Ah, it's so unbearable! This walking stuff doesn't do any good but increases your problem. Beware! You will hurt yourself if you continue." Only by remaining calm and continuing with your walk will you see that, in fact, the problems are far from unbearable, and in reality, your health is improving and you are having less and less trouble.

The *Lotus Walk* procedure is effective for almost every known kind of health problem, and manifests some amazing effects. For instance, someone who needs to walk with a cane due to stroke, injury, or old age (provided she or he is willing to invest some time and faith in the effort), may well find that the condition improves so much in a few weeks or months that he or she is able to do away with the cane. There may be a small cost: When the diseased energy of staleness, numbness, and weakness become apparent in the down-and-out process, the recovering person may feel numb, weak, and heavy. In some cases, he or she may feel unable to continue walking. Do not panic, as the walking effort would be wasted if the diseased energy gets absorbed back inside by the panic. (Should the diseased energy get reabsorbed, the person will then be able to walk again but only as before and without any improvement).

Individuals practicing the lotus walk should remain calm, rest as necessary, and avoid paying too much attention to the problem. They should be detached from it and should continue to walk as much as possible. When the adverse symptom is over, s/he will find a tremendous improvement in the problem. Some people may think that this kind of walking lacks challenge and excitement, compared to rapid walking, jogging, or other forms of strenuous physical exercise. "You don't even sweat in the slow walk and therefore it will not give the normal exercise effect nor help to reduce weight."

Precisely, it is the lack of challenge and excitement that gives rise to peace and joy, which are more profound and lasting. With challenge and excitement, you fabricate tension, which is detrimental to overall health, and when you get old, the strength you built in your muscles might well become the source of weak limbs. You pay a price for it.

You should therefore learn to appreciate peace and joy, rather than challenge and excitement. This manner of walking, by the way, is also excellent for weight reduction, which depends on smooth drain-off passages enhanced by the lotus walk. With smooth drainage the body is unable to trap excessive fats and fluids. The loss of weight in this manner is more profound and lasting, compared to the loss of weight through the usual sweat-and-burn technique which is often quickly restored when the person stops exercising furiously. The exercise process itself fabricates tension that blocks the internal draining-off ability. Even though the lotus walk is not strenuous at all, during the time when the initial opening effect takes place (say after a few weeks), you will find that you can sweat profusely because your sweat pores become opened and their healthy functioning is restored. This will be reduced over time to a light perspiration and warmth.

When properly performed with a whole-body looseness, the walking process may give rise to involuntary swinging of arms, weird movements, or a tilting of the body. Do not control the movements but allow them to happen naturally. The release or unwinding of tension in this manner is extremely beneficial to your health as it can rapidly sort out and clear the binding forces.

The process may also involve periods of no improvement. This is due to the natural ability of the disease energy to hold on, in order to obstruct the letting go process. Such a holding-on ability is a built-in feature in varying degrees for every individual. It can be considered part of one's character. When you come face to face with the problem, you are powerless to command a release in order to let-go. When this happens, you might become frustrated and reluctant to continue walking. Practicing CFQ exercises together with the lotus walk will help to open out your system so that the diseased energy will be unable to hold back. CFQ movements also help to deal with a limitation of the lotus walk procedure, that is, owing to the location of the feet, it takes a longer time to deal with some problems centered up the head or the body.

Retirees who choose to invest a lot of time in this procedure, can be reasonably assured that they will live to a healthy old age. After all, karma will reap what a person sows. If a person has so much time but prefers to use it in other ways, he or she will be rewarded in other ways, which might include ill-health and a shortening of life due to inappropriate sensory pleasure. For others who take time off due to ill-health or holidays, this walking technique helps to fill up time which might otherwise be spent on idle resting, or other activities which promote health problems.

Meridian Sitting: Butterfly Shake *(yao jiao gong)*

This is an excellent relaxing exercise for those who are so weak and frail that they can hardly do any exercise at all. They may, for example, be inhibited by partial paralysis due to stroke or injury. Others may just need to pass time, as happens with some cancer patients. The leg movements of the Butterfly Shake create a downward process in line with the disease-curing path. Such movements also cultivate a karmic cleansing practice.

Instructions:

1. Sit on a reclining chair with a head rest for maximum whole-body looseness.

2. Place the feet on the ground at shoulder width and shake loosely and continuously at the rate of 60—100 repetitions per minute.

3. Both knees should draw inward and outward at the same time. Allow the movement to spread throughout your legs all the way down to your feet.

Purposes & Effects. This is an excellent relaxing exercise, especially for those who are quite weak. It is also helpful for patients incapacitated by an illness such as cancer. The movement of the legs creates a downward process in line with the disease elimination path advocated by TCM(Oriental traditional medicine). Karmic cleansing, as mentioned above, is also promoted. When the knees open outward, the feet yin meridians open out to enhance bioenergy flow. When the knees draw inward, the feet yang meridians open out to enhance return flow of energy. However, there should not be any attempt to visualize these flows. The explanation serves only to clarify why such a simple act is powerful enough to treat various diseases, including severe, irreversible or medically incurable cases.

All major meridians form into a network and are mutually influential. There are six meridians that run through each leg—3 yin and 3 yang. By making full use of these meridians, one is able to gradually enhance smooth bioenergy flow along all the 12 major meridians to bring about a whole-body repair effect. Care is needed to ensure a whole-body looseness to facilitate such repair and rejuvenation. The most important act is to simply carry out this procedure without any attempt to visualize or make anything happen. This enhances the downward flow of bioenergy, which according to Chinese medicine, makes hundreds of diseases vanish. The "not doing" mental attitude enhances peace, the all-powerful healing force.

It is an effective treatment for Alzheimer's, Parkinson, senility, and dementia as the simplicity of this exercise does not demand any form of memorizing, yet provides sufficient activation to the whole body to dilute the gripping-binding force of diseases, helping to free the patients from such problems. However, such patients often require reminders from other people since they shift their attention to habitual thoughts and forget about butterfly shaking. Noticeable and speedy improvements occur in a matter of a few weeks or months for those who voluntarily and willingly participate. The crucial factor is to spend time at it, even as much as eight to ten hours daily, not just 10—20 minutes. But time is often what such people have in abundance. Without proper activities being encouraged they might spend time in idle thinking and self-pity, which only exaggerates their sufferings. It is also not a good idea to spend too much time on those activities requiring excessive mental usage, for example, reading, watching TV, crossword puzzles or playing chess. These are often contributors to their problems.

To enhance the effects of the Butterfly Shake, explain to the patient the importance of meridian-shaking as a way of shifting functional patterns from the mind to the body, from being physically passive to being more active. For those who participate reluctantly, the healing effect will not be good. In the first place, they appear to prefer their thoughts, which, of course, give them pleasure and pain, happiness and anger, fear and excitement. They are not willing to let go of their thinking habits, which, after all, have accorded them some enjoyment. If you talk to them, they will deny such an imprisonment. The thoughts occur naturally and they are just taking them as they come, often forgetting those thoughts as soon as or immediately after they occur. They may also be so trapped in the dreaming world that they become totally dissociated.

The butterfly shake will naturally trigger thinking, and will make the compulsive nature of the thoughts more obvious in the dissolve and release process. Take care not to follow the thoughts, focusing only on the leg-shaking. In time, when compulsive thinking is corrected, significant improvements may occur. However, it takes a great deal of effort to free oneself from the grip of the thoughts, to be able to proceed with butterfly shaking. Do not fight to stop the thoughts, as this would activate them more furiously. Take the attitude that they are entitled to exist but you have no business with them. In this way, you will be able to continue with the shaking.

This technique is also good for people with just about any problem, who want to make good use of their time for healing. The opening out and dissolving of disease energy forces inevitably causes discomfort including pain, numbness, heaviness, stiffness, heat and cold. These should be treated with understanding. A cure from disease comes from clearing out debased forces. Clearing out is experiential, and must occur and be felt as it happens. A right attitude and understanding help to alleviate the natural tendency to hold back and obstruct the process. It is a good idea to take short breaks to stretch, loosen and walk about.

Some people may protest with disappointment, "This is so simple! It can't be very effective!" But this is precisely the core of effective healing. A truly effective method must be simple and universally good. Complex and sophisticated methods may serve to satisfy the desire for excitement. Take for instance the act of breathing. That simple breathe-in and breathe-out sustains life. If life chooses to depart, sophisticated machines could not hold it back. At best they provide assistance to the patient, supporting enough in-and-out-breathing to provide time to enable the patient to pull through.

You may have noticed that many people have the butterfly shaking habit. Your colleagues in the workplace, people waiting for a table in restaurants, and others often do it. By shaking their legs they are able to deal with their stressful states of mind or emotions. Otherwise, they might walk or move about restlessly or shout out their frustration. However, the manner and speed with which they shake often does not help them go beyond dealing with the present situation.

Modifications: Those who are highly stressed, the weak, the elderly, or partially disabled, may not be able to shake loosely and slowly. They either shake quickly or not at all. Initially, it is okay for them to shake improperly. Check and help them to gradually reduce the speed and strength of their shaking. Their ability to slow down often means that their condition is improved. Some people may not be able to shake evenly. One leg might shake more easily and loosely than the other. Do not deliberately try to balance the movements, but check to make sure that they put equal attention on each leg. Eventually, natural forces will bring balance to both legs, which will mean that conditions have improved. Similarly, for those with partial paralysis, it is OK for the paralyzed leg not to move at all, but the patient should try to put equal attention on each leg to ensure progress. When the paralyzed leg starts to move, it often means that it is loose and strong enough to practice standing and walking.

For bed-ridden patients, it may not always be practical to move to a sitting position to practice this procedure. They can place their legs straight on the bed and shake their feet to move their entire leg. However, this position is less effective as it lacks a clear downward direction. It is also more difficult to maintain awareness, resulting in frequently forgetting to shake. To enhance progress, move them to a sitting position as much as possible.

A Case Example: *The male patient, in his late fifties, discovered that his abdomen was swollen. Medical tests revealed he had liver cancer that had spread extensively. The diagnosis was that he was at the critical terminal stage. His doctor disclosed this prognosis to the patient's wife and children but withheld it from him. Medication to induce urination was prescribed but did not help to reduce the swelling. No further treatment was recommended. The patient was not told of the diagnosis by his family. He blamed his condition on an auto accident that had occurred the previous year. He became depressed, lost his appetite, and refused to see visitors at home. On a relative's recommendation, his wife brought the cancer victim for my energy treatments. His family pleaded that I should not reveal his true condition to him, with which I fully agreed. On our first meeting, I simply mentioned that the problem was caused by an injury and that it could be cured. Healing sessions were scheduled twice weekly.*

After the second session, his appetite improved. After five sessions, the swelling began to subside and he stopped taking medication for urination. Subsequently he took the medication on occasion when he felt that his abdomen was swollen, as he believed that the medication could rapidly reduce the swelling. After the eighth session, his appetite returned and he consumed enormous amounts of meat that he was fond of (His wife and children tried to stop him from excessive meat eating but that made him very upset).

He resumed his morning walks. I tried to introduce the lotus walk, but he preferred his usual forceful walking and arm-swinging. Since he was a retiree with excessive idle time, I advised him to spend more time outdoors walking and resting in-between. He declined to do. I also suggested evening walks but he was disinterested. However, one change surprised his family. He grew fond of receiving visitors and spent long hours talking with them cheerfully. After 16 sessions, his condition had greatly improved. Since he lived quite far from the center healing was reduced to once a week.

Fourteen weeks passed. He found out about the liver cancer diagnosis. He refused to come to the center to consult or for further treatment. Instead he switched to some herbal treatment. Several months later (slightly over a year after the medical diagnosis) he passed away.

9

The Heart Sutra: Prajna Paramita

My unusual experience in 1993 and subsequent meditation experiences encouraged me to renew my earlier interest in Buddhist Dharma. During this period I joined my Buddhist friends in chanting retreats. But I gave up when I found that I could not get myself interested in chanting Sutras. Attending then to the insights achieved in my meditation experience, I was inspired to look for the possible source of those insights, which I joyously found in the Heart Sutra.

The Heart Sutra: Translated Text

The Bodhisattva Avalokita, while moving in the deep course of Perfect Understanding, shed light on the five skandhas (basic elements that constitute the body)and found them equally empty. After this penetration, he overcame all pain.

"Listen, Shariputra, form is emptiness, emptiness is form, form does not differ from emptiness, emptiness does not differ from form. The same is true of feelings, perceptions, mental formations, and consciousness.

"Hear, Shariputra, all dharmas are marked with emptiness; they are neither produced nor destroyed, neither defiled nor immaculate, neither increasing nor decreasing. Therefore, in emptiness there is neither form, nor feeling, nor perception, nor mental formations, nor consciousness; no eye, nor ear, or nose, or tongue, or body, or mind, no form, no sound, no smell,

no taste, no touch, no object of mind; no realms of elements (from eyes to mind-consciousness); no interdependent origins and no extinction of them (from ignorance to old age and death); no suffering, no origination of suffering, no extinction of suffering, no path; no understanding, no attainment.

"Because there is no attainment, the Bodhissattvas, supported by the Perfection of Understanding, find no obstacles for their minds. Having no obstacles, they overcome fear, liberating themselves forever from illusion and realizing perfect Nirvana. All Buddhas in the past, present, and future, thanks to this Perfect Understanding, arrive at full, right and Universal Enlightenment.

"Therefore, one should know that Perfect Understanding is a great mantra, is the highest mantra, is the unequaled mantra, the destroyer of all suffering, the incorruptible truth. A mantra of Prajna Paramita should therefore be proclaimed. This is the mantra: "Ga-te, ga-te, pa-ra-ga-te, pa-ra-sam-ga-te, bodhi, svaha."

General Commentary. Quantum physics has provided evidence that all matter is made up of atoms and are, in their core, essentially empty. Sub-atomic particles are, by nature, light manifested either as particles or waves. The basis of all matter is therefore energy. All matter exists as it is. There is no "why?" The "why" is irrelevant. Matter has a definite lifespan and will return to the energy state. That is the law of impermanence.

Our point here, however, is not science. Rather, we are talking about human suffering. The very fact that we exist means that the sufferings of birth, aging, disease, and death are part of our existence. None of these can truly be isolated. Although isolating and treating disease as done conventionally is as natural as eating and working and although we have a duty and responsibility to ensure that we carry on existence in the best possible manner, without an integrated picture of suffering that includes the other components, and without an appreciation of the law of impermanence, the solution will be partial and incomplete.

The need to expand beyond the conventional perspective is much more obvious now, due to the pressures introduced by material progress. The comfort and enjoyment brought by such progress comes with a price, which may involve suffering. Indeed, some people may find that the challenge of coping with progress itself reveals a sense of something missing. The human experience of life requires a balanced mix of the physical and the spiritual, the God presence, which may often be missed in the face of physical pursuits. But humans are not robots, they have hearts. The displacement of the heart by material possessions creates a great vacuum. Despite the promises proffered by medical and scientific progress, we face increasing threats of new diseases. While many of the old problems remain partially or unsatisfactorily solved, there is the danger of a re-emergence of some extinct diseases. There seems to be a cruel trick being played by nature: in the developed countries the rate of contraception and infertility appears to be increasing and population growth is predicted to be below zero. Is nature is trying to tell us that the stresses of modern living are unsuitable for human existence?

Despite new scientific inventions and genetic engineering, human suffering does not end. Even if all diseases could be cured, there remains the incurable problem of old age and death, the fear of which is something many people can identify. Fear itself means suffering. It is therefore justifiable and timely to make a more serious exploration into that aspect that human life that has been brushed aside to make way for scientific advance: the spiritual aspect, which deals with the heart.

Science has in many cases assumed that humans are no more than their physically observable body. Some may protest: "Humans have at no time neglected the metaphysical domain. We have many religions to cater to this need." True enough! That is the area of the religion. But religion should not be confined to principles, ethics, codes of conduct, or just reading and admiring the stories of ancient saints. There must be a way to enter and feel close to God, to be sure of ultimate existence. There must be ways to achieve our own experience of what the ancient saints discovered.

The Importance Of Insight. At present, we exist in the world of physical reality, with a physical body and a consciousness (consisting of the five senses, the brain and the psyche), which are attracting (drawing-in) by nature. The mind (sixth) consciousness is the most predominant in terms of registering our experience of existence and our relationship with the physical world. Every thought and action is cumulatively assimilated and processed in the light of existing memories. New perceptions are influenced by the patterns and limits of previous memories and by the restrictions of the mind consciousness. This consciousness, called the discriminating mind, processes, sorts, and discerns information according to its limiting patterns. The reading of dharma or religious literature, listening to dharma talks, or reading of this book cannot bypass or erase pre-existing conditions. Neither can a new set of conditions cancel out a pre-existing condition (for instance, the introduction of good karma does not cancel out an existing bad karma). Any attempt at understanding the dharma and thus changing life's conditions for the better will be futile if our efforts are limited to such attempts to understand.

In view of this, Buddha encouraged his disciples to develop insight into his teachings. "*Ehi passiko,*" *he said*—come see for yourself. It is of utmost import to go beyond and to by-pass the faculties of consciousness, particularly the mind. How can that be done? Within the deepest level of consciousness, in the depths of *alaya* (eighth consciousness), lies the purest consciousness; a consciousness that has not been affected by the tendency to absorb and draw in. It is called *Tathagata garbha* (Buddha-seed) or God-consciousness. It is an energy vibration constituting clear, transparent light.

Find the way to access, release and radiate the innermost Heart light, and its transparent beauty will shine out into the eternal and neutralize the effects of fabricated memories of existence. It will gradually dissolve, dilute, and free us of the burdens of fabrication. It is a process of Metta (loving-kindness) whereby memories and the ego-centric grasping within the memories (the fundamental source of "suffering beings"), are freed to return to Emptiness. Thus, we should not be talking about understanding the Heart Sutra but rather about materializing the reality of the Heart Sutra.

Only by radiant intimacy with the transparent light of the *alaya* can one truly be free from the grip and boundary of one's human instincts and the fabricating and absorbing tendency of one's consciousness. That intimacy involves a letting-go and undoing process, which liberates the ever-present reality of the Heart. Using any other way burdens you with your fabricating and absorbing instinct, since such ways rely on normal consciousness, particularly the mind.

Insight Through CFQ. The unique method of meditation taught in CFQ allows the transparent light of the deepest consciousness to shine out and merge with the pure energy vibration of the cosmic universe. It follows the Zen tradition of Mahayana Buddhism by not relying on dharma literature or explanations, but by trusting direct experience and insight.

One paramount technique that facilitates access to this deepest consciousness is a process of direct transmission from a teacher to student, that is, initiation. Initiation has been traditionally called "*impartation of the heart.*" This is metaphorically equivalent to using the fire from an oil lamp to light up other lamps. Without the first fire, the lamps of others will not be enlightened.

After initiation, a student moves spontaneously in the freeing, burden releasing process. Those initiated also learn to deal with their own problems (and even other peoples' problems) without any conscious effort. Such moving is different from the spontaneous, free-flowing movements practiced in various Qigong methods which are based on a qi-power that is motivated by desire (seeking strength). Gradually the novice's physical movements diminish, to be replaced by meditative states whereby she or he directly sees and feels the activation and purification of energy forces, and arrives at a new way of understanding through *prajna-paramita* or direct intuition. This wisdom opposes that generated by the normal discriminating mind.

When all forms fabricated by memories, which stand out as impurities, are completely dispersed, the Heart reveals itself as luminous, transparent, Boundless Love. The meditator arrives at the state of samadhi (perfect Stillness) with perfect understanding. The transformation process goes from forms to Emptiness (void of forms); from bodily senses to the extinction of such senses; from thoughts, emotions, consciousness, feelings and sufferings to luminous transparency. Boundless Love occurs in reality, not just conceptually. It is seen to be happening as it happens. It brings about a complete transformation in both the body and the consciousness. This change in the physical state, as well as the mind-state, eradicates all disease.

Even a new initiate can, while in the meditative state, escape from entanglements and burdens by watching the dissolving process with a detached attitude. The transformation process and encounters along the way are, however, too lengthy and will not be described in the present book.

The transition from the habit of fabricating and acquiring with the mind, to a letting-go and undoing process using pure consciousness is too great and bold for most people. Learning about something not within the grasp of ordinary minds can be both burdensome and painful, even if the truth is evident. Facts can be cold and harsh, even if they can solve some personal problems. At some stages of development, a blissful ignorance may be the best a person can achieve. There may also be a constant struggle to retain and enhance the fabricating-absorbing tendency of "I want" in response to the tension being eroded by the letting-go process. This struggle may be all a person can handle at the moment. Even with proper initiation, if a lay practitioner does not have the sincere motivation (in actuality non-motivation) of seeking spiritual truth, he or she may readily switch back to the normal thinking mind, even while in the meditative process, instead of allowing the transparent light to shine out in the letting-go process. The prospect of progress in the purification process can thus be sabotaged.

As described in Chapter 6 above, to avoid a full encounter but at the same time help to remove the sufferings of disease and life's problems, I have developed the CFQ seven movements exercise system, together with the four complementary techniques. These are practices that enable a process of letting-go and undoing. To arrive at the best results, do not forget about *xin fa,* the way of the Heart. The practices are not for the purpose of achieving or receiving anything, but rather to enable peace, which must occur unconditionally, without objectives, or doings. It is a *"doing something in order not to do anything."* The practices are merely tools to arrive at "non-objectivity," without which no transition will actually occur. When peace reveals itself, you realize that you have become familiar with the contents of the Heart Sutra, even though you may not have experienced the complete metamorphosis. The advanced cultivator comes to realize the peace, purity and the transparent light of *alaya* with her or his own heart's share of ultimate intimacy.

The Spiritual Journey. The spiritual and the physical realms are so united that to deal with the spiritual is to simultaneously deal with the physical. We may view the human body as existing because it is required by spirit. The bodies of living creatures are different from inanimate objects, since the moment life or spirit no longer exists, decay sets in. Spirit thus exists in a complementary manner with the physical body. If you remove all the possible explanatory systems, spirit is right there. Just sit back and close your eyes—you know you are alive, you know you have a spirit.

Just sit back. Do nothing. You must really do nothing. That doing-nothing will unveil all the doings of the past. Do not be carried away, but rather be detached and non-judgmental. Wanting something is, at best, being stuck in the superficial layers of your energy system, merely able to watch the games played by the different forces in the superficial layers. These layers must completely leave you before you can move deeper.

To do so you must learn the appropriate skills—use purity to dilute the impurities of the darkness; use detachment (non-conceptual wisdom) to dilute ignorance; use Metta (loving-kindness and compassion) to dilute self-centeredness with its negative emotional traits.

Layer after layer, fold after fold, scene after scene, message after message—dilute, dissipate, and out they go, back to Emptiness. Since each cleansing is actually physical, there may be physical pain and discomfort. Endurance is more than worthwhile. You get to know what your disease problems are. They are all part of you and could never leave you in any other manner. There are perhaps millions of layers and folds, but that does not matter. Clearing off a small fraction of the layers will rid you of many of your problems. You learn to accept things as they are, and accept your responsibility in dealing with your problems: You feel the presence of Boundless Love in and around you. You accept the fact that your body is not made to last forever and that God has the perfect place for you in the future. You let go of your fear and feel peace. You reduce your conflicts and disharmonies. This further eliminates the physical pain and disease problems, and, at the same time, gives you spiritual comfort and the ability to better cope with life.

For those determined enough to pursue the course and utilize the entire opportunity offered, the eventual outcome is Perfect Awakening, Perfect Understanding and Perfect Illumination.

The Heart Sutra: Commentary

Perfect Understanding brings absolute peace, joy, detachment and transparency. Every space is filled with magnificent, clear light. When the layers and folds (karma) are completely clear, the physical body appears to be non-existent. The mind and five senses are completely replaced by the pure instinct called "wisdom." The seeing of things as they are is called, *"full, right, and universal Enlightenment."* Once this stage is achieved, the cultivator is no longer subject to the cycles of rebirths.

Bodhisattva Avalokita. Bodhisattva means *"awakened seer."* A transcendent bodhisattva is one who has actualized the perfections and has attained Buddhahood but has postponed entry into complete Nirvana. Bodhisattva Avalokita is the bodhisattva of compassion and is portrayed by the Chinese in female form as the Goddess of Mercy or *Kuan Yin.*

Five skandhas. These are the five aggregates or elements that comprise the human body. Only by completely doing away with attaching karma, can Perfect Understanding be attained. Without any attachment, the body, the mind and the spirit are completely harmonious and in this condition, there should be no pain, no disease.

Form is emptiness, emptiness is form. Seeing from the perfected state is to see with purity and transparency. As said earlier, all matter remains as matter but originates from pure transparency. Seeing with the eye of wisdom reveals the true nature: that things simply are what they are, but without real existence. Perfected seeing is a kind of acceptance with detachment.

Feelings, perceptions, mental formations and consciousness. These exist because of the natural functions of the body. Once we detach from them, we realize that they do not correlate with being, and are therefore empty of existence.

All dharmas are marked with emptiness. Dharmas are the methods or the laws of the existence of matter, forms, and phenomena. Seeing them with detachment, and accepting what they are, reveal their true nature. They happen to be what they are, but have no true existence. Detach, be unmoved by them and observe that they dissipate into emptiness and eternity. Attainment becomes irrelevant.

No attainment, no obstacles. Cultivation is a path undertaken without conditions. Motives and conditions are obstacles that prevent our liberation from illusion. Thus, if someone were to try to become a Buddha, he or she could never become a Buddha. The acquisition-intention would block the way.

The destroyer of all suffering is incorruptible truth. If the true nature of all matter and existence is empty, by being detached and independent we resolve the suffering arising from entanglements with cravings and ignorance.

Gate gate paragate parasamgate bodhi svaha. This can be translated as *"gone, gone, gone beyond, gone completely beyond, awakened, so be it* (the Heart Sutra is also called the *Sutra of the Wisdom Gone Beyond*)."

Spirituality and Divinity

Whatever the reason for your involvement in spiritual development, whether you want a cure for diseases or you want to fill up that hollow feeling or find the missing part of you, you must be seen to be involved. You must follow specific ways and spend time. The path of cultivation, however, is full of obstacles, hindrances, and obstructions. You are what you are, to some degree, because of your past knowledge and the life experiences that have shaped your patterns of thinking and behavior. Spiritual development means going beyond that, to be present to your true instinct. The first hurdle, ordinary thinking, is hard to overcome. The true instinct is deep within and surrounded by many false instincts. The pains and confusion found within the spiritual way demand great bravery. There are real life problems you have to handle, living in society and dealing with the people you have to face. Many people and books have focused on how. This book of life tells you more. Which methods to follow? How to make sure that you continue with your pursuit diligently and consistently?

Divine Blessings. Simply trust in the Ultimate source. This source is much more powerful than we are. It is utterly beyond comparison with anything we experience or know. This ultimate source, God, cares for and loves you. The pure vibrations of the Absolute help you decide on your pursuit, guide you along, and facilitate removing your problems. During "down times" you can know you are in safe hands, and that the hardships you encounter are opportunities for utilizing the gifts given you. During the "ups," praise God that you might face the truth and not flatter your ego. In time you will know that God is ever with you.

This does not mean that having faith and praying to God is a sufficient act of trust. God lovingly shares with us the privilege of responsibly participating in our lives, making our way to Love. You must spend time to manifest your sincerity. The puzzle of wanting to know where we come from, and the fear of facing death at the end, are common experiences. Some people may not admit to having such fears during times in their lives when they are feeling successful and safe. The unknown danger is remote and does not cross their minds. With faith in God, we know such problems have been taken care of. God makes sure that we live the life that is given to us, and decides where we should go when your time here ends. Faith is true power, capable of great miracles, when we learn how to make use of it.

Pure Land Buddhism. Karma and rebirth are the basis of Buddhist teachings. A departed person will be born in any of the six realms (modes) of existence. They are the *"three good"* as in gods (further subdivided into 26 realms), titans, and humans, and the *"three bad"* as in animals, hungry ghosts, and infernal beings. Rebirth and the course of existence bring suffering and confusion. Even the most determined cultivator will find that his or her pursuits will at times be obstructed. On the other hand, for those who are not cultivating this level of spiritual awareness, life will probably be understood as a simple cycle of rebirth.

Shakyamuni Buddha taught of a Pure Land created by Amitabha Buddha by means of his Buddha-field *(buddhakshetra)* under his vow to eliminate suffering brought by karma and rebirth. Those with an absolute and sincere faith that they will be reborn in the Pure Land, will have their wish granted if they have even for one day (perhaps even for one moment) in their life-time made a sincere and truthful wish and recited the Buddha's name *"Namo Amitabha Buddha."* They should also recite the Buddha's name as often as they can to ensure that they do not forget their wish in the midst of life's distractions.

This is a most appealing destiny. Rebirth in the Pure Land means an end to the cycles of rebirths in the six realms and fears of Karma. The Pure Land is a heaven where existence is completely without suffering. There is only joy. Every being there will progress along the path of cultivation to perfect wisdom. The recital of Buddha's name is easy enough to be done by anybody. Even the sick and old who can hardly do anything else, can realize peace if they recite Buddha's name in full faith. Amitabha Buddha is worshiped by Mahayana sect of Buddhism as the *"supreme king of healers."* Should you have reached a stage of development beyond bartering for divine gifts, you will know that Heaven and the Way there has been at the core of your being all along.

A Case Example: *The male patient, in his late forties, was diagnosed with advanced nasal cancer. The cancer had spread to the lymph node behind his jaw. He was given 20 radiation therapy treatments over a one-month period. Three months later, his CT scan detected isolated cancer cells remaining in his right lymph node. A booster dose of radiation was administered. This had the effect of hardening tissue on an extensive region from under his right ear. His right arm became rigid as well.*

Two and one half years later, cancer had resurfaced again in his right lymph node. He was given a course of 15 treatments of radiation therapy. A month later, someone brought him to my Center but he was reluctant to disclose details of his condition. I proposed that he learn and practice CFQ

as an overall health maintenance activity. His wife also joined in the prac-
tice.

After the third week of meridian practice and having learned five move-
ments he informed me that his right arm had become more flexible. The
arm had been stiff for the past two and half years. He was, as yet, unable to
stretch his arm out completely. The stiff feeling was gone and he could easily
raise his entire arm. He also felt that his whole body becoming more
relaxed.

By the fifth session he had learned all the seven movements. I asked him to
join the meridian exercise group. I elaborated on the principles of CFQ
with regards to the treatment of cancer and expressed reservations on the
conventional "search-and-destroy" approach. He then requested direct
energy healing sessions, and I agreed. Treatment was arranged on a once-
weekly basis. After six weeks he told me that he felt good. But he feared a
relapse and wanted to continue with more healing sessions. I increased the
treatments to twice weekly.

He has since been practicing CFQ daily without fail. During treatment, he
experienced various sensations and reactions. Some reactions lasted several
days, including: numbness and heat running through his arms, muscles
twitching, numbness on his face, heart palpitation, blisters on his mouth,
and a spreading and resurfacing of the previous hardened region. The dark
patch on the skin from radiation therapy began to spread, fade and finally
peeled off.

He said, "People in my condition never feel really safe. You have to tell me
that I am all right." He confessed that since he was diagnosed with cancer
over three years ago, he had been constantly worried. He had no confidence
in his body's healing and was suspicious and doubtful of all treatment.
Each time he came I allowed time for him to express the reactions he had
experienced and to air his worries. I would reassure and console him. I also
explained that the healing reactions meant that the symptoms of the disease

were releasing and the crisis had reversed. I said these can be felt as flowing out. He agreed that he usually felt the sensations flowing out.

He received a bonus benefit. From his teenage years, he had had occasional involuntary shaking and twitching of body and limbs. He had not found any remedy for the tremors. After twenty energy treatments, he discovered that this problem was almost gone. His frequent sore throat, present since receiving radiotherapy, had cleared up.

PART III

Healing Applications:
Freedom from Disease

10

Becoming A Healer

When I started my Healing Center, I hoped to rescue people from their illnesses and cure the incurable. Reflecting on this goal, I see the underlying ambition as heroic, trying to have the power to do the impossible, almost playing God. Reality, however, manifested another picture. The struggle to save people required long hard hours of treatment and exhausting, painful hours of practice. I experienced frustration, sweat and tears of helplessness, often with the sense that, "If I could just break through the problem at hand, this hapless being could be saved," or "If this fellow had come earlier, his situation would involve a straight-forward cure. But after multiple unsuccessful treatments, the problem is already too messy, and yet the demand is that I instantly fix the patient."

Treatment is indeed hard work but, in my experience, it is much easier than helping people understand and accept the treatment. The patient can't be blamed for the confusion. My energy method is indeed *out of this world.* But most patients do feel the changes that occur during the treatment itself, and they actually want the treatment. Frustrations come from many directions but if the healer takes the attitude that healing others also helps one's cultivation and improves one's level of proficiency, the healer will not feel bad. The healer wakes up to the reality that he or she is not God's greatest creation, nor a savior, but just a plain human being. Still, there are sweet rewards as well. One is able to cure what is considered incurable by others, and seeing the work accomplished is worth all the pains, sweat, and tears. Saving the incurable gives the energy healer a satisfaction worth more than all the treasures of the world. Peace and a clear conscience are wonderful. With that, you can stand firm and have compassion for the many who choose to slander and condemn. They are stuck with a worldly wise attitude that tries to prove that they are superior to this *out-of-the-world stuff*.

The majority who come are obviously satisfied with their treatment, but too often discontinue before I'm satisfied with the fullness of their cure. On the bright side, if I had too many continuous patients I would perish from exhaustion. Others return once they encounter new problems. Diseases certainly cause a great deal of anxiety. As a healer, one often becomes deeply involved with people whose anxiety level is too high. It is all too often the case that one, in addition to being greatly appreciated finds oneself a convenient outlet for their anxiety. Since Master Wong Kiew Kit(1995) mentioned my work in his book, *"Chi Kung for Health and Vitality,"* I have received hundreds of letters from all over the world, inquiring about training. I have not had time to reply, nor did I know what to say to them. I did not want to burden them with bitter sweet stories, more often than not, of the pain, sweat and tears involved in becoming an energy healer. I hope these friends out there everywhere read this book and forgive me for not having the heart to reply to their letters.

The Healing Source

Your call to heal others is dependent on your ability to generate Metta (loving-kindness) and share peace. This is evidenced by your ability to heal yourself to effect improved health in others. For anyone who practices CFQ diligently, the development of healing abilities is a natural outcome.

For those who wish to become healers, the practice of CFQ meditation is strongly recommended. Such training will enable you to generate Metta and penetrate deep within your patients, bringing about profound cures. At the same time, CFQ can help you be sensitive enough to detect the true cause of problems. It further enables you to clear off disease-making energy from your patients.

For those with a nurturing heart and an open mind, meditation practice readily manifests their gifts even within the first one or two months. Spontaneous movements show methods of releasing tension via self-acupressure, tapping, massages, sweeping and clearing off, prayers and mudras (hand symbols). Previous knowledge of acupoints and massage work is not necessary for the manifestation of such effects. Neither is religious belief relevant. A free-thinker or a Christian may spontaneously perform Buddhist prayers or mudras, as in Tibetan Buddhist practice. It turns out that certain prayer procedures and manipulations of hand signs also regulate the meridians and are remedies for ill health.

After initial manifestations, some students turn to fellow practitioners or onlookers and work on them using similar techniques. They are now truly relaxed and the inability of others to relax stands out and gives them confidence. They become inspired to work on others. And, although they have no idea of what is wrong with them or what they are doing, they seem spontaneously to know what to do and where to work. Anyone who manifests in this manner shows good potential to become a healer. They should be cautioned, however, to avoid self-flattery. Allow the manifestation to occur naturally without any interruptions by thought or emotion, but rely completely on the Mantra. Only by complete reliance on spontaneous movements can the risk of overdoing, use of excessive strength, or working on the wrong places be avoided. After treating people, they spontaneously conclude, break-off the rapport, cleanse and regulate themselves.

Manifestations during practice sessions should be allowed naturally with an open, kind and generous attitude, but without the slightest ego involvement or pride. However, unless necessary, emerging healers should not voluntarily treat other people until after they have had three years of practice. Their healing ability will still be weak and their ability to protect themselves will be inadequate. Although what they do now obviously appears to work, it is still far from being good enough to qualify as healers. Even after three years of practice, were they to volunteer to treat others, they should confine their involvement to one hour a day and spend more time, say two hours, working on themselves. Only after seven years do the letting go, relaxation, and radiant features become sufficiently built into their systems so that they can reasonably be able to protect themselves against debased energy from other people.

People with healing inclinations may consider becoming professional healers after seven years of practice. By then, they will be able to trust the Mantra completely and allow whatever needs to be done to occur naturally. However, as they become progressively more advanced, there will be less external physical "doing". They gradually become more familiar with Metta, which is a boundless and pure source that literally feels like a sea of water that floods the patients and melts away any impurities. Those without healing inclinations and manifestations can still consider becoming healers by relying on the CFQ meridian exercises and at the same time continue with their own meditation practice.

Benefits of CFQ Meridian Exercise

CFQ meridian exercises are designed for the purpose of healing. The skillful use of the energy channels (meridians) provides rapid loosening effects that clear blockages and drain off pent-up conflicts, disharmony, negative emotions and undesirable self-sabotaging energy trapped within the body. These are replaced with peace. Undesirable traits, however, know how to play their tricks to consolidate their existence within the person. This is experienced as a kind of reluctance to perform the exercises. The problem-causing traits, normally thought of in terms of "I" prefer excitement and stimulation. The belief is that by taking action against what bores you or what you are reluctant to do, you clear your problems.

In contrast the healing source from meridian exercising is peace, and from meditation is Metta. However, in the advanced stage, they are basically the same—radiant, pure, and boundless energy. In the initial stage, the meridian exercises can provide a rapid comforting effect to reduce pain and distress, but their effect on karma is unpredictable. They begin at the energy, physical-consciousness level and gradually go deeper. To make sure that the process works well, you need full sincerity and trust. Trust God. Trust CFQ. Trust whatever you do.

Those who diligently practice the exercises become progressively relaxed and healthier. Different problems require different periods of time to be reduced and cleared off. It is important to look at improvements in terms of overall well being, rather than focusing on certain problems which appear to be more stubborn, while ignoring those that have already been improved. This latter approach misses an important part of the experience. With a fair and open attitude, improvements may be seen within days, weeks, or in one or two months. Some students of healing may become sensitive enough to feel others' problems and sense what needs to be done to clear those problems after only six months of practice. If they wish to work on others, they can simply follow what their instincts tell them.

Those who are not sure of what to do, can simply let-go on the others' behalf. To exercise on someone's behalf is to have the intention that, as the helper does the exercise, the patient will improve. Once the helper starts the exercise, this intention must not be kept in conscious awareness. Rather, the helper should proceed with the motions in exactly the same way as usual. Those who are sensitive will feel a kind of rapport and feel that they are doing something on behalf of the other. But this feeling is not required for the exercise to be effective. The effects can be equally good even if there is no such feeling. One should not be over-concerned about this.

For those with family members and close friends that need healing urgently, they can start dedicating the benefits of their practice to the patients as soon as they are familiar with the exercises. This normally takes a few days to two to three weeks. At this point, it does not matter whether the exercise is actually helping people, it is the heart that matters. When there is good will, there is a way and God will help. They should not be calculative in getting results. The patient need not be present or be informed of their dedicated help. They can be hundreds of miles away. Just do it rather than indulge in worrisome or idle thinking which is futile. Helpers must take care of themselves at the same time. Perhaps they could exercise two sets for themselves and two sets dedicated to the patients. The three and seven year criteria systems discussed in the preceding section are relevant.

Even the *"lotus-walkers"* and energy *"butterfly-shakers"* can help to heal other people. If they have used these techniques to heal themselves, they can be equally effective to heal others in the same manner by dedicating their practice. To be really powerful, they must have spent a lot of time in their own practice.

The Heart Sutra is revered by the Mahayana Buddhists as the Sutra that eradicates all problems and disasters. With consistent and diligent recital, it can be a powerful healing tool. Similarly, all other Buddhist Sutras can serve this purpose. Their effectiveness is dependent upon many years of unconditional and devoted recital. The human tendency to seek a reward results in obstructing the radiant effect of Sutras used as sources of power. With sincerity and complete submission, recital awakens the letting go phenomenon: and allows for spontaneous movements, reactions, and sensations. Eventually every word recited comes to be seen and felt as radiant.

Types of Healers

Dependent Healers. There is a traditional Taoist teaching called *"invoking the assistance of the Masters."* Practitioners of this kind are initiated by performing a ceremony and chanting certain verses, until they lose their normal consciousness and shift into a trance. In this state, they are able to perform certain acts which they normally are unable to do, and know about things of which they were previously ignorant. In some cases, the effects of these interventions can seem miraculous.

This method can be adopted by CFQ users, to help those who need to work as healers before they are fully ready. The CFQ system can easily bring about similar effects, but may not facilitate a deep trance. Begin by making a prayer (to God in your belief system) for the ability to heal. Within seconds or a couple of minutes, practitioners may experience a surge of energy sensations, and a displacement of normal consciousness by a kind of detachment governed by spontaneous actions. They remain fully conscious and are able to come out of this state any time, at will. If a clear sense of what to do is absent, pray to connect to CFQ. If so moved, the reader may use this book as a medium to be connected to CFQ energy. Once the healer feels connected with a Higher Self or being, allow what happens without forcefully controlling or directing movements or activities. Act in such a manner until the work is completed, and then conclude and return to your normal self.

Even beginners who have spent one or two weeks practicing CFQ and have developed some energy sensations and a sense of mental detachment can be successful in using this method. You are therefore encouraged to try it out. If you have no one in particular to work on, you can work on yourself. Full and complete faith and sincerity, with purity of motive are necessary to get good results. Abuse or misuse will corrupt the manifestations and make them ineffective. In time of real need, any habits of wrongful use will undermine the necessary faith and sincerity. Therefore, it is advisable for you to heal in this way only as needed, for example, to quickly arrest a life-threatening problem affecting yourself, your spouse, children, relatives, or close friends. Use this method selectively and only in matters of urgency.

Becoming A CFQ Energy Healer. Only those with a genuine concern and interest in humanity should consider becoming professional healers. Healing should be taken as a pursuit both to help people and to facilitate an understanding human behavior, in order to improve self-cultivation, which eventually leads to the *"illumination of the Heart."* Money-making should never be the main concern. Healing with energy involves a heavy involvement and interference with other people's karma. The best way to ensure that this does not bring serious repercussions to the healer is to optimize the healer's purity of motive. Healing is hardly a financially lucrative endeavor, as those who are rich tend to prefer recognized treatment and are often reluctant to pay for healing services. Those who are poor need a discount or pay whatever they can afford, and sometimes your service needs to be free.

Normally, a person is only ready to become a professional healer after at least seven years of both meditation and meridian exercise practice. Prior to this, she or he should have practiced diligently for one to two hours daily, and have volunteered at healing work to gain proper experience and understanding. Initially, the novice healer relies on much spontaneous "doing" by using massage, acupressure, tapping, and sweeping, always with complete reliance on the Mantra. With experience, this will gradually settle into a kind of meditative healing where the healing energy comes out as a boundless mass, to engulf the patient completely. The time required to become an ideally purified and matured healer is approximately 10,000 hours of involvement in practice. Healing becomes truly supreme only after 7x10,000 hours, which is beyond the ability of anyone to reasonably achieve.

Healers should teach their patients CFQ techniques, to help them better deal with their own karma. Karma is an individual's own responsibility, and up to a certain point, nobody else should interfere. Strictly speaking, healing is futile if the patient does not have the desire to get well. Those who commence their CFQ practice after 50 years of age (7x7) are not encouraged to become professional healers. At this age, they should spend more time on their own karma-cleansing rather than on helping others. However, if they wish, they may learn other methods of alternative medicine and use CFQ as a complement.

Complementing Alternative Medicine. Alternative medicine providers, including herbalists, acupuncturists, massage therapists, chiropractors, and energy psychotherapists who practice CFQ, will benefit from a gradual increase in their sense of what to do, precision, location and use of strength. They will be open to incorporating techniques about which they have yet to learn, and over time will achieve greater effectiveness.

Under any circumstances, the problem of absorbing disease-producing energy from patients is real. With the proper practice of CFQ, this problem is easily resolved, and undesirable impacts on the well-being of providers is avoided. Practitioners can also teach CFQ techniques to their patients, both to speed up recovery and to provide a form of post-treatment maintenance. Those who have the ambition of becoming healers, would do well to consider starting off as providers of other forms of alternative medicine. This may prove to be a more practical approach in any case, since CFQ healing will take time to be widely appreciated.

The practice of CFQ will bring obvious benefits to medical doctors, nurses, nursing home operators and care providers, social workers and volunteers of organizations like hospices. At the very least, it can provide a cleansing off of diseased energy, absorbed through the course of their work.

Amateur Healers. There are many people who wish to help their loved ones (spouses, children, parents, brothers, sisters and friends) recover from illnesses. With CFQ, this wish can be granted. They can now put their kind thoughts into action. This is much better than merely thinking and worrying about helping, neither of which is helpful, and, in the case of worry, may even jeopardize one's own health. Volunteers and child-care givers will also find CFQ useful.

All such caregivers should learn CFQ starting from the meridian exercises. Once they are able to perform the movements properly, they can teach them to their loved ones or persons under their care. Much patience is needed to do this, as people who are sick, especially the chronically ill and old, tend to be impatient and find the exercises boring or difficult to remember. A proper explanation of the principles and benefits is therefore necessary, before teaching the steps. In some cases, one might have to practice hundreds of times with the patients until they can fully remember and perform the exercises. Monitoring may be necessary to ensure that the patients keep up with the practice.

Amateur healers can dedicate their practice to their patients. However, a good sense of rapport and visible results can only be expected after they have practiced for six months or more. Effectiveness comes from prolonged practice, and beginners are, of course, limited. That does not mean that their efforts are worthless. What matters is that they do whatever they can with a good heart.

For those who are not in a position to help the patients directly with CFQ, their practice is still useful as a form of self-protection. Disease energy moves freely back and forth in the context of normal care and handling, touch, proximity and even sight. The mental agony of thinking about or worrying about the loss of loved ones may cause health problems for helpers. By practicing CFQ, any disease making energy that may be absorbed or mental stress that may be fabricated can be readily cleansed.

CFQ Treatment Not a Panacea

CFQ cosmic healing has been found to have at least some impact on every known health problem on which it had been tried. However, special care should be taken in considering treatment for the following cases:

Emergency & Acute Problems. Such cases should first be given proper medical attention. CFQ treatment is more suitable for chronic problems. Although it also helps in acute situations, one often lacks the expertise and equipment required for emergency cases. There is also the risk that some problems will deteriorate rapidly without proper medical treatment.

Infectious Diseases. Proper care and precautions should be taken when treating highly contagious diseases. Your CFQ practice would make you less vulnerable to infections, but it does not give full immunity. Therefore, you should spend extra time in your practice for personal cleansing after treating such problems, as well as continuing to take precautions appropriate to the particular situation.

Diseases of the Aged. For the very old and frail, with bodies that are highly stiffened, compacted, and deformed by long years of tension accumulation, intervention may require more time and effort than is possible. Some elderly people also lack interesting activities and as a result may turn their attention to their failing physical condition and other problems. Therefore, unless they are willing to listen, learn some of the techniques recommended in this book, and spend time in practicing them, you should consider limiting or simply not offering treatment. Treatment for such cases, no matter how minor the problem, is most likely to be effective only in providing limited improvement, as such problems have been thickly compounded and usually require many treatments. In such cases, patients are likely to protest, "Why must it take such a long time to fix this simple problem? CFQ must not be effective." They may be more contented with any form of "doing" rather than with CFQ, which does not involve doing anything tangible.

It may also be the case that the unwinding and cleansing effect may give rise to more pain and discomfort than some elderly people are able to face. Other problems are treated simultaneously in CFQ, but since the elderly tend to have accumulated so much debased energy, treatment may stir up too much for rapid improvement. The healer in these cases may be blamed and not appreciated, even though the patient's overall well-being is vastly improved, and the original complaint has been greatly ameliorated. Treatment, however, is justifiable if patients are open-minded and are willing to accept the treatment with the right attitude. The acceptance of their problems, together with the treatment itself, greatly reduces their symptoms and discomforts. Refer to Chapter 13.

Cancer. This is a unique problem because of the social stigma, common knowledge of what the "big C" means, and medical propaganda related to its supposed incurability. CFQ treatment is very effective for this problem, but the excessive fear generally associated with it may complicate the cleansing abreactions as the illness is reversed. Therefore, unless the patient can understand the principles of this treatment even before its commencement, the healer should refuse treatment rather than run the risk of being caught up in a difficult and blaming situation. Refer to Chapter 17.

Heart Disease. In some cases, it is difficult to loosen the congestion in the chest and heart region. Therefore if you are unsure of what to do, do not try to move through a blockage forcefully. It may be better not to treat people who are weak with severe chest congestion and heart trouble, especially those who have undergone bypass surgery.

Organ Transplant. Most recipients of organ transplant, e.g., kidney, heart and liver may require long-term medication to control their condition and prevent rejection. They tend to be very cautious about pain and discomfort. Treatment should therefore be avoided as the healing abreactions may cause panic.

Psychological Disorders. Included here are schizophrenia, clinical depression, anxiety, chronic fatigue, insomnia, and psychopathic tendencies. Persons with such problems are often sensitive, may lack self-confidence, and may easily become suspicious. For those who are unwilling to accept themselves and their problems, the results of treatment will be unsatisfactory. Similarly, the treatment outlook is not good for those who need a lot of persuasion and who lack initiative. There can also be a problem with a lack of patience, as some expect almost instantaneous cures and will stop after only a few sessions. Even with much improvement, they will not have the patience to pursue the full benefit of CFQ.

Pregnancy. Some expectant mothers may be susceptible to miscarriage. CFQ treatment brings about an improvement in blood circulation to the lower body including the womb. Although such a change is beneficial, it may increase the risk of a miscarriage for those in the 8-16 weeks stage. Such an incident has not yet happened, and this risk is at present merely speculative. Nevertheless, it is better for pregnant women to seek well-tested, more regular, and routine pre-natal care.

Close-minded Non-Believers. Do not hesitate to refuse to treat those who come just to "try you out" or who display the attitude of, "I will only accept and believe in you if you fix my problem." They are not open enough to allow the treatment to be effective, and their attitude often creates a distrust and withholding pattern which magnifies the discomforts of the healing abreactions. When that happens, they unfortunately tend to become angry with the healer. One possible response to this is to tell them that you do not believe that your treatment is the best solution for their problem at this time.

CFQ Direct Meditative Healing

A standard healing session normally lasts half an hour, though it may take more or less time than that in other circumstances. When you feel it is time to conclude, do not forcefully try to do more. That additional treatment may put you in a situation where, since you have bypassed the right time to conclude, unnecessary discomfort is experienced, both by yourself and by the patient.

My standard appointments are once a week. I make an exception for cases of rapid deterioration, in which daily treatments are necessary. Such treatments often reverse the situation in a matter of two or three weeks, after which the sessions can be spaced out. Depending on the situation, for example, for those who travel from out of town, the spacing of healing sessions is arranged on a case by case basis. For acute problems, two or three sessions a week is often justifiable.

The healing effect does not occur only during a session, however, but continues for at least three to four weeks after that time. Weekly sessions tend to produce optimum results. A more frequent arrangement may speed up the effect, but does not give the best time-cost results. For chronic problems, you need to allow the body to change physiologically. Such a change may become obvious over, perhaps, 100 to 300 days or more. Spacing the sessions to less than weekly, say fortnightly, makes effectiveness less obvious.

Find out for yourself what is the best interval. For new professional healers, perhaps twice a week is best, while for amateurs and volunteers perhaps daily sessions may be preferable. New professional healers should restrict their healing work to three to five hours daily and increase gradually.

Cooperation with Physicians. Cooperation with medical doctors and other alternative medicine providers should be sought as often as possible. Pride should be swallowed for the sake of the well-being of patients. Co-operation is particularly important for disease like cancer and leukemia since, with proper conventional treatment, without the complications caused by an over-kill approach to cancer therapy, chances of full and complete recovery are good.

This is the area I have thus far been unsuccessful. Some of my patients who told their doctors about their CFQ practice or treatments received, along with the apparent benefits, were treated in negative and discouraging ways. Most of my patients (with good reason) prefer to keep their energy treatments secret from their doctors. In a case of a patient with hypertension, whose periodic medical check-up showed improvement, the physician was obviously pleased, "So you have been managing yourself properly. I think I will reduce the medication for you." The patient was so delighted that he told his physician about his CFQ treatment. Immediately the doctor changed his tone. "Something has gone seriously wrong. I will send you for a thorough medical check-up." Hopefully, somewhere, in some part of the world, there is more objectivity, more openness, and less need to protect status and territory.

Compassion. The prerequisite for helping people with their problems is to be truly concerned, to love, nurture and care for them. This prerequisite serves as a good means of gaining the rapport that allows for healing, One must, however, be emotionally detached and remain unmoved by any circumstances. The detachment is what makes healing work. To practice with too much concern and sympathy risks becoming personally involved with the patient's problems, which tends to prevent the healer's doing what is necessary to remove their problems. In such cases, healers become overly involved, which can also cause other problems for them. By being detached, the helper creates the contrast in the situation which is required to clear it out. By being unmoved, the healer projects the image of a person free from the problem, where concern and sympathy have been lifted into compassion. True compassion is non-compassion or love.

But we are human and have feelings. To be so free and boundless is a difficult thing to achieve. You can only try your best to follow the Divine cosmic example and get beyond weeping and worrying about outcomes.

A Case Example: *The male patient, aged 43, had depression severe enough to cause him to lose interest in working. This had gradually developed over a period of ten years. He saw a psychiatrist who gave him medication every six months, when he had a bout of severe depression. Some three months prior to seeing me, he had another relapse. The medication dosage was increased without effect. A week later medication was changed.*

The day after my first healing session he telephoned saying he felt well enough to work. He also asked me to help with his constipation, a side effect of taking the new medication from the psychiatrist. I suggested that he resume using the old medication. Three treatments later, he felt he had recovered almost completely.

I then started him on the CFQ meridian exercises. After five lessons over three weeks he reported further improvement. He felt confident and agreed to reduce the prescription from three to two tablets. Three months later he took only one. He feels completely normal with one tablet. I told him he could stop when he wished, without concern about any relapse.

11

CFQ For Children

o o o o o o o o o o o o o o o o o o o o o o o o o o o o o o o

CFQ Interventions: *The unnecessary load and burden that a human carries constrains life, bundles the spirit, causes physical deformations and obstructs healthy physiological functions. The solution is therefore very simple. Let go and unload. This approach cannot be confined to lip service but must actually be carried out. If the individuals do not play their part and make the effort, Nature seems unwilling to carry on alone. To work on health problems is to let go and undo the cause in which cure is the only outcome.*

Endangered Children

The high-stress component of modern society not only pressures adults but, I believe, even more destructively victimizes children. This results in children being subjected to an extensive range of health problems. Geneticists are producing increasing evidence that suggests that many diseases are in fact genetically predisposed. Not only are problems like thalassemia, leukemia, Down's syndrome, and cancer traceable to genetic causes, but also common diseases like hypertension, heart problems, stroke, arthritis and asthma. The likelihood of middle-aged adults' having health problems is increasing. Similarly, children are showing this tendency. The speculation is that when children grow up they, too, will be at high risk for having the diseases that afflict their parents.

Mental and Academic Development. Current workplace demands impose rigorous learning standards, creating a high demand for mental and academic development. Not only does the average adult find it necessary to keep up with the explosion of knowledge, but children, too, are compelled to join in the race. Academic syllabi are constantly updated to meet this demand. My daughter in elementary school carries a school bag twice as heavy as the one I used to carry as a child. My Grade 3 son's school syllabus is much more sophisticated than what I used to study in Grade 6. On top of that, in urban areas, competition to excel compels children to enroll in various academic study outside normal school hours. This kind of exposure naturally leads children to become over involved with cognitive activities including school work, reading, hobbies and other cerebral and sedentary interests. The most important aspect of child development, the physical aspect, is neglected. For enduring health to be possible, a proper balance between physical, mental and spiritual development must be ensured. Physical activities help to develop the physiological body. Meridian development and healthy energy flow is especially important before 14 years of age. The heavy emphasis on mental development makes it difficult to have time for and interest in physical development, even for physically active children. The less physically active ones (the majority) stand an even greater risk due to unbalanced development.

In the course of my work as a healer, I frequently hear about normal school children, and university undergraduates, excelling in their studies, who suddenly experiencing anxiety, depression, and psychiatric illnesses that make it impossible for them to continue with their work. Such incidences are alarming, and may be more common than is recorded officially. The demands for mental and academic excellence made by educational authorities, parents, and society is increasingly pushing children to a point where they can no longer cope.

Treatment for such problems is actually quite simple: Open the energy channels and flush the mental and emotional load down and out, and change the children's attitude and that of people around them so that neither they nor their parents feel so pressured. Encourage those who lack exercise to spend some time in physical activity, thus counterbalancing the heavy pressure for mental activity. Usually, new patients with mild to moderately severe problems, can return to almost normal condition after one, or perhaps a few healing sessions, finding themselves capable of a balanced study and normal life program.

Unfortunately, although I've been told of many such cases, few turn to me for help. Rather, parental stress is alleviated by parents' turning, on behalf of their children, to commonly accepted treatment from psychiatrists, counselors or temple mediums. Parents exhibit great patience in these cases, spending years and large sums of money to little avail. The delay causes the children's problems to become deep-seated and habitual. Their difficulties are further complicated by the prolonged suppression accomplished by drugs, as well as speculative treatment suggestions that often confuse the patients. These complications make CFQ healing slower when the children are finally brought in. Unfortunately, in cases where obvious improvements take place, parents are often impatient and expect instant results, and even when problems are successfully treated, parental understanding and appreciation are often missing.

Parental Neglect. The current trend toward families where both parents work seems to increase the risk of child neglect. Love, care and attention establish the bonding and trust between parents and children which is needed to solve children's problems and monitor their behavioral, mental and physical progress. Remedies are more effective if implemented at early stages of development, rather than after problems have develop to the point where little can be done to solve them completely. Children are sensitive by nature, and require love, care, and concern. Lack of these causes psychological problems that may manifests as problems with physical health.

Food and Nutrition. The need for food is basic to survival. In underprivileged, impoverished societies, the lack of this basic necessity results in malnutrition and severe health problems. Children growing up in such conditions may suffer long-term damage even after conditions eventually change for the better.

In more affluent societies, the problem of malnutrition is equally real, albeit artificially created. Providing plain, simple, basic, nourishing food is not as lucrative a business as that of marketing mass-produced, fanciful, "junk foods." Corporate profits are the driving force for the development and the widespread sale of various junk foods aimed at children. While the adult market is less pliable, children, lacking discipline and knowledge, are easily lured into consuming non-nutritious products, and their caregivers often feel powerless to refuse these demands. Not only are many juvenile health problems directly caused by the consumption of unhealthy foods, but the absence of normal meals can bring about its own set of health problems.

The current obsession with nutrition in affluent and middle-class strata of society can easily be manipulated. Researchers financed by the mega-multinational pharmaceutical companies come out with ever-increasing claims of nutritional benefits. The resultant market often assumes a "the more the better" attitude, and few people appear to question the validity of this mentality. In the first place, it fits our acquisition and fabricating instincts. Nutritionists who have any reservations may find themselves suddenly unemployed. If we were to use common sense observations, we would realize that the older generation, even in the not-too-distant-past, appears to have lived a fuller and healthier life. (This observation, of course, excludes special cases where starvation and contagious diseases prevailed). Those grand old men and women who are still alive today are often ignorant about nutrition. All they need is plain, simple meals. The body can use such foods to satisfy all its nutritional requirements, provided that we do not lose balance in our enthusiasm for simplicity. Being overly zealous about nutrition fabricates a heavy burden for the body. It can also deposit excessive amounts of undesirable elements in the body, block and hinder physiological functions, and produce excessive waste products and toxins which the body may not be able to properly release. Everyone becomes a victim of this problem, but children suffer the most. They have more years to be exposed to this threat, and imitating adults makes them more likely to consume excessive amounts of inappropriate food.

Childhood Trauma

Trauma arising from severe natural disasters as well as acts of violence such as wars, famines, crime, fighting and internment can result both in emotional and psychological disorders as well as physical illness. However, few people suspect that trauma can be caused by much less dramatic occurrences, including, in some cases, normal daily events.

Any event which creates physical distress, agony, mental or emotional anguish could be a trauma. The energy-spiritual response to trauma is a sudden drawing-in and upsurging of consciousness. The energy upsurge in the brain may hinder its normal communication with the body and its sensory organs. The traumatized mind, in order to shut off the pain, can become dissociated from the external environment. Trauma creates a kind of energy blockage or shield, that misaligns and deforms the physical body and deflects vital organs from their normal physiological functions. The trauma victim is refocused from normal consciousness to an altered, disoriented state. In extreme cases the patient loses consciousness and falls into a coma.

The severity of a trauma also depends on the nature of the traumatic event. A sudden shock or bizarre occurrence tends to bring about more harm than the gradual accumulation of tension promoted by expected stressful events. Tension accumulation can be fabricated by repeated or continuous exposure to emotional arousal of all kinds, including ordinary excitement. The consequences produced by trauma vary with the emotional stability of the victim as well. A highly anxious and stressed-out person will suffer more severely than a calm person.

Trauma produces alterations and misalignments at the physical, mental, emotional and spiritual levels. In severe cases, such as combat trauma, the victims become profoundly disoriented. In other cases, their personality and behavioral patterns can be affected. Victims may never become completely free from their altered state and may remain unable to return to a normal state, though with the passage of time the altered state may become less apparent.

CFQ involvement can be effective in these cases, since it works on all consciousness levels (mind, body, and spirit). In severe situations, time and perseverance are necessary to slowly do away with the alterations and misalignments, which result from continuous psychological conflict, and replace them with peace and harmony. In less severe cases, significant results can be achieved within days or weeks. However, if CFQ involvement is delayed and the trauma is given time to take root, complications often set in and cure becomes more time consuming. Benefits are more rapid in patients who are expressive and willing to share their problems than in those who are withdrawn and socially isolated. In dealing with difficult clients, special tact, patience and imagination are required.

CFQ involvement is useful for preventing and treating trauma arising from the problems of life, such as exploitation and interpersonal conflict that produce stress reactions and negative emotions. Children, who are normally sensitive, may be more affected by minor trauma than adults but often the disturbances appear to be mild and consequently go unnoticed. All trauma problems are caused by either a sudden or gradual build-up of stress, arising from events fabricating anxiety, excitement or emotional arousal. While some problems in children arise from events beyond parental control, many are in fact driven by parents themselves, as they inflict a stressful environment on their children. The outcomes of one or a series of stressful episodes can affect children's subsequent development, and the results may become problematic years later. When children show noticeable symptoms, the normal solution is medication. But a prolonged use of drugs compounds and aggravates the problem.

A Family Case Study: A CFQ student narrated to me how he managed to help his anxiety-stricken son. In the past, verbal and physical assistance took time to be effective, and the child appeared to be confused even after getting over the problem. With the CFQ remedy, the problem stopped and his son again became his normal self. There has been no relapse into an anxiety attack since.

There was one occasion when the father was unable to help. His son had a fever that continued for three days even with medication. One night, the child complained of severe headache and became so dissociated that his parents were unable to reach him. At that time there was an outbreak of a fatal viral epidemic of Japanese encephalitis. The father panicked and sought my advice. At 10 p.m. I told him to take the child to the hospital immediately. I promised to soon go and see the boy.

Meanwhile, I began meditating and performed a remote healing. At 10.10 p.m. his wife phoned in great alarm. Just as they were getting into the car to drive to the hospital, the child developed a nosebleed. I sensed that the pressure on the child's head was reduced. Trusting this perception, I assured the parents that the boy was all right. I said that he should have calmed down. The mother confirmed this. I told her to take the child for medical help anyway. By the time they reached the hospital, the child was cheerful and active. His temperature had returned to normal. He was discharged from hospital after observation.

Further, my student had severe psychological problems. Since his teenage years, he had had haunting nightmares in which he felt himself being strangled. He had vivid and frightening images in his nightmares, including that of the childhood house where he grew up. Despite psychiatric treatment and the intervention of shamans, the problem became even worse. He converted to Christianity and consulted his priest who was also an exorcist. During the exorcism, he became unconscious. His condition continued to deteriorate. The problem looked hopeless. He was unable to continue work, sleep or drive. He was frightened of people and was afraid to stay at home. He kept calling his wife at work and the strain was affecting her as well.

It was at this stage (in 1993) that he came to see me. It took nearly 50 sessions of energy healing to clear the problem, which we had traced back to his childhood. There were strong manifestations of his problem during the treatment. But he persevered. Two months later, he had recovered sufficiently to return to work. In 1995, he joined my CFQ class and has since been one of my most dedicated students. He is determined to become a healer. I believe he will be able to help people greatly. His wife and two young children have also become CFQ students.

Summary. All trauma problems are caused by a sudden or gradual build-up of stressful events which produce anxiety, excitement or emotional arousal. While some problems result from events beyond a parent's control, many are, in fact, driven by parents themselves. Even when problems crop up, few people notice them. Pressure, excitement and stress are often considered desirable due to the fact that the feelings they engender are often pleasant and there is a general ignorance of the possible deleterious results of such experiences.

The CFQ Remedy

Problems affecting children arise from complex social and hereditary influences. They are not confined to the realm of mental and physical health, but are closely connected and inter-woven with social, economic and political circumstances. Remedies for problems must be visibly effective within months, profound and lasting. They must be realistic, able to be implemented on a widespread scale, and economically viable. They must also create a physical and psychological transformation for the children in need as well as for their families and health care providers. CFQ is a potentially viable solution.

Teaching CFQ. Volunteers, social workers, health providers and parents can learn the CFQ exercises and complementary techniques along with the children. A helper can understand the principles, teach them to the children, and practice with them regularly. The drain-off effect clears blockages and repairs the body's systems, as well as reducing the mental and emotional burden that accompany healing. Counseling children with the principles of CFQ can help them to accept themselves and their problems. It does away with disharmony and conflicts arising from the struggles of life. With the help of CFQ, both children and adults can learn to deal with life's problems, or learn to forget them. Acceptance itself can often bring about an immediate and obvious improvement. The complete eradication of existing and future problems comes with regular practice, a health promoting activity which provides a proper outlet. Time out from mentally reviewing problems as well as tension reduction is achieved. Children given this kind of guidance can grow up as harmonized persons, well equipped to heal every injury inflicted on them. The practice of the CFQ exercises—two or three complete sets, two or three days per week; or daily in needy cases—will yield rapid results.

Dedicating CFQ Practice. This method is suitable for parents working with their own children or for health care providers working with small groups of children or adults. Refer to Chapter 10 on how this can be done.

Direct Healing. My healing work on children shows that CFQ works on every known physical or emotional problem. However, it is impossible for me to help most needy children because I am overwhelmed by the numbers. Healing requires time and personal attention. Training qualified healers takes years. I have about a handful of students who could be ready but the prevailing hardships present in promoting healing abilities and the lack of recognition for an alternative medicine approach makes it unjustifiable for me to encourage students to give up their careers to do healing.

I encourage all of you to help people who are in need of healing. Do what you can with what you have learned. Practice. Good results may well be evident after a few months. Results will improve further over time. Nothing should deter you from your effort to help people with full sincerity. In case of real and urgent need, please use the techniques described under, "Dependent Healers" in Chapter 11.

CFQ Classes For Children. The calm (lack of excitement) nature of the CFQ exercises is often less than appealing to children. Parents may find it hard to compel their children to participate in the slow practice. In such circumstances, it is easier to teach them in groups of similar age and to modify the meridian exercises. Other tai-chi exercises can be added to increase the appeal. Children can do "exchange hands" sparring *(dui shou)* techniques from martial arts while practicing in pairs. Such techniques should be carefully selected to avoid violent and offensive movements. Emphasize, rather, loosening, sinking down and hip movements. In this way, the playful instincts of children can be utilized to create enthusiasm. At the same time, the practice encourages mutual respect and co-operation. The loosening, sinking down and hip movements increase flexibility and promote healing. This can also be used as an effective self-defense training for children, aimed at protecting them from disease. It is certainly better than offensive techniques, which require strength for proper execution.

CFQ Self-Help Technique

The use of CFQ techniques as self-help is effective in providing remedies for the multiple problems that I will list below. It does not mean that you should suddenly and completely dispense with normal medical treatments. For acute problems, of course, continue with them for the time being. For those on long term medication, it is advisable to continue taking it. Gradually reduce or eliminate it in consultation with your doctor.

For those of you who are new to CFQ practice, I would encourage you to exercise patience and perseverance instead of being overly enthusiastic about possible outcomes. As you are limited in your ability to heal, results will be less noticeable and will take longer to become obvious. Undue eagerness in seeking visible results will only bring frustration, and may cause you to distrust and stop using CFQ.

The need here is that you learn the exercises and practice regularly with the children. You need not be too particular about the children's correctness or precision in their movements. Correct them gradually, instead of trying hard to ensure their accuracy in execution. Avoid frustrations and irritation. You must, however, try to closely follow the exercises as formulated. Check regularly to improve on your own performance. Your own improvement will bring about greater healing effects. Encourage your children to follow you closely in terms of timing, looseness, and speed.

Many parents and helpers will find it difficult to convince their children to practice the exercises. In such cases, perhaps you could try to do lotus walking with them. For children with physical handicaps (spastic behavior, cerebral palsy or Down's syndrome) or mental retardation (arising from brain damage, or fever, or pre-natal trauma), it may be very difficult to teach them. In that case, you could try teaching the butterfly-shaking technique and supervise them to ensure that they do it. You can also assist them physically if necessary in doing the lotus walk or the butterfly-shaking.

In all cases, keep the children occupied. (I'm thinking here of handicapped children who are unable to perform normal activities.) For those who are physically unable to do the butterfly-shaking, you could spend time moving their legs loosely and easily (say for a half hour each day). When doing so, encourage them to experience and participate. Your effort will be well rewarded. You will find that within a short two or three months, they will be able to do it on their own. Then, recovery of physical ability may gradually take place.

Those children with agonizing or life-threatening problems are likely to be less willing to cooperate unless you take the trouble to explain the benefits of CFQ practice. However, children with severe problems (e.g., leukemia) often seem to be more mature and cooperative. For those with physical disabilities, teaching them a few movements rather than all the movements will still help them greatly. It is quite acceptable if they move clumsily or crookedly. Do not try to forcefully correct them. After some time (this can extend to two to three years), their physical movements will be greatly improved.

Parents who practice CFQ themselves, even without involving their children, may notice a gradual improvement in their children's health, although this alone may be insufficient to clear more severe problems. For genetically induced problems, CFQ may not work well unless both parents are involved in the practice. I'm thinking of juvenile problems and diseases such as leukemia, thalassemia, and Down's syndrome, asthma, and even emotional and behavioral problems. Sinusitis and digestive problems show indications of genetic patterns as well. For families with a child suffering from one or other of these problems, it is advisable for both parents to be actively involved in the practice.

Parents can also dedicate some of their practice to their children. If they develop some healing ability, they can also work on their own children. Their efforts will help the children greatly by speeding up recovery. This might provide a solution if their children are unable or unwilling to participate in the practice. They can also turn to "dependent healing" in time of real need. Teaching CFQ to children below kindergarten age is difficult, but infants and toddlers can benefit from dependent healing methods.

In succeeding chapters, I shall refer generally to the practice as "CFQ involvement." This includes the use of any CFQ actions which can be logically and reasonably applied. Treatment leading to recovery from disease is certain, if you fully appreciate the reason behind all personal well-being problems.

Therapy for Childhood Pathology

Depression, anxiety and violent behaviors may be occasioned by a single traumatic experience, or by prolonged exposure to stress, sensation-seeking and undesirable behavioral patterns. By far the most challenging children are those with such severe problems that they are unable to attend school or carry out normal activities. The energy patterns of these children show severe misalignment, with strong folds and crosses. The face and head region are tightly held in by strong stale energy forces, which can cause disorientation, insomnia, restlessness, altered states of consciousness or hallucinations. A gripping force in the chest region causes chest congestion, fear, and heart palpitation.

CFQ practice replaces disharmony, conflict, confusion, and anxiety with peace and harmony. It also re-aligns the energy-physical-spiritual systems by opening out and removing the folds and misalignments. The majority of cases will be resolved within a few days to a few weeks. Therapy begins with acceptance from caregivers. First, we must unconditionally accept the children with their problems. They need to be comforted and consoled so that they too can accept themselves. Tact and sincerity are crucial. With acceptance, the continuous conflict, confusion, anxiety, stress, and the tiredness arising from fighting to get rid of the problem are removed. In some cases, acceptance itself will be sufficient to eliminate the problem. The complete eradication of these problems comes with regular CFQ practice (two or three sets of meridian exercises twice or three times per week, and use of the lotus walk and butterfly shaking as frequently as possible). These provide a proper outlet and activity whereby "time-out" from their emotional and tension fabricating activities is increased. The children can thus grow as harmonized persons, well equipped with the resilient ability to deal with life's difficult realities.

For those children who are withdrawn, uncooperative or have behavioral problems, it may require a longer time to see positive changes. Children with hyperactivity or attention deficit disorder have excessive stress that is often genetic or fabricated by trauma in early childhood or infancy. Children with behavioral problems are less likely to participate. Caregivers must move in to lovingly drain off the stress and energy blockages. All involved can help by dedicating some of their own practice to the benefit of these children. They will, of course, be limited by their abilities. Habits are difficult to change. Moreover, the children will probably not understand how their behaviors produce problems. Tact, perseverance, and patience are necessary for dedicating help may require some time to produce positive changes. In severe cases, both parents must also practice CFQ for more efficient results.

To prevent relapse, it is a good idea to continue with the CFQ practice even after the problem has been cleared. For children on medication, gradually reduce the dosage with guidance from the doctor. Sometimes, it is necessary to help re-establish self-confidence in the patients (see Chapter 11).

Poor Academic Performance. Children who receive CFQ healing for any problems often show improved academic performance. When stressed is reduced, the mind becomes more alert and flexible. However, initial responses may manifest as a memory lapse if large chunks of stale energy forces form into a shield in the head region before leaving. Parents, of course, would have no way of knowing if that were to be the case, but would be well advised to continue practicing, have patience, and give the CFQ time to do its work. The younger the age of commencement of CFQ treatment, the better the effect. The apparent memory lapse should pass in due course, leaving the child much improved.

Attention Deficit Disorder. The source of hyperactivity and of poor concentration is often excessive stress, which compels children with this diagnosis to be on the move all the time. Such excessive stress can be innate, or fabricated by trauma in early infancy. Treatment therefore involves draining off the stress in their systems. This can be done by the dedication method. Patience and perseverance are necessary, as it takes time to see results. The younger the child's age at the beginning of the CFQ treatment, the better the effect will be. The initial response to healing often includes increased restlessness, but this will gradually decline.

Mental Retardation. Mental retardation can be energetically felt as a kind of hollow, hardening, or glue-like sensation in the head region. Whether the problem is caused by birth defects or disease, much can be done. The earlier the commencement of CFQ involvement, the better the effect. When begun before seven years of age it is possible to bring about normal intelligence in less severe cases. Do not emphasize the head region but always work in general. By paying attention to the lower abdomen and hip region, the opening and flushing down effect is enhanced.

Brain cells can be generated or repaired simply by de-stressing and opening. This can promote proper physiological functioning. The normal medical conclusion in the face of its inability to rejuvenate brain cells using drug treatment stems from the assumption that the problem is too deep and sophisticated for drugs to have any effect. By de-stressing the pure or resilient spirit, you can surpass medical limitations. Intimacy with God, who does not have such limits, has produced amazing results in many peoples' lives. If the problem is caused by disease, the spiritual response includes eliminating the re-appearance of the disease and its symptoms.

A Case Example: *The child, a girl, aged thirteen, had excess fluid in her brain at birth. This problem cleared up with medical treatment. Her mother, however, became concerned that she was not normal. She was undersized and complained often of headaches. In elementary school she did poorly. Socially she was shy and withdrawn. She came along with her family for CFQ practice, and initial attempts to teach her the seven movements were frustrating. She was unresponsive and her movements were uncoordinated and clumsy. But over a period of five months of practice, the frequent headaches disappeared. She had also grown by two inches in* *height. In her school exams, two months after she started CFQ exercises, she was placed twentieth in a class of forty. Prior to that, she was near the bottom of her class.*

Obesity. Obesity is not necessarily caused by overeating. In many cases, even normal eaters are overweight. Those who have other problems like asthma, muscular dystrophy or a need to consume steroid-based medication also tend to be overweight. This is due to the retention of body fluids. Practitioners of CFQ often experience weight reduction after a six months to one-year period. The effect is quicker for children. It is, of course, slower than commercial slimming programs or diet pills but the implications are different. CFQ practice is beneficial for overall well-being and weight reduction is a fringe benefit. CFQ is a natural way, whose effect comes from relaxing and clearing passages so that there is no room for trapped excessive fats and body fluids. Diet programs and slimming drugs do not work to prevent fats from being absorbed by the body, and may have undesirable side effects. It could also renew accumulation of fats and fluids after the dieting program is completed.

The regular practice of CFQ also does away with cravings for excessive food by reducing stress and anxiety. The weight reduction achieved is also sustainable as it comes with an overall sense of well-being, and a profound sense of mental and emotional peace. In some cases, the transitional response causes an increase in appetite and yearning for food, but that dissipates after a while.

Hearing and Speech Defects. Some speech problems are caused by hearing deficits from under-developed auditory nerves or defective connections. In spite of this fact, however, it can happen that the installation of hearing aids to improve hearing does not result in speech problems improving. The cause of some speech and hearing defects can be energetically explained. From this viewpoint the problem is seen as stale energy, which forms into glue-like shields in the middle of the ears and throat. The obstructions can spread into the head region, neck, and chest, causing energy folds and deformations. Patients often have short or bent necks (forward or sideways) due to the constrictive or shortening impact of the stale energy, although more popular explanations might suggest that this is the result of strain or attempts to hear.

What matters is whether the children can have their problems solved. Yes! For children below ten years of age the chances are excellent that they can be brought to normal levels of hearing and speech. CFQ involvement can often bring some response within the first few tries. The effects include increased vocalization, restlessness, and sensitivity to seemingly disturbing distant or faint noises. In some cases the dissolving of stale energy forces from the head region can temporarily form a shield causing dreaminess and poor memory. Often a satisfactory result comes after a year or more of treatment.

Asthma & Sinusitis. Most children will outgrow asthma problems though they may recur in late adulthood. The current medical remedy is confined to relief and control of the asthmatic symptoms. This, of course, is necessary since severe asthmatic attacks can be fatal. Asthmatic children are often sensitive or allergic to foods, emotional arousal or external factors like smoke and dust and should avoid such agents to minimize attacks. Cold food, drinks, fruits, strenuous exercise, partying, excitement, and emotional arousal of any kind should be minimized.

Asthmatic and/or sinusitis children show strong tension formations in the head and chest regions, which squeeze on the respiratory tract. They often have short or curved necks, and hunched or stiff shoulders. When sitting in a relaxed position, many of them show a clear depression across the abdomen, indicating the presence of strong binding forces. During an attack, tension forces fabricate a spasm that squeezes on the respiratory system, resulting in breathing difficulties.

CFQ involvement effectively reduces the tension, thus resolving the problem. When practiced over a period of six months to a year, obvious visible changes in posture will occur. The transition may trigger attacks due to the excitement manifested by tension forces in the dissolving process. Such attacks are often milder than normal attacks, as the forces responsible for the attacks are thinning off. Nevertheless, medical attention is necessary.

Arthritis. Incidences of childhood arthritis are much fewer than adult arthritis but they can have severe implications. If improperly managed, normal deterioration or the frequent use of pain-killers may gradually lead to death. Isolated joint pains during the normal rapid growing period between ages 10—15 years is not arthritis. This problem is dominated by stiff and shortened muscle formations, which can be traced to emotional origins. Arthritic children are often highly imaginative, sensitive, and withdrawn. Encouraging positive emotional habits and reducing pressure on them can be of help. They tend to have low pain threshold and their sensitivity, while genuine, is all too often regarded by others as an exaggeration. Be careful when seeking massage, physiotherapy, or orthopedic help for these children. If the child expresses great pain when stretched or moved, let him or her relax, allowing the pain to pass. If the moving or stretching is continued, the excruciating pain can effect unconsciousness or throw the child into a coma, which may be fatal. If a child is reluctant or unable to exercise, do not be too forceful. Strenuous exercise could result in injury or tiredness and require a long recovery time.

CFQ exercise can be reasonably practiced within reasonable limits by these children. In the beginning, take it easy on them. The emphasis should be on looseness, without concern for correctness or elegance. If they get exhausted easily, allow sufficient rest. For difficult cases, Movements 1 to 3, ending with the conclusion, are sufficient until they can comfortably repeat these movements for half an hour. Then teach them the other movements. Use the dedication method in severe cases.

Both parents may also be required to practice. Persevere in practice, as this problem may take a few years to completely clear.

Cerebral Palsy. Strong and irregular energy formations are the basis of distorted physical shapes and spastic behaviors. CFQ appears to be the best solution as it is able to dissolve the tension. In severe cases, where the children are unable to practice, direct healing or dedication appear to be the only available measures. In such cases, it will be useful to encourage the afflicted children to do energy butterfly-shaking. If unable to do so in the beginning, shake their legs for them. Encourage them to loosen and to feel the movements. When they gradually are able to do this for themselves, their conditions will have improved tremendously. The practice of one or a few movements from the CFQ exercises, depending on their responses, will help greatly. Occasionally, instruct the children to use visualization to stretch the physically tensed or weak spots or irregular formations. Stretching this way is preferable to using physical strength, and will yield good results.

Down's Syndrome. This is recognized as having genetic origins, but the problem at its core is still tension. Pre-natal tension forces form a pattern of basic energy crosses, which hinders the physical body to the extent of creating the problem. CFQ is well-equipped to resolve this problem as a gene-altering tool.

If CFQ treatment commences before the age of five, the chances of complete normalization are good. Visible effects (including changes in facial features) occur within one to two months of treatment over five to fifteen healing sessions. For commencement of energy treatment after the age of five, improvements are normally less impressive. The greatest problem is parents' belief that the disease is untreatable by any means.

A Case Example: *The infant girl had severe Down' Syndrome with typical facial features—a nose completely without a ridge and ultra-thin lips. She also had congenital heart defects. At four months, she could hardly* *move her limbs and could barely turn her neck. The first healing session was for twenty minutes. The infant's mother informed me that on the night after the first session, the baby had strong movements in all her limbs and could also lift her head up. When supported under her arms, for the first time, she could stand up.*

I noticed a remarkable change in the second visit. Her nose had a noticeable ridge, amazing considering that treatment only started two days previous. Her facial features also appeared to be more normal and she indeed could move her limbs with ease. After the session, I sense that she could develop a fever as part of the healing response. I told the mother to expect it and not to worry. She could wipe the infant with a wet cloth and give an aspirin to subdue the fever.

The mother rang up the next morning and confirmed that the infant had had a fever and the baby was fine. She, however, did not show up for the third appointment nor provided further news of the baby. It was not until more than two years later that I saw the mother. She came to my Center for treatment of a neck pain. When I inquired about her baby, she disclosed that she had stopped the energy treatment for corrective heart surgery on her baby which was successfully performed. The toddler, now over two years old, apparently was developing normally and was walking as well. However, there was a hearing and speech problem which the physician said was due to her auditory nerves.

Afterward. It was a year later before her mother brought the child back for treatment. She was 38 months old. Her mother gave the excuse that a temple medium had assured her that he could treat the child and ridiculed her for the CFQ treatment. Finding no change in her baby, she came back as she wanted me to help the child who was now deaf.

The doctor she consulted earlier explained that the child had a bad auditory nerve connection. Nothing could be done in one ear while a hearing aid could be installed in the other at a future date. Her deafness meant that she did not learn to talk. My observation was that the child had many other problems observable from her physical and behavioral deficits.

To date, I have done a total of seven weekly healing sessions of 15 minutes each. Since the child disliked being held, I left her to play freely while I meditated sitting at corner of the hall. Below are the observed physical and behavioral changes, which have been verified by the mother and grandmother:

After two sessions the baby was able to lift her head up and move her neck freely (previously she always looked down). After three sessions her body posture had straightened where before she had been walking with an obvious tilt forward. She could drop her right hand to the side and move it freely, and after six sessions also drop her left hand. Previously, she had held both hands rigidly against her chest and had slapped her head continuously. Also, she began to walk and move about on her own. Previously she needed to be supported as she toppled easily. Her eyes, once rigid and up-turned, now moved freely.

She could play, and she moved around freely in my Center touching and grabbing at objects though when she first came she sat pretty motionless with a book in front of her, without doing much else. Her grand mother complained that she was unable to cope with her.

After session 4, she began humming on different tones continuously. Previously she had sucked air into her mouth in order to vocalize. After the next session, she went from walking heavily with wide-opened legs, needing to be held up, to walking lightly with a bounce, and running. She enjoyed being stroked and massaged, where previously she would move away even from the touch of her mother and grandmother. She became very upset if anyone touched her on the face. After session 6, she was observed to turn her head to investigate loud noises and she responded when her name was called. Previously she did not respond (could not hear) at all. Her nose bridge was more prominent.

Her grandmother (who is the main caregiver) added the following about the child's behavior at home:

The baby cried with sounds and tears for the first time since birth(after the third session). She could cry for attention, and climb up and down the staircase for the first time. The baby could no longer be confined to her crib (after five sessions). She would cry and climb out of it. Previously she could be kept there for the entire day. Now she moves around the house all the time and reaches for things she wants. She is interested in food and knows how to ask for it. When down with a flu she had a runny nose, while in the past her nose had remained dry, no matter how sick she was.

Her speech and auditory failure is clearing gradually. I believe it came from the inherent tension knots in the head and throat that obstruct speaking and hearing. I am optimistic that with continued CFQ treatment, she will continue her now normal development.

Muscular Dystrophy. This disease of the muscles is genetic in origin. The energy formations of these patients typically display a kind of weakness or "cut-off" pattern from the lower back down to the legs. The cut-off forces are debased energy with strong sensations of weakness, staleness, hollow numbness, and lethargy. Above the cut-off point, particularly in the heart region, there is a sensation of compactness and rigidity. With further deterioration, the disease gradually spreads upward. That gives rise to weakness of the arms, breathing difficulties, abnormal heartbeat, and sluggish mental functions. When the cut-off point shifts up to the chest and heart region, death is inevitable.

CFQ treatment involves the downward and outward release of the weakness, which is often clearly experienced as a numbness during the release process. This is no easy task, as the amount of disease energy is tremendous. As is evident in every kind of disease, the body is capable of absorbing an amazing amount of disease energy before showing even minor symptoms. For life threatening disease such as muscular dystrophy, the amount of disease energy is almost unimaginable. Yet, it is treatable with CFQ. The patient, together with the support of family members, including parents and siblings, should embark on CFQ practice to neutralize the genetic energy traps and family karma. Most patients, however, can not be expected to be able to stand and practice CFQ exercise for even five minutes. Even for beginners who have little problem in walking and moving normally, the downward release of such a tremendous amount of weakness and numbness will temporarily produce an experience of weakness. Their legs may be disabled when following the CFQ meridian movements. As the numbness flows away, everything will be all right.

Take care not to struggle to regain mobility. This is the usual tendency, but it is counterproductive. Doing it involves absorbing back all the numbness. This rule applies to all the other cases of illness in this and all other chapters. Please do not allow the patient to try to outsmart him or herself by fighting back and resisting physically. Encourage a little mobility and loosening at a time. Then stop completely to allow the numbness to clear off. Maintain a calm, relaxed, and reassuring attitude.

In the beginning, practice the Movements 1—3 as a complete set with the affirmations and conclusion. Repeat from the beginning and rest completely in between each set as the situation warrants. While resting, take care not to be carried away by a sense of reluctance or a temptation to discontinue with the practice. When a patient is able to exercise continuously for 30 minutes (about five sets), the overall condition should have improved tremendously. In that case, he or she should learn the remaining movements to ensure completeness of the exercises.

Even for those patients in a severe stage, cure is often far from hopeless. They should do the butterfly-shaking or lotus walk, whatever their condition permits. For those immobilized in a wheelchair, parents and friends should assist. Shake their legs for the patients while encouraging them to take notice. In such cases, great patience and perseverance is necessary. Their condition is already critical, but such children still have a good chance of recovery. They must be involved with CFQ in whatever manner and for whatever time they have. In severe cases, two or three hours of daily practice is necessary. In other cases, one or two hours daily is reasonable. This deadly disease must never be treated lightly. Even for those who can practice the exercises, they should also do the lotus walk and butterfly shaking to complement the meridian exercises. Most people will not want to practice the meridian exercise for more than an hour. When doing the lotus walk and shaking, the same rule applies—rest when overwhelmed by numbness.

Noticeable improvement can be achieved within one or two months, but the unwinding reactions of the healing response are also tremendous. There are times when numbness seems to be oozing out from the entire body extending beyond the body. The patient feels numb and the energy discharged fills up the entire environment, to the point that anyone coming near will feel the numbness and cold. There may be bouts of depression, disturbed thoughts and nightmares as the stale energy, deep within, moves out. There will be pain and discomfort as the muscles rejuvenate. Please be prepared and willing to face the reactions. They are worthwhile sufferings that restore health. A major breakthrough and cure may come after a year or so. MD patients who overcome such a difficult traumatic healing process and symptom release should continue CFQ practice as a life-long opportunity.

Cancer. If the prevailing ideas and conventional treatment approaches change, cancer might well claim fewer lives. Children with cancer often fare better than adults. They are generally more resilient, less suspicious, less frightened, less panic stricken, less rigid in determining what will work for them, and their systems are still in an active growing phase.

To help children with cancer, their parents would do well to be open-minded to energy medicine. Please read Chapter 17 on the nature of cancer carefully. This will enable understanding and facilitate choosing the best treatment approach for any given child. It will reduce the risk of being over concerned, which might in turn lead to actions and remedies which might hasten deterioration.

Do CFQ meridian exercises from one to two hours daily. An overall improvement in well-being should be noticeable within a several days. Please do not be overly concerned with a particular lump or supposed problem area. Overall health is much more important. There will be reactions, discomforts, and various other responses in the healing process. Please view them with the realization that they are symptoms which evidence the disease is going away. Give yourself one month to decide on whether you should use other methods of treatment. One month is the normal interval between the first diagnosis and the commencement of a radical treatment. CFQ's effectiveness is less certain in cases where the diagnosis suggests that the disease is in its terminal stage, or after other treatment approaches have been used.

A Case Example: *A boy, aged fourteen, suffered a painful knee, which was diagnosed as bone cancer. This was confirmed by a second specialist. After a month, the teenager was scheduled to travel to a hospital out of town for further oncological tests and a determination of treatment procedures. The possibilities included amputation, if the cancer had spread beyond the knee.*

The father, a factory manager, was acquainted with a CFQ student. On hearing about my healing he expressed great interest. The boy's mother, a nurse, however, resisted, accusing the father of relying on "quacks and such nonsense." The father delayed the appointment with me for four weeks. The family finally came to my Center four days prior to leaving for the hospital appointment.

The first healing session had a dramatic physical effect on the boy. He displayed a variety of involuntarily movements, his neck twisted from side to side, his shoulders jerked and pulled back, and his limbs quivered and shook. His father sat quietly at his side watching with fascination while his mother stood by with a frosty face. I offered a second appointment for two days later, which his father happily accepted. However, they did not show up for the appointment nor did they telephone.

Three weeks later, my student who had introduced the family excitedly informed me that the boy had returned from his hospital trip. Tests had not detected the expected cancer and he was discharged without treatment. The knee pain and limp had gone earlier, just after the second day of receiving energy healing.

Comments. Clearing a cancer problem with just one energy treatment is too good to be true. But then, children have better regeneration abilities. Their bodies have less trapped energy forces that stiffen and block up healthy energy flow. I had fully expected a dozen weekly treatments to ensure that the problem would be completely cleared.

Leukemia. Leukemia patients generally have strong energy congestion in the chest and heart region. It can be traced to genetic origins. The congestion and constrictive effect on the heart region probably fabricates more conflict and disharmony. This suggests to the immune system that it respond with the production of large quantities of white blood cells to fight an alleged threat. Such excessive production can also be triggered by frequent occurrences of common infections like the colds, flu, sore throat, hidden infections (not be easily diagnosed), and a prolonged use of drugs or antibiotics. CFQ treatment works on the cause that triggers the excessive production of white cells or leukocytes. By opening and clearing up the trapped energy, CFQ flushes out the body's excessive infectioun-fighting agents as well. By regulating and releasing the conflicts and disharmony, the body no longer has to produce excessive numbers of leukocytes to defend itself.

Be involved in CFQ exercises with the afflicted child. Do whatever is possible to get the patient to practice. This includes family support (both parents must be involved to help clear the disease promoting genes), by dedication, or direct healing. Use the exercises and complementary techniques for an hour or more daily. Improvement will show in the form of increased appetite, better sleep, positive blood test results, and a healthier physical appearance. Healing reactions might include heavy perspiration. This is in contrast to the slowing down and elimination of sweating seen in the later stages of the disease or as happens when chemotherapy is administered. Perspiration is evidence of a reversal process that shifts the patient to wellness. Other possible reactions include muscular pains in the thighs and lower back, urine with a stench, occasional vomiting, and fever.

From the spiritual perspective, the medical approach does not seem to deal with the true nature of the disease. The immune system of the leukemia victim produces an excessive numbers of leukocytes because this system "thinks" the body needs it. To take the leukocytes as the enemy to be utterly destroyed leads to more problems. Not only are the leukocytes sacrificed but the treatment also destroys healthy cells. In the end, conventional medicine wins the battle but loses the cancer war (see Chapter 17 on *Resilience to Overcome Cancer*). Is there a better way? I suggest a cure by making peace.

I know that CFQ can maintain a sustainable cure, as evidenced by the many cases that I have treated. I ask that CFQ be given a good and fair try, at least as a complementary treatment to conventional medicine. Do CFQ, say for six months, for one to two hours daily. Meanwhile you can continue to see the doctors. Perhaps the leukemia patient needs regular blood and platelet transfusions as well as medication to control symptoms. After the leukemia is declared "cured" continue to use CFQ for at least an equivalent amount to that given to medicine. This ensures that the problem does nor reoccur.

A Case Example: *A young patient, aged fourteen, was first diagnosed with leukemia two years before I met him. He was treated with chemotherapy, injections, and oral medications. His condition improved but a year and half later, the leukocyte count was on the increase. He had frequent bleeding from his eyes and gums. He also required blood and platelet transfusions every two or three weeks. His condition was monitored twice weekly. Finally, his doctor expressed the opinion that the leukemia could no longer be controlled. A final chemotherapy treatment was proposed. The strong injection would be a make-or-break last resort.*

It was at this time that a family friend of theirs recommended that they should bring the patient to see me. They decided to defer the chemotherapy. The boy appeared extremely pale, his limbs were cold, and he was diminutive in size. He had blood patches under his eyes and darkened gums. I gave him a half hour healing session. He had been unable to perspire for a considerable time. At the end of the session, his shirt was wet. He felt hungry and wanted food. Appointments were scheduled every second day.

He did not come for the third visit as it conflicted with his routine blood transfusion. He showed up seven days later. After the third session, he perspired even more heavily. For two days he felt intense heat at night but with no fever (he normally felt cold even when he had fever). On the fourth and fifth healing, he appeared to be more alert, active, and cheerful. His limbs had regained their normal warmth, his appetite and sleep improved. Even though he continued to perspire heavily and needed to change his clothes several times a day, he felt comfortable.

By that time, the doctor had become alarmed by the delay in the chemotherapy. He insisted on going ahead with it, since the leukocyte count was still high. The boy's daily dose of medication increased from six to twelve tablets. Within a week the boy was admitted to the hospital with severe body and joint pains. Blood tests showed that he had negligible or no leukocytes and had become extremely anemic. He was placed on drips with antibiotics. He received four packets of blood and platelet transfusions and put under intensive care.

His mother pleaded with me to visit the boy and I willingly agreed. Despite my two last attempts to save him, his fate was sealed. On my final visit two days before his death, his face and body were full of black patches indicating severe hemorrhaging. He was also hallucinating. Yet he did not forget to thank his mother, grandparents, visitors and me. He was so sweet and well mannered that seeing him suffering and overwhelmed by the disease was heart breaking.

Afterward. Two weeks after the boy's death, his mother visited me at my center to express her gratitude. She remarked on the many positive changes observed on her son since the energy treatments were performed. She felt confident that he might have recovered fully if not for the complications. She suspected that the final chemotherapy treatment and double dose of medication caused severe irreversible damage.

12

Psychological Disorders

Mind as the Root of Disease

All of life's experiences, actions and reactions are energetically stored within the body. Once stored, the energy forces gradually seep beyond the sixth consciousness (mind) into the subconscious (or Unconscious) which is conceptualized here as *mano*-consciousness and *alaya*-consciousness. These deeper sources of self-identity continually influence the mind in the interpretation of events and in decision making. Memories are further influenced by temperament and inherent traits, which interact with the environment. Gradually these stored energy forces, or memories, give rise to behavioral tendencies, habits, likes, dislikes, and perspectives. These energy forces co-exist internally, but are constantly pressing to expand into reality. They attempt to influence and dominate the mind, and are easily aroused by external stimulation and thoughts. These forces stimulate physical growth, give rise to every action, and eventually lead to old age and death. They exist in bundles in one's whole being (not just the mind as is often imagined) and have their imprint in every cell. The authority that puts them under control and allows the strongest among them to speak out is the ego self.

Time and action give rise to a continuous absorption of energy forces which, once absorbed, become the basis of mental functions. They are as alive as any physiological organ carrying out normal functions, and do not stop even for a second. When a person is engrossed in some physical involvement, however, mental activities are ignored and do not appear to cause disturbances. If the person thinks deeply on a personally involving subject, energy forces that are irrelevant to this subject become temporarily subdued. When one is not physically occupied, all energy forces fight to be heard. The more stressed a person is, the louder the voices of these energy forces are, and the more disturbing they become.

The differing strengths of the various energy forces determine how influential they will be. The strength is dependent on its connection with evoked emotions. Events or incidences (for example, trauma that causes excessive emotional arousal in the form of anger, fear, anxiety, depression, or despair) tend to repeat continuously in the mind, so that undesirable behavioral and emotional traits, once habituated, become easily aroused. They pick up momentum with each arousal, until a person loses control of them. Fundamentally, compulsive negative thought patterns and undesirable behaviors are external manifestations of internal emotional and spiritual-energy pain, which results from memories and experiences that occur in normal life. In addition, pain evolves from information and beliefs that are non-harmonious and that therefore engender conflict. Stressed people, especially those inclined toward mental passivity, are more prone to uncontrollable, undesirable emotional experiences than those with a well-balanced mental-physical lives.

Contemporary society places a high value on the acquisition of knowledge and mental stimulation, even though these things may produce pain in the long term. Even underachievers feel deprived of opportunities to catch up with the realm of knowledge. Those who feel left out in any way can therefore become discontented, angered or frustrated. They store up stress that can then make them vulnerable to even more stressors. Thus, stress is a burden that causes emotional and spiritual pain, which finds its outlet in behavioral and psychological problems. In addition, people suffering psychological problems may fail to understand their own distress. They may regard problems "in the mind" as either non-existent or inconsequential. Few, however, including experts, understand the mind's image-making nature. Or the fact that imagery has real energy, which can disturb people naturally and which therefore cannot be ruled out or ignored. Social stigma may isolate people with psychological problems and is often interpreted as weakness. People with such problems generally lack self-confidence, are afraid of themselves, and fearful of losing control. Their struggle to face themselves and to hide their problems makes them withdraw, fabricate further conflict, and compound problems in a vicious cycle.

Subduing the Counter-Productive Mind. Energy forces that are the basis of undesirable behavioral traits are often highly compacted and linked to emotions. They can be distinguished as explosive or implosive. The explosive person reacts strongly when triggered by external stimulation, and flares into a rage or tantrum. The outburst is so reflex-like and natural that the person may not be conscious of it until it has occurred. The implosive type is also easily hurt and embarks on a self-destructive process of withdrawal. When the withdrawal becomes unbearable, it may flare into an explosion. The relevant energy forces pick up strength with every reoccurrence until the person feels helpless. Every attempt to control such emotional tendencies leads to more frustration. As this painful pattern progresses, its victim becomes more sensitive and vulnerable to further provocation.

Negative and undesirable behavioral traits cannot be subdued by mind control. All too frequently, attempts to do so simply provoke a more powerful reaction. This pattern leads to a spiraling of psychological problems. Fighting and controlling the thoughts provide the fuel for stronger thoughts and, in time, the person becomes hopelessly entangled and bullied by them. He or she loses confidence and tends to submit to the prevailing thoughts. As these thoughts become stronger, their victim moves into a spaced-out state of consciousness. As the process goes on, switching to these painful thoughts may provide a sadistic satisfaction and become habitual or addictive.

As low esteem builds, the sufferer becomes suspicious of others and withdraws. She or he may lack the energy to change their daily routine even to get well. For the chronically ill person, treatment is often not successful if he or she lacks initiative, endurance, and a real intention to get well.

Energy & States of Consciousness

Memory-housing energy can gives rise to excessive and uncontrollable responses, that are quite strong and easily activated. When triggered, energy forces within the five senses become aroused and cause muscular tension. This biases perception and spreads out into a field that extends into the subconscious. This information field manifests as a dark energy cloud, replete with imagery and color characteristics (e.g., red is often connected with anger). Such clouds can function like a shield. When this occurs, the victim becomes dominated and controlled by this field and ceases to have normally flexible and adaptive thinking functions; indeed the person's actions are increasingly dictated by this field. If one sees images or hears voices within the reality in this energy field, he or she hallucinates. In drug-induced states, the drug effects a surge of energy, shielding off normal consciousness. If the person is addicted, then his or her usual consciousness and control can actually be obstructed by the energy shield.

Such an energy field usually dissipates its forces in time. But it wreaks havoc before partially wearing out. The remaining dysfunctional energy tends to be reabsorbed into the energy field. After the energy field settles back into appropriate levels of consciousness, the person functions normally again. But with each outbreak, energy forces become stronger and the next outbreak can occur more easily and with greater power. While such outbursts occur readily in stressed people, they may also occur in people who are normally relaxed, though in the latter, it takes a much stronger upset to provoke an outburst. Outbursts can occur in response to extreme emotional arousal causing such feelings as excessive anger, fear, or despair. Once such an outburst occurs, it needs to be dealt with properly, or it can become a habit within the person's consciousness that can be more easily triggered the next time.

Even normal healthy people can switch into an altered state of rage if sufficiently aroused. In such cases, the person feels agonized by the gripping effect of the energy force field. At this point, he or she is in an altered state and their normal flexible mind is shielded off. Actions are dictated by energy field forces, seeking to relief the agony. If one becomes deeply involved, there can be a loss of responsibility and morality.

Trance & Hypnotism. Trances, whether self-induced or induced by the influence of others are commonplace examples of hypnosis, or the achievement of altered states of consciousness. By way of auto-suggestion or assisted suggestion, an energy field is created around and in a person, which displaces normal consciousness. This force field can be fueled by imagination and influential beliefs (e.g. a positive belief in the value of hypnosis). When a person reorients to normal reality, the trance energy forces may continue to co-exist within inherent energy forces in the consciousness. It is possible for a person to become so habituated or even addicted to a trance state that reorienting to a normal state can be challenging.

In societies with a strong cultural belief in the supernatural, any psychological or behavioral problem is readily explained as a supernatural phenomenon. Superstitious beliefs provide a convenient system for explaining things beyond our comprehension. In such societies, when psychological problems are beyond someone's ken, they are often attributed to underworld spirits. Remedies for the problems experienced are therefore sought from temple mediums and shamans.

I have spent a good deal of time studying the practice of mediums who claim to be able to communicate with ghosts or departed spirits. My conclusion is that such spirits exist only in the mind as "thought entities." Here, every type of existence occurs but does not really cross over to the human plane to influence and control life. It is humans who imagine, create conflicts, and lose control over themselves. There is an advantage to blaming ghostly figures for one's problems. When the problem episode is over it is less embarrassing to blame one's bizarre behavior on someone or something else, than take responsibility oneself.

I have successfully treated a number of persons who blamed their troubles on possession by evil spirits, charms, potions or spells. Some of the cases were so severe that even reputed shamans were unable to help them. I found that most of the problems were caused by erroneous beliefs and suggestions that stimulated confusion and conflict. Charms and spells appear to have power largely in a person's mind. To be more specific, they are empowered by the imagination and suspicions within one's energy field. If the person's background beliefs are strong, their suspicions and paranoia attribute the psychological symptoms present to a charm or spell. People who are at a low ebb of confidence easily fall victim to speculative auto-suggestions.

Casting a spell on someone does not require discipline or training. All the person needs is to understand human weaknesses such as fear, greed, self-centeredness and ignorance. Equipped with some basic understanding, at least 50 per cent of such attempts will be successful. Even those who specialize in sorcery need to rely on trickery. A powerful sorcerer can manipulate another person's energy field to fabricate problems. But a truly powerful person knows the adverse consequences of such interference and will never do it.

Case Study of a Sick Family. A boy came from a poor rural family. At age seven he moved in with a relative, to enable him to go to school. He was required to work in the grocery store operated by his uncle. At age eight, he started having backaches and was sent back to his parents' home. Coming from a superstitious and uneducated background, the parents consulted numerous temple mediums or shamans. They suggested that the cause of the child's pain was due to evil spirits and spells. The mother blamed the relative for casting an evil spell on the child.

The pain became more severe spreading over the boy's body and to his legs. The parents took the child to Western doctors who diagnosed it as "childhood arthritis," which the parents doubted. As the child's condition deteriorated, the family blamed the villagers for colluding to harm the family through the boy. By age 14, the boy's condition became so severe that his whole body, particularly from the hips downwards, was excruciatingly painful. His skin was red and burning. Moving or touching him caused extreme pain and he would not allowed others to so touch him. His legs were weak and he struggled to walk with the support of a cane. He had been hospitalized for a year, but no treatment seemed to have worked.

At this stage his grade school teacher (one of my students) recommended that the boy be brought to me. His energy field was so thick and extended that my treatment had dramatic effects. During each treatment session, he responded to every thought of mine with vigorous jerky movements, twisting and turning on the couch. His arms and legs followed my specific healing movements like a puppet, even though he could not do such movements normally, and his eyes were closed.

After about ten sessions, twice weekly, his condition was so improved that he could walk unaided. He walked clumsily supporting his thighs with both hands. He still could not bear being touched or assisted by others. After 20 sessions, I stopped treatment as I was away on a six-month meditation retreat. The parents continued to rely on temple mediums exclusively, even though they were of no real help. The parents felt good about these consultations as their suspicions were confirmed by blaming a supernatural cause. During the CFQ treatment, the boy had reduced the number of pain-killers he needed, but now he fell back to this medication again.

Almost a year later, the family contacted me again when the boy's condition took a rapid turn for the worst. By then, he was completely paralyzed and bed ridden. He was also starving, as he refused to eat and barely drank. His hallucinations were frightening. He claimed to be inhabited by wild spirits and babbled about vengeful ghosts. His hatred was terrifying. He cursed his whole family, neighbors, and threatened to kill them all. He demanded human blood to drink. Their residence was in a remote place, up on a hill, inaccessible by car. His parents could not move him to the hospital. He was dying. Thus far, the only treatment that had helped him was CFQ. The parents called me pleading for help. I met the father at the foot of the hill and was taken up on his motorbike. The boy failed to recognize me. He vented hatred, struggling to breathe at the same time. He seemed to be going fast.

I tuned into him to clear and sink the stale energy. It appeared to be solid and impenetrable. I exhorted him to accept himself and not to blame others. Within ten minutes, he regained normal consciousness and asked for water. After the session, he shifted his body, complained of hunger, and asked for food. The next day, he had a relapse and became delirious again.

I returned for another treatment. He regained consciousness and that night asked to be admitted into a hospital. He told his mother, "Make sure Sifu Yap comes to the hospital to treat me." The next morning he could walk unassisted downhill to the car waiting below, and was driven to the hospital.

X-rays of the hip area found that his flesh had blackened from the surface to the bone. The doctors said that nothing could be done except to prescribe pain-killers. He was allowed to stay in hospital for two months. During that time I made fifteen visits. He shifted between agonizing bouts of pain and trance states. His body remained burning hot and his skin was bright red. In the first five sessions, he unleashed a tremendous amount of hatred in my presence. I spent long hours after each session remaining with him in meditation. I then initiated him in CFQ meditation. He developed strong spontaneous movements while lying down reciting the protective mantra. By the fourth week, after eight treatment sessions, he was able to get up and walk clumsily.

After his discharge, I advised him not to return to his remote home. He had developed a fear of his home, making it an unsuitable place for him to rest and recuperate. He moved into his grandparents house. I kept him occupied by doing CFQ meditation for eight or more hours daily. During the initial three months, there were frequent recurring pains. These were significantly reduced over a period of two years. Another problem involved high body temperatures. A feverish heat would break out in his body. His mother would wipe him down. She would wash the towel out in a bucket of water, which quickly turned thick, sticky and viscous. Three buckets of water were needed for the heat to clear off. The searing body heat returned two dozen more times before it finally stopped.

Follow-Up. He was taken to my Center for treatment thrice weekly for six months and then for bi-monthly treatments for another 18 months. I taught him, his siblings, and his mother CFQ exercises. He is now close to normal except for some stiffness in his body. Since he cannot work or do anything else as yet, I have advised him to practice CFQ for ten hours daily.

Comments. This is a family victimized by misleading and superstitious beliefs. Their home was a dark, old, run-down ancestral house in an isolated region. The siblings claimed they saw ghosts and nightly apparitions wandering in their house. One of the sisters fell into a trance and demanded human blood. The extreme superstition, suspicion, fear, and hysteria could have wiped out the entire family. Strange things happened daily during the crisis but have now cleared up. The most difficult task was to change their attitudes and beliefs and to accept their problem as one explainable by natural causes. Every one in the family had health problems.

Medically, it was clear that the boy could not have survived without my intervention. Other family members were also successfully treated. His grandfather had an enlarged prostate gland and was incontinent. His grandmother had glaucoma and suffered from hallucinations. Both were healed. They have learned the meridian exercises. The boy's three sisters and a brother each had their own problems, which were alleviated while practicing the CFQ exercises. His mother suffered from dizzy spells, chronic body pains and flatulence. With a month of CFQ practice, these problems vanished. The father did not join the family in CFQ practice initially. However, he watched his family practice at home and secretly began to practice on his own. Two months after his attempt, he proudly announced to his family that his distressing back and leg pains were gone. His left leg (previously stiff and lumpy) had completely healed.

Trauma, Misfortune & Resilience

Every psychological problem has an emotional component. When a person is a victim of a sudden or prolonged traumatic experience or stressful event, mishap, violence, injustice or loss, a permanent emotional impact is formed. She or he can become disoriented as the emotional pain and suffering lingers. Natural responses, then, are dictated by energy forces and memories of the incident. These responses are of two types, either to:

1. Dwell in and follow the negative thoughts and emotions which in turn aggravates further pain, hatred, anger, and fear, thus trapping the victim in an undesirable psychological state, or

2. Attempt to reconcile and suppress the incident. The victim in this case becomes deeply entangled in emotions and feels powerless against the compulsive undesirable thoughts.

In either case the victim is dragged down with haunting memories or compulsive negative thoughts. A better alternative is to learn to accept oneself. Accept the fact that the incident has happened and is now in the past, regardless of what may have gone on or what damage may have been inflicted. The wiser path is to pick oneself up and move ahead, to claim one's rightful entitlement to health. By moving forward in love, the negative thoughts have no chance to catch up.

Resilient people are wonderfully able when it comes to getting over a trauma, misfortune or despair. They have an optimistic and cheerful outlook, and are more relaxed. They tend to live by the positive human values of love, kindness, generosity, responsibility, self-worth, and spiritual faith. An ability to accept oneself and uphold a strong sense of responsibility and commitment to others make a person resilient.

Some people present a strong facade, which can often obscure undesirable attitudes. These individuals are more likely than others to succumb and fall apart when faced with psychological problems, traumas, adversity, misfortune or even normal life hassles. They may interpret minor frustrations or incidences as major pressures. Undesirable forces that undermine resilience include self-centeredness, pride, worrisome thinking, perfectionism, having unrealistic expectations, lacking in emotional expression, hostility, and over-reacting to problems.

Most psychological problems would not develop with a proper understanding of the nature and functions of the brain and the mind. Science no longer uphold the notion that all memory resides in the brain. We now know that the organs and muscles also contain some of our memories. This can explain the effects of emotional trauma. I experience memory being stored energetically throughout the whole physical body, in every cell, and in the mind and spirit. The assumption of memory storage solely in the brain implies that all memories could be altered or erased. This belief counters experience. The more one attempts to control or forget memories, the stronger they bounce back. In times of mental distress, this no-win "remedy" aggravates the situation. Further, it is an ineffective strategy to encourage a psychologically or physically fatigued person to rest to get over their problems. By resting, the person is spending more time fabricating fatigue.

For example, if chronic exhaustion causes a person to be unable to handle his normal workload, this suggests that the person has little interest in work. He or she has become more concerned about fatigue. A few days off from the work routine might prove helpful if the person comes back soon after the time off. But if the disinterest in work persists, something else should immediately be found to occupy the person. Normal rest or inactivity is really no rest, but is rather more time for a counterproductive dwelling on one's problems. The same holds for depression, anxiety and unhappy emotional states. The best way is to move ahead and carry on with life; being meaningfully busy so that negative thoughts cannot catch up.

Absence of Diagnosable Symptoms. Psychological problems are often distinguished from physical illnesses by the nature of the symptoms. Thus a person who suffers chronic tiredness, without, say, the physiological symptoms of diabetes, may be diagnosed as having chronic fatigue. The basic assumption of energetic healing is that the cause of every problem is debased and drawn-in tension energy. The stress-illness link manifests in different ways depending on a complex mix of a person's habits, attitudes, lifestyle, physical condition and activities. When fatigue persists or chronic, the original stress becomes is combined with added stress. The mind's inclination to be anxious, suspicious or speculative drives the body to produce excessive blood sugar. Eventually the chronic fatigue victim may even be diagnosed as diabetic.

Now the person has a tangible or "real" problem that seems to explain the distress. In many cases, such a switch from the original non-physical problem to a physical problem seems to make a person feel better. The physical problem is accepted, the victim forgives the past conflict, and is freed from the psychological dilemma. The person in our example takes medication for diabetes and accepts the fatigue, even though it persists. Similarly, a depressed person will be sad but experience relief if she or he eventually is diagnosed as having a physical disease, even cancer. The person can now be busily involved in the treatment of the cancer. Without such a physical distraction the person refuses to accept the depression which then continues to escalate.

Finding physiological symptoms that fit disease criteria indeed deflects many psychological cases into physical treatment. But is that a good idea? Can better or more effective things be done? Yes, because the fundamental source of all disease is tension. Why not work on its elimination? This would not be difficult, provided that one is willing to tone down the public's love affair with the brain and the belief that the mind alone fabricates, controls, and conquers everything.

Scientists would do well to pause in their relentless pursuit of complete understanding of the brain, and in their drive to find a way to use 100 percent of its power. They are not satisfied with the two percent that is claimed to be normal brain usage. In fact, no human being can or should be satisfied with such an impoverished utilization of natural gifts. Humankind will likely, however, become extinct long before the halfway mark of 50 percent usage is achieved. More importantly, however, we need to utilize our other assets, for example, the talents of the resilient spirit with which we are endowed.

Working on stress is relaxing, spending some time each day lowering the risk of brain burnout. To relax means to do something that is not in the normal thinking, doing, fabricating, or idling behavioral systems. In normal relaxation there is no time off from mental activity. That means using the time to facilitate the brain in continuing to burn itself up. This could be more harmful than keeping stressfully busy!

Not only does every biological disease have an equivalent psychological component but the reverse is also true. However, many physical symptoms of psychological states are unfortunately not medically understood. Even if detected, they often are not seen as harmful. I observe, generally, that people with psychological disorders have raised chests hunched at the upper back even when relaxed. Their shoulders and necks are stiff. Their faces are often rigid with little expression. They manifest little elation. They express pain or sadness readily. Their eyes are dreamy. They often complain of stiffness in their jaws and of body pain. But all these are medically classified as relatively insignificant.

Take a moment to consider what is causing these physical effects. They stem from psychological problems related to pressure and inflexibility within the head and upper torso. Be sensitive, and connect with the pain and discomfort created by the body pressure. Connect with the deprivation of blood and oxygen supply due to poor circulation. Internal blockages may produce wrong or inadequate nerve or information exchanges. There may be a helpless internal struggle going on. Then the outcomes called depression, withdrawal, anxiety, restlessness, fear, palpitations and pain become more understandable.

It is also evident that such patterns common to people with psychological disorders are increasingly evident even among many with normal health. This implies that psychopathology is on the rise.

Acceptance & Moving On. Dealing with people with psychological disorders may be extremely complex and requires a good deal of tolerance. Their attitude and mind-set may make it difficult to please them; their mood swings can render their behavior unpredictable; they may be over-sensitive and over-react to petty or unrelated issues. These problems, together with the general public's discomfort of mentally ill people, isolate them from society. As their social contacts dwindle and they become isolated, relatives and loved ones who are close to them not only suffer with them but become a convenient outlet on whom they vent their frustrations. The family and care-givers may suffer even more than the patients. Psychological problems are unique because the mind is capable of repeating a compulsive thought with such intensity that normal work and activity can be greatly disturbed.

Generally, people have little idea how the mind operates. It does not stop for even a second. When a person is thinking, the mind absorbs and is absorbed by the subject matter, whereas when one is involved in physical activity, the mind functions along with the activity. When resting, without any particular thought (idling), the mind wanders and becomes trapped in thoughts with strong emotional attachments. When a person sleeps, the mind becomes dissociated from both the senses and the external environment, leaving the mind to carry on its own sorting, processing, and assimilating of energy memories.

Thus, at no time does the mind stop. Neither can thoughts stop. They revolve around some object of incessant thinking. If the person is focused on something of great interest, he or she is able to side-track other interfering thoughts. Otherwise, if allowed to function on its own, every memory fights to be heard. The ones that speak most strongly are those with deep emotional involvement or events with great physical impact. Traumatic episodes are, of course, the ones that tend to cause deep emotional involvement. Similarly, objects of preferential mental activity have deep emotional roots and any attempt to fight or control such thoughts only fabricates stronger thoughts.

To minimize being controlled by the gripping and suffocating effects of psychological problems requires moving ahead with normal life and activities. This reduces the available time within which the mind is allowed to "fool around" with the victim. Whatever the problem, real or imagined, the victim must be brave enough to leave it behind. The past cannot be lived again, differently. Once one has learned the truth of the past event, there is absolutely no need to recall it, or to think about its right or wrong, good or bad qualities. Do not allow the problem to drag you down, depriving you of your rights, privileges, and entitlement to a happy future. Willingness to change your attitude is crucial if you are to leave the psychological problem behind and proceed with normal life and enjoyment. Such a change in attitude is often sufficient to greatly reduce the problem and enable a return to normal life. It is also crucial to help a former victim return to a normal state of consciousness.

However, more often than not, patients continue to suffer low efficiency in work, and to lack interest and initiative. This is understandable. Normal work and activities are mundane compared to the thrills and chills of mental adventures. Moreover, some patients have developed the habit of enjoying the benefits of being fearful. To overcome this, they need to develop a strong sense of responsibility, backed by positive values. These values promote actions that create or renews healthier functional patterns. To completely eliminate the disturbing thoughts that exist as energy memories, embarking on CFQ practice is a truly positive action.

Undoing Psychological Problems

The practice of CFQ is recommended as a positive tool to dissolve any pathological behavior, trait, emotion, or compulsive thought through the letting-go approach. This approach removes the problems from deep within the spiritual realm and out through the mental-emotional and the physical body levels. It enables shifting from a pathological state of consciousness to a normal state. It anchors this achievement of balance in a beneficial state of consciousness. Psychiatric patients who are taking medication should continue to do so until their condition improves, after which they should discuss with their physicians the possibilities of a gradual reduction in dosage.

Meridian Exercises: These facilitate a whole-body unloading of the problem from within to liberate your own essential deep peace.

Butterfly Shake & Lotus Walk: These are practiced to complement the CFQ meridian exercises. An average person might be able to practice the 7-movements for about one hour, which might involve three or four sets. This hour program might be repeated two or three times a day for those with psychological problems. More repetitions of the meridian exercises can be beneficial. When encountering compulsive thoughts, avoid them by butterfly shaking or lotus walking (say, half hour for each) until such emotional spells dissipate.

Meditation is discouraged here. It tends to go too deep too fast, without requisite skill and strength to deal with the problems. On principle, CFQ discourages any form of meditation for psychiatric problems as it might expose them to the risk of strengthening their psychological disorder. In meditation, if the meditator becomes side-tracked by strong undesirable thoughts, problems begin to intensify. Those who have, however, eliminated these problems by first using the

7-Movements, butterfly shake, and lotus walk may meditate if they wish to gain better insight.

Cleansing Reactions. In most cases of deep psychological difficulties, sufferers experience severe weakness during their initial tries of CFQ practice, due to the opening out and releasing of the problem. Some clients can hardly stand up for five minutes to practice the 7-movements. Severe weakness and numbness in the legs disables them, despite having no normal problem walking. Perseverance with a strong intention to get well will ensure that they gradually improve. After two or three weeks, they are able to exercise for as long as half hour at a time. This means that they are also experiencing great overall improvement.

The nature of psychiatric problems is such that compulsive and recurrent thought patterns cause internal exhaustion, weakness, and staleness in the mind, emotion, and spirit. When these are cleared out in the release process, the weakness and staleness flood the whole body. Willingness to face abreactions is crucial to ensuring full recovery. Severe weaknesses may be experienced within the first three months, though they are greatly reduced after that. This also means that the presenting disorder has been reduced. However, complete eradication of the weakness may take two or three years.

Similarly, the outflow and unloading of spiritual and emotional pain from CFQ therapy, together with the muscular opening and realignment, result in the client's experiencing physical body pain, particularly around the neck and shoulders, and lower back. This will gradually dissipate through the hands and feet. The process of moving out might be felt as pain in the arms and legs.

In the healing process, there will also be a reversal of symptoms in the form of chest congestions, headaches, dizziness, indigestion, cravings for food, constipation, purging, perspiration, insomnia, and nightmares. Attempts to remain calm and peaceful without avoiding such flushing away of debased energy will bear good fruit. Dissociating from a fear of the symptoms will ensure that every bit of the problem will be fully unloaded and eliminated. At times, practitioners may also experience strong and compulsive thoughts, emotional explosions, and even temper tantrums. Although these may be disturbing, they are part of a releasing process. A close scrutiny will reveal that they are different from the original problems. They are not deeply connected to the emotions and appear unreal or "artificial." Practitioners who remind themselves of their responsibilities and positive values in the face of these experiences, will note that they fade away quickly. Cooperation and social support from others will help greatly.

Insomnia. Many people with psychological problems have trouble with sleep. An over-active mind is unable to switch-off and allow sleep. In some cases, the person may be happily snoring away, yet upon awakening may think that sleep never came. The natural response when tired is to try and catch up with sleep at the expense of day time work and activities. This becomes the start of a vicious cycle–long hours of half sleep and sleepiness by day; night time insomnia, or too much alertness to sleep. With long hours of poor sleep, the mind may become caught up in a spree of negative thoughts, suggestions, and imaginings further compounding the psychological problems. Sleeping at the wrong time to overcome tiredness provides fuel for more tiredness. In time, the person becomes consistently tired and can become disinterested in anything but sleep.

There is widespread misconception about sleep. Exactly how much sleep is needed is still controversial and varies from person to person. If someone misses sleep for a day, the general notion is that they should catch up. CFQ counters this idea. Missed sleep need not and can never truly be replaced. What is more important is to move ahead so that, in the future, the insomniac can enjoy deep restful sleep. Problems often start with over-sleeping. Observe school children who wake up late during school holidays and see for yourself how lethargic and inactive they become throughout the entire day. Try to sleep more during the weekends and observe your Monday blues.

Inability to sleep is only a big problem if someone wants to sleep but is unable to do so, and envies others who can. It becomes a lesser problem if s/he thinks, "So what? OK, I'll catch up with some work." If the person changes attitude in this manner, the likelihood is that she or he will fall asleep soon. Try forcing the insomniac to do something disliked and you may find that the person falls asleep in the middle of the task. Why is this so? One has a choice between doing something reluctantly and doing what is interesting (sleep). The person will unknowingly switch to the one thing that is of interest, and soon dozes off without being aware of what is happening.

In contrast, if you tell the insomniac to sleep, the person's interest is often in continuing the waking thoughts or dreamy mental functions. He or she is then unable to fall asleep. The difference, while relative, is beyond the ability of the insomniac to consciously control. Such interests and preferences took a long time to develop into habits, and exactly when and how they got started is most likely untraceable. Those with sleep problems must first eliminate the general idea of the need to have seven hours of sleep per night. In most cases, quality sleep of five (or fewer) hours is sufficient. By giving yourself less time you are more likely to have deep sleep. Note also if there is a habit of carrying the mental load of unfinished work, worry, or plans to bed. Develop instead, the habit of acting on and doing necessary thinking instead of idle thinking. With such changes, sleep should improve and any related psychological problems should be eliminated.

In the event that sleep problems occasionally arise or persist, you should get up to do some work. A better thing is to sit up on a reclining chair to butterfly shake (shaking in bed is often less effective). If you do this and avoid trying to sleep, you will eventually doze off to a deep, sound sleep. That kind of micro-sleep, even for only minutes, is equivalent to a full hour of light sleep.

An Instant Quick Fix

Psychological problems can be healed by direct CFQ energy transmission, which dissolves and unloads fundamental causes. However, clients often have finicky minds, are suspicious, and lack perseverance. They may stop coming for treatments even though improvements are noticeable. Their paranoia may make them speculate negatively about pain and discomfort. These responses further aggravate the discomfort in the cleansing process, making successful and satisfactory healing difficult. The crucial criterion is whether the individuals are truly sincere in wanting to get over their problems. With such sincerity, proper cooperation, mutual feedback and counseling to overcome the problem is possible. Such criteria do not occur easily. The majority of people simply avoid coming face to face with their problems. They may not even want to discuss them.

For those who genuinely wish to get over their problems, and if the mental disturbance evolves around specific issues, CFQ healing offers a way to quickly eliminate the disturbance.

The Procedure
Instructions

1. Ask the patient to think deeply on the problem, to activate and arouse the energy involving this matter. Get the client to note the degree of perturbation using a SUD scale from 0—10 (Subjective Unit of Distress scaled from 0 to 10).

2. Ask the client to say aloud the following affirmation:

   "Even though I have problems and faults, I deeply and completely accept myself." (Repeat three times).

3. Allow the client's eyes to close to relax while the healer uses auto-tracing (a technique developed by CFQ meditation to be sensitive to the energy pattern). Undo the energy problem by tapping, slap-

ping, massage and plucking off. For those who lack the auto-tracing skill, they may gently tap the whole scalp, rub the forehead and eyebrows in an outward direction from the center. Also massage the neck and shoulder out through the hands in a soothing manner. Finally massage the back and slap down gently all the way to the legs and feet. This process can last about ten minutes.

4. Ask the patient to think deeply about the problem again, to note its perturbation level. In a successful treatment, the thoughts cannot be formed and neither do they cause any emotional arousal. This is rated as '0' and the problem is cleared for good. In most cases, the problem is reduced to 2 and 5.

5. Investigate whether the client has other, related issues that are disturbing, and repeat the above procedure. In most cases, some related problems will be presented. When they clear off, all will be reduced to 0. In a successful treatment, a half hour session often eliminates the problem. Otherwise repeat the procedure for several sessions.

A client healed in this way should be encouraged to practice CFQ (particularly the 7-Movement exercises) to further relax. This is to change the physiological structure and reduce development of future psychological problems. Otherwise, the client's physical, emotional and energy patterns may still be prone to such problems.

I have used this technique successfully to rid clients of haunting thoughts of a dying person, shortness of breath, job anxiety, allergic reactions to smoke, and fear of losing control. It is also effective for most cases where specific psychosocial fears, or traumas can be easily identified. In all cases, successful treatment is dependent on a genuine and sincere desire of the client to overcome the problem.

A Case Example: *A female patient, aged 49, had a history of chronic fatigue, depression, anxiety, gastric problems and fainting spells (for five years). She had two grown children, but as a parent was so over-controlling* *that it caused great disharmony in the family. She became paranoid, fearing that she would become violent and kill someone. She had medical tests done, searching for cancer. She thought of this possibility because of gastric pains that had bothered her for six months. None of the medication she took had helped. She was quite upset that the cancer tests were negative. Her sister brought her to the Center for treatment. For the first three sessions, I used the "quick fix" method which got rid of most of her discomforts. Teaching her the meridian exercises was difficult, as she was uncooperative and disinterested. It took 12 lessons instead of the normal five. For the initial three lessons, the release of stale and numbing disease energy disabled her from standing for longer than five minutes. She refused to practice at home and even on the fifth lesson, she could not carry out the first movement. She stopped complaining of her problems by the sixth lesson (on the sixth week). I changed the teaching strategy by getting her to follow each complete set without explanation. This was followed by a ten minute rest interval before continuing in this manner for three sets.*

By the twelfth lesson, she was able to complete three sets without resting in between. However, she made no effort to practice at home and her daughter had great difficulty persuading her to come each time for treatment. Occasionally, her sister would visit her house to work with her. (Two of her sisters were committed students after their problems had been healed). They continued to persuade the reluctant patient to come to the Center for further treatments. This was a clear case of a person who refused to be well. I suspected that the healing effect would not last. She had no household chores to keep busy, and much idle time which she spent sleeping. That, experience told me, would bring back all her problems.

13

Healthy Aging and Rejuvenation

o o o o o o o o o o o o o o o o o o o o o o o o o o o o o o o o o

Tension informs the life process. Debased energy manifests an upsurging and suspending nature. Stiffening human tissues result from the enfolding of debased energy. Thus the inward-drawing and gripping effect, like sticky glue, obstructs bioenergy flow flow within. Disease unfolds and manifest.

Transition: Age of Retirement

Senior citizenship is the period of time when normal roles, responsibilities, duties and obligations have been lived through. The need to work ends with retirement and there is now time for true relaxation and the bliss to play catch-up with all the things you have most wanted. But many seniors face problems that undermine their human right to the joys of fulfillment. I will suggest solutions, hopefully viable, that can help make the golden years shine with the glow and twilight glory of the evening sun.

An aging body with sluggish physiological functions and slow regenerative abilities is inevitably plagued by a number of possible health problems. Impermanence is the rule of every sentient existence. The earth and even the immense universe are not spared. The difference is in duration. If we temporarily disregard disease symptoms and their medical names and examine the true nature of aging instead, we discover that aging itself, as a physiological event, can be considered a disease. It hinders bodily functions, causes pain and disease, and eventually leads to death. From the ancient past until today, from primitive shamans to learned wise-men, between East and West, within underdeveloped societies and advanced societies, many individuals, groups and organizations have been trying to come up with a cure-all, a fountain of youth, in a bid to overcome this disease. But so far, no one has achieved success. It is not my ambition here to describe a full solution but I will discuss the subject of longevity. Much can be done that can insure a ripe, full age with few problems. We can take the necessary actions to reduce, manage and control such problems as do arise.

As I discuss the problems faced by the aging, I will be concerned about their continued well being. It should not be limited to providing physical care, amenities, and treatment. There are many individuals, groups, and organizations which are doing a good job in these areas. I hope to contribute relevant suggestions that may be widely useful. I believe that the psychological patterns of aging, though often problematic, are extremely important. I will share ideas and suggestions that require a willingness and acceptance on the part of seniors. This involves changing attitudes and courses of action. Often an improved state of well-being at the psychological level can bring about a desired physical transformation.

Retirement Blues. Retirement often means a complete change both of normal activities and a personal mind-set. Without the ability to deal with the change, develop new activities to fill the gaps left by bygone days, as well as to achieve a fresh mindset, retirement can cause multiple problems. I have personally witnessed many people, once active and healthy, fall into deplorable conditions soon after retirement.

Idleness brought about by too much wasted time can be depressing. A sense of no longer being needed shatters self-confidence. A lack of activity encourages staleness and makes the mind and body lethargic.

The lack of interactions with others brings about withdrawn behavior and suspicious attitudes. All these participate in a chain reaction which brings about undesirable physical, mental and psychological consequences.

Self-Sabotage. For those whose lives do not keep them busy, fully occupying their time, the trap of idleness looms large. They run the risk of enslavement in self-pity, negative thoughts, and counterproductive emotions. Life is a continuous process within which nothing stops, neither the body with its physiological functions, nor the mind, emotions, or spiritual functions. When a person is not physically occupied, the mind naturally wanders. A wandering mind stirs up dysfunctional emotions risking pointless restlessness, anxiety, depression, anger or hatred. Thoughts are drawn from past memories, experiences, knowledge and events colored with distorted emotions and projected into an imaginary outcome. In old age, when there is literally little future ahead in the physical or material sense, consciousness falls back and revolves around the past. The elderly can thus become prey to fond or bitter memories, analysis of what should or should not have been done, who was right or who was wrong, and what alternative outcomes might have been. Such ruminations can cause emotional disturbances and awaken fear. This easily turns into a fear of the future and a fear of death.

Scientific evidence increasingly points toward the influence of certain mental and emotional states as aggravating existing health problems and creating new ones. If we could devise appropriate methods for reducing the mental and emotional influence of dysfunctional states, many physical health problems could be reduced, managed, controlled or prevented. Mental and psychological well-being is health protective in the true sense. Everyone born goes through aging, disease, and death. Physical fulfillment is but a part of the picture. Ultimately what matters most is ending life in this world with acceptance, dignity and peace.

The mind is not something that can be controlled in any absolute sense. The more a person tries to control his or her mind, the more powerful the thoughts become and the stronger the emotional disturbances activated. In the end a person can become tired, depressed and frustrated. The mind continues functioning even in sleep. During sleep memories of the day's events and thoughts are organized and stored in a self-sorting manner. It is a busy process as evidenced by changing brain frequencies and eye movements. In an average person the time of deep, sound sleep comes during several periods each lasting a few minutes. Perhaps the sleep time required for adults is five to seven hours daily. This is ample for the self-sorting process freed of interruptions from conscious thinking. When a person oversleeps, the mind proceeds to be engaged in thoughts and imaginings drawn from existing stored memories. This gives rise to wasteful daydreaming.

Retirees and those with too much time (including working adults during weekends, or school children during holidays) are likely to oversleep. The dreaminess caused by over-sleeping makes the body and mind lethargic and brings on undesirable health effects. Such undesirable effects are more profound in the retirees and elderly who make a habit out of daydreaming as a replacement for normal daily activities. Over-sleeping is not confined to the time spent in bed overnight but also includes morning and afternoon naps. For those who need to recuperate from illness (including adults and children), the speed of recovery is increased when they occupy their time with waking activities rather than mere resting. The stale energy produced by the dreamy state occurring at rest is dense and sticky causing undesirable effects which hinder recovery from illness. Moreover, over-resting prevents truly restful sleep and can cause the vicious cycle of insomnia.

Mental activity is a natural function coming from an energy source drawn from memory and experience. It is futile to try to stop it. It is a bad idea, however, to be busy meaninglessly just to avoid it. This merely fabricates tension and boredom. When a person gets tired, mental activity becomes disorganized. Focusing and concentration techniques practiced in some meditation methods may provide a shift of direction and attention. These methods can help cut off compulsive mental activity. But focusing and concentration are also mental activities which can be a burden in their own right. Thoughts do not dissolve, dilute and clear off the existing energy memories. Moreover, when mental energy is strong and compulsive, as in some elderly or diseased people, the ability to concentrate becomes limited. Meditation can become ineffective and frustrating, requiring considerable endurance. Positive thinking, in these circumstances is futile as it cannot beat negative thoughts but may awaken them instead.

There are those who spend a lot of time reading, watching TV or busying themselves with mental games such as chess. Such activities excite, activate, and thus burden the mind. Over-doing creates an imbalance by speeding up the upward suspension process and quickening the deterioration of various physical functions. Such excess not only compounds physical problems but may lead to mental problems like Alzheimer's disease, dementia and senility. What constitutes over-doing is a person by person issue. For those with a low tolerance for mental work and a hardened body state, two hours daily is excessive. For others who are generally healthy, eight hours daily is tolerable provided that they also have sufficient physical activity.

The elderly are often limited when performing physical exercises and sporting activities. Their muscles can be stiff and lack endurance. They can become exhausted easily, prone to injury, and require long periods of rest to get over tiredness. Their range of activities can also be restricted. With the progression of age, further deterioration is normal. This itself is not only evidence of failing health but creates frustrations and further attacks self-confidence. Thoughts of personal worthlessness that spring up are not only difficult to deal with but compound health problems.

Some people may be so overly concerned with their health that they obsessively search for remedies and treatments. While some problems are real and need proper treatment, others are imaginary. When a person gets caught up with the "business" of seeking treatment, he or she easily becomes confused about the real needs. Over-treating a problem may lead to side effects and cause more problems. Obsessive treatment seeking can become mechanical and an occasion for the invention of rationalizations. This brings about more confusion, makes a person feel lost, fabricates conflict and obliterates peace. Problems become aggravated and complicated. The more intense the search, the less the peace available, and the more physical and psychological problems the person promotes.

The Normal Remedy. The normal care and treatments (medical, physiotherapy, and alternative medicine) undertaken are of course remedies that are necessary for the well being of the sick. The physical perspective, however, predominates in all these disciplines. The mind's connection to distress further challenges our desires to help. In relation to healing, help depends greatly upon a person's willing acceptance of help. This may be difficult to achieve when one is in a state of emotional upheaval, anguish and physical disturbance. Excessive therapy, care and assistance gives rise to dependent patient attitudes and this too becomes counterproductive.

Introducing appropriate activity to the elderly is therapeutic and makes life more meaningful. They can be encouraged to participate actively in household chores, mutual support, hobbies, group activities, voluntary services and community recreation. All these keep them busy, utilizing time in a way that slows down physical and mental deterioration. Such activities instill a sense of pride, usefulness and fulfillment. Some elderly people are so fragile and their motivation so low, that their range of possible activities is limited. There are also problems related to facilities, personnel resources and organizations that are costly.

Call of the Spirit

"There is neither form, nor feeling, nor perception, nor mental forma-
tions, nor consciousness, nor eye, nor ear, or nose, or tongue, or body, or
mind, or sound. No smell, no taste no touch, no object of mind, no
realms of elements (from eyes to mind-consciousness), no interdependent
origins, and no extinction of them (from ignorance to old age and
death), no suffering, no origination of suffering, no extinction of suffer-
ing, no path, no understanding, no attainment. "

Heart Sutra

Time spares no one and we all discover at some point that age
catches up with us and we are no longer as young as we were. This is
the time to discover or deepen that very important part of ourselves
that we have been minimizing or missing all along. When failing
health restricts our activities, or deprives us of treasured enjoyments,
we can turn attention to our spirit, a part of life that needs none of the
activities mentioned above. Perhaps this is the way our Maker wants
things to be. For those who can relate to what I'm saying and switch
their attention to this higher opportunity much can be gained.

Peace. When you follow your calling and identify a viable direction in
life, you soon realize that you no longer require much of the sensation-
seeking activities, attention, care, support, and involvements you
thought you needed. You minimize the basic urges for doing and wanting. You do away with despair, frustration, disappointment and conflicts arising from trying to fulfill what you think or imagine you need.
You begin to calm down and relax with inner harmony. You find peace
when you discover that you really do not need or miss the so called
necessities of the past. Neither positive nor negative events in life nor
your inner urges can truly disturb, threaten or pressure you. Spiritual
life is eternal and joyous. God has always been lovingly with you and
has been helping all along.

This is truly a significant change. You begin to feel blessed with a kind of wellness, a true peace of mind, emotions, and spirit. Use whatever names are meaningful for you. This sense of well-being will quickly permeate you and bring about many positive changes in your physical body and consciousness.

Miracles. The experience of this change differs from one person to another but is often significant and profound. In some cases, it gives rise to great joy and expanded consciousness described as a transcendent state. With spiritual sensitivity many physical and psychological problems can be removed or reduced instantaneously. A cure radiating from a person's own inner resources is much more profound and lasting than many so called "miraculous" cures effected by spiritual healers or prayer. Such personal healing comes from the willingness to let go of and stand free from yearnings, conflicts, disharmonies, and burdens.

Miracles may occur when paying homage in sacred places, in prayer sessions or visiting spiritual healers. When a person is in a state of despair, she or he often feels the need for some kind of divine intervention. We actively seek out opportunities that result in a breakthrough. In pursuing a last hope, we can put full faith into it. It is this faith that creates the right conditions for astounding miraculous effects that, for example, make the blind see or the paralyzed walk. However, for such an amazing miracle to occur absolute faith is required. Such a miracle is also conditional upon the type of problem. If the problem is due to strong psychological or emotional obstructions provoking physical problems, the miracle is possible. If the physical problem is too severe, it takes time to gradually clear all the difficulties.

Faith is a strong force to be reckoned with. Trusting God with full faith has the potential for overcoming any obstacle. Such power arises from open-heartedness reinforced by a willingness to let go of existing ideas, burdens and attitudes. Without this letting-go miracles become scarce or short-lived.

This explains why miraculous cures connected with devotions, prayers or faith in evangelists, psychics or healers may be temporary. Miracles arising from a person's belief system and regular practice are profound and long lasting. Faith in God has to be unconditional. You cannot be dependent upon whether your belief brings you the expected benefit. You cannot trouble yourself with your own expectations of how you want or imagine outcomes to be. If you do so you won't find peace. You obstruct the Absolute from helping you.

The greatest miracle is the person who finds peace that radiates a true sense of well being, bravery and joyousness. Even when physical conditions are deplorable, acceptance diminishes the pain. The spiritually attuned person can be composed and dignified even to their last breath. This is what really matters. It means having achieved intimacy with the Divine. In terms of karma, a person's acceptance and inner harmony eliminates much of the negative karma. It also creates lots of radiant helping energy and the merit for good karma. One is thus assured of having a good rebirth.

Spirit. When a person lets go of an inclination towards and identification with physical existence, and the desire for material possessions, and replaces these with a pursuit of peace, the way opens for a realization that there is a part of existence that can even be more real than the physical body. The person learns that physical existence is only possible if spirit exists. He or she becomes more aware of the workings of the mind and emotions and the driving force behind them. One feels and sees images, information, designs, shapes, and forces which give rise to one's thoughts, emotions, and actions.

These are but the impurities, burdens and shallow manifestations of the spirit. Beyond them are the purer, finer forces that eventually lead to a boundless, non-physically-existent reality. This is the realm of the Absolute. It is beyond your sense of identity and form. It is utterly magnificent and real. The perfectly purified spirit merges with the eternal.

There are people who report seeing God, the Divine or demonic beings. This they must approach with caution. The Divine is so great that seeing this incomprehensible reality would be like claiming one can see an infinite number of planet earths together in one unit. You cannot see the Absolute in that way. You can only feel the unmistakable Presence. Neither can a person actually see other spiritual beings so easily. It is not difficult, however, to see images and forms that exist within a person's thoughts, memories, and imagination. Buddhist teachings refer to the seeing of forms and getting attached to them as a "kind of deviation" called an "entanglement in forms." The consequences can be extremely negative. The solution is to help a person understand the "true path" and the "true knowledge" needed to do away with self-flattery and egocentricity. Thus with pure instinct (from the Heart Sutra), there is Emptiness, there is true reality.

CFQ Energy Elixir

CFQ offers a viable way for the elderly to occupy their time. It helps to do away with all kinds of self-sabotage, bring about psychological and physical well being, find peace and spirit, and be intimate with God. It is equipped with the necessary strategies and principles to clear out disease. At the least it reduces disease symptoms to bring about improved physical, mental, emotional, psychological and spiritual well-being.

The Meridian Exercises. These exercises are designed to establish a smooth bioenergy flow, clear the body of dense disease energy, open out to repair the body's systems, and reveal peace. The non-exertion or tensionless, loose, and slow nature of these exercises is extremely beneficial for physiological repairs. Though the exercises may be considered by most thrill-seekers as boring, their slow rhythm is precisely what makes healing possible. The exercises shift the cultivator in a new direction. The normal excitement of fabrication, action and stress-provoking activities which become increasingly difficult for the elderly, is shifted to a calm and blissful state of spiritual, mental, emotional and physical harmony. Peace is hidden beneath boredom. To find it simply be willing and happy to be bored.

The aging body increasingly may be so stiff, misaligned, or restricted that doing the exercises in complete accordance with the recommended patterns may be difficult. Do not be over-concerned with elegance and correctness. Do not forcefully correct the postures. Frequently check on the important features of looseness, slowness, easy breathing, relaxation of the hamstrings, and releasing inner strength. The whole system is simply a tool to facilitate peace. Peace is the objective. Gradually, when the movements become loose and coordinated, obvious health improvements occur.

Many elderly people find it difficult to remember the exercises properly even though their normal memory is more than adequate. This is because they are used to effort and focus in their experience of the recall process, whereas the CFQ exercises are effortless. The CFQ focus is the reverse of normal functions and therefore the elderly, especially those suffering high stress, or serious disease problems, find it difficult. There is a secret: Try to do the exercises naturally. Do not try to remember by thinking hard with the brain. Let the body remember. When the body remembers, it means relaxation. Peace energy has come to the body and physiological functions are being restored.

It is worthwhile to help those with trouble recalling the exercises by doing the exercises with them. In this case it suffices to perform Movements 1, 2, and 3, ending with the affirmations and conclusion. By the time they can remember and perform these on their own, their health conditions will have improved. It may take hundreds of repeated sets taking one to two months of guided practice for them to do the exercises on their own. Once they can remember the first three movements, the remaining four can often be easily taught without memory problems.

The exercises release disease energy. The elderly often have tremendous amounts of disease energy with weakness, staleness, and numbness. When that passes through the limbs, particularly the legs, they may feel weak and unable to stand for even a few minutes. This can occur even though they have no such problem in normal situations. Watch out for such an occurrence. Be patient and encourage them to rest allowing the weakness to pass. At rest, check to ensure that they are not struggling forcefully or resisting impatiently. The weakness will be re-absorbed back into them with such action. They should remain calm and relaxed if the weakness is to leave. When they can exercise for half an hour, health improvements will be visible. Repeat for at least two sets for health maintenance and three sets for health improvement (each set lasts 15 minutes). For those with time and those who are more interested in health, repeat three sets two times daily. In some cases (particularly those with dizziness, high blood pressure, and problems of balance) perform Movements 6 and 7 for five repetitions instead of the normal ten.

Meditation. CFQ meditation is for those who wish to explore their spirit, develop intuitive wisdom, and illuminate their heart leading to enlightenment. For the elderly, with many physical and psychological problems, starting meditation is discouraged. Life's facts may be cold and cruel. Karma has no mercy when you come face to face with it.

Lotus Walk and Butterfly Shake. For those who find the meridian exercises difficult or impossible, there are alternative exercises. The practice of lotus walking and butterfly shaking promotes physiological and psychological repairs to the body's system. Disease energy is released and cleared and physiological functions are enhanced. These exercises can be conveniently and readily practiced for hours. They help utilize idle time that otherwise might be wasted on negative thoughts and emotions. If you do not kill the dysfunctional use of time, it kills you! A good use of time can add up to five or ten hours of daily CFQ involvement for those who have few other activities. By being CFQ involved, the normal excitement-seeking instinct is restrained. It may give rise to boredom initially. By overcoming boredom, however, peace, calmness and relaxation are revealed.

Maintain a relaxed, peaceful, and "not-wanting" attitude when practicing. Do not be forceful or overly eager to see improvement. Health improvement is certain. By means of your practice you lay a claim to your health entitlement. By taking this action you say "yes" to the ever offered Divine help. By contrast, if you think and dream idly for good health, or anxiously seek treatment to make yourself healthy, you are distracting yourself from affirming and resonating with the Supreme Energy already being offered to you.

Some support may be necessary initially. For those who are unable to walk properly, someone should help. Do not be overly concerned about walking straight or with balance. It is just fine to appear to be walking in an ungainly or slow manner if that is what one can do. Rapid progress occurs normally within one or two months when one realizes the importance of looseness and walks as naturally and loosely as possible. For those who are unable to stand, count on butterfly shaking. Sit with a back support, loosen the whole body, rest both feet on the ground, and shake loosely and naturally. Initially the shaking may be rapid and stiff as this is all some can manage. Gradually, loosen and slow down with generous movements. When one can actually do this, it may well be the sign of enough strength to stand. Standing and walking exercises then become possible.

For those with a paralyzed side, shake the other side. Be balanced when shaking by de-emphasizing the paralyzed leg. Gradually it becomes loosened and will start to shake. Those who are paralyzed in both legs can be assisted. Shake their legs while holding their knees. They can participate in both by attempting to sense the movements and with a willingness to inhabit the movements. In that way, it will not normally take very long before they can move on their own.

Those who are bed-ridden should be carried to a sitting position to do butterfly shaking. If this cannot be done (sometimes no one is available to lift the patient) try shaking the feet with both legs straight. When the disease energy unwinds through the legs it can produce an overwhelming stiffness, heaviness and numbness. Pause and relax calmly with a whole body looseness. Do not try to force the disease energy out but let it leave naturally.

As soon as the person is well enough to practice and exercise on his or her own, she or he should be encouraged to do so. This will speed up recovery. During the practice, the mind and emotions can initially cause a disturbance. Remain calm. Do not be frustrated or try to stop such disturbances from happening. You have a job to do. Your job is the walk or the butterfly shaking. The mind is not your job. It continues to be active but you do not have to be carried away by it. If you do, stop and come back to the practice as soon as you realize what happened. Gradually, you become detached from the mind and emotions and feel they are distant and unreal. Butterfly-shakers may frequently doze off. This is often a beneficial deep sleep and should be allowed to happen. However, even if a hint of consciousness remains, continue with the shaking rather than wait to fall asleep.

Heart Sutra. Those who wish, may recite the Heart Sutra with an attitude of infinite openness. Repeat it calmly and peacefully for say one half to one hour. When doing so, be leery of the inclination to absorb power. Avoid yearning some superhuman or Buddha's blessing. This is a common human shortcoming. In fact, the recital of most holy scriptures from any religion should give rise to peace and a healing but that may not arise in an acquisitional spirit.

By remaining calm and composed, breathing settles down. Awareness comes naturally to the lower abdomen which becomes the center of the recital and of radiant Metta. The practitioner gradually feels and sees the breaking up and departure of dark, dense disease energy. With prolonged practice the energy of radiant, bright colored and magnificent loving-kindness can be felt and seen.

Healing. Direct energetic healing treatment is effective for most kinds of diseases. However, healing for the elderly is complex and time consuming. Their bodies have been in long and perhaps unbalanced use.

Now that the body is slowing down, it may be approaching a breakdown. CFQ works not on a particular symptom but on the whole system. That means there is much to deal with like the enormous proverbial forces below the tip of the iceberg. There are uncountable numbers of disease symptoms. Even if treatment removes some, it is unlikely that most will be fully cleared. Thus healing might not seem effective. After a period of treatment a patient normally forgets about the discomforting, painful symptoms that drove the person to seek treatment. Despite many positive changes, however, other symptoms arise to cause dissatisfaction and as is true with most people, the painful events attract much more attention than the peace-filled ones.

There are many patients who remain grumpy yet cannot identify what is wrong. In one case, I pointed to the grandchildren the patient brought to the Center. "You can't be like them." I noticed an immediate flash of understanding. Getting old for some is too hard to be swallowed. For those who are still very much in search of thrills and stimulation, the healer cannot meet their expectations. They need to be willing and able to practice CFQ and gradually cultivate peace and calmness. Then healing becomes meaningful and produces a tremendous impact. Then it helps them greatly.

CFQ Principles. Proper understanding of the CFQ principles, as discussed in this book, helps self-understanding, the acceptance of oneself and the right use of problems. When that happens, conflicts and struggles are reduced. There is an instantaneous reduction of disease symptoms. Proper understanding is dependent on open-mindedness and the freedom to look at various options. Be willing to avoid being dogmatic and over-protective of preconceived or prevailing beliefs about treatment and cure. Reading over this book every few months can enhance understanding and verify the correctness of your practice. For those unable to read for themselves, occasional reminders and an elucidation of CFQ principles helps greatly. I sincerely wish that this book be an occasion for healing for open minded readers.

Responses and Reactions. The predominant disease energy of the aged shows characteristics such as staleness, weakness, numbness, dryness, and coldness. These can be clearly felt in the flushing out process. Cure is a reversal of disease. The original symptoms of the disease being flushed out are re-experienced. They rarely, however, manifest strongly and do not pose any threat as they do during the original disease occurrence. Even though the clearing symptoms are similar (but milder), they move in the opposite direction. Clearing opens out, releases and repairs whereas the disease occurrence closes in, absorbs and damages. In the flushing experience, however, care must be taken to maintain calm and peace. Excessive anxiety caused by suspicion and speculation aggravates discomfort, obstructs and slows down the releasing process and brings undesirable effects.

Longevity & Disease

The human lifespan can be as long as 120 years and geneticists believe that life extension can be doubled or tripled as demonstrated with simple life forms such as insects and worms. While the limit of life expectancy remains controversial, it has in fact just about doubled in the last century from about 45 to roughly 80 years. In the same period, the human population has exploded from two billion to 6.5 billion. Inevitably, questions of depletion and the destruction of environmental resources abound. One may well wonder if we are rapidly heading for planetary annihilation.

Many breakthroughs have been achieved in the combat against disease. There has been an explosion of innovations to reduce, manage and control symptoms and physical distress. These innovations come in the form of corrective remedies, life support devices and life sustaining systems utilizing ever more complex and powerful high tech machinery. The contributions are undeniably tremendous. How much more or what else should be done is an urgent concern. Previous and current emphasis tends to be focused on the physical aspects of life. There has been a recent shift in the biomedical model to include the role of the mind. To further the quality of human existence, we need to examine the distinction between the physical body and psychological (mind) aspects of our existence to determine relevant values. From what viewpoint is one aspect more important than the other?

Physical pain and suffering are easily perceptible, while psychological pain and suffering can hide in the mind. Impermanence or mortality is the unwavering physical rule, and thus the body is obviously not meant to last forever. One might arguably be moved to support psychological well being and the absence of emotional disease as much more significant. With a healthy self-concept and enhanced self-acceptance, one is better able to see the nature of suffering, accept the decline of the physical body thus achieving peace. Such a health-protective consciousness can replace fear, suspicion, restlessness, conflict, disharmony and emotional pain arising from the struggles of life, aging, and illness. I try to help people deal with the core of their sufferings. On the other hand, prolonging life artificially when the body has deteriorated beyond use and provides little but pain, becomes morally unjustifiable and meaningless.

The absence of a scientific study of the mind until the past few decades, means that our present understanding of human consciousness is relatively shallow. Our present psychological paradigm does not include the spiritual side of consciousness since the empirical method of science is inept for its study. Spirit is too fine in terms of vibrational quality and too lacking in physical and objective features to be verifiable with physical instruments. The bioenergy that is measured presently seems to be an electromagnetic field correlated with physiological functions. Spirit is so fine and vibrational that it is empty of all physical attributes and thus appears to be physically non-existent. Yet it is boundless and fills the space of the universe and more.

Scientific inquiry collects objective data in order to use it as evidence or fact. However, it is unreasonable to assert that what is immeasurable does not exist, is a fiction, or at best a philosophical issue. The CFQ system promotes an awareness of the spiritual side in the human being.

It clarifies what the spirit is and its relevance to life and existence. Spirit is critical to mental, psychological and emotional behaviors as well as physical existence, health, and disease issues. Unquestionably it is a bold step to integrate body, mind, and spirit to understand life itself and achieve solutions capable of resolving human problems.

CFQ Module. Life begins from the basis of the absolute purity of God that is ultra-fine homogenous vibrations. Since there is physical existence, the faculties of mind and body exist as a mechanism with pathways for internal action and adaption to the external environment. Every experience, memory, and thought is energetically stored in the body and this consciousness stimulates growth and continuity of existence. However energy residues of mental functioning stored in this manner also become a load and burden on life.

Diseases are caused by strong energy burdens and disharmonious and conflicting energy. There is obvious body misalignment and physiological functions are obstructed. Death occurs when such burden shuts them down. The shut-down process also naturally occurs as the organism ages when energy burden accumulates and becomes excessive. Energetically seen, the burden forms into folds, shields, and wrinkles within and beyond the body. Healing is the dissolving process that isolates and converts the debased energy substance, the basis of physical deformations. This is a glue-like substance obstructing physiological functions. When further diluted it is freed off from the body. The freeing-off results in its experience as sensations and memories.

Research on disease and aging in cell division and metabolism has revealed a similar glue-like substance. The theory is that this glue is produced by the conversion of glucose and other chemical compounds, as well as by the consumption of oxygen, damaging DNA and mutating or destroy cells. However, research on removal of this "rusting and glueing effect" to keep cells healthy has not so far been effective. Without such a scientific breakthrough, longevity remains out of reach.

In CFQ energy healing, all forms of this glue-like substance are cleared off thus eliminating disease. At the same time it leads to the prospect of reversing aging. It dilutes impurity with purity from the inside out. The opening-out is the most important in bringing peace which is the bottom line of well-being. Without that, no amount of effort can truly solve human suffering. With peace within, one lives in peace. The person feels peacefully connected with others. This transforming experience turns into a commitment to help others to have peace.

Theoretically speaking, complete clearing of disease energy forces brings about a restructuring and realignment to arrive at perfect physiological functioning. This however cannot be realistically done. Every person has endemic fears and weaknesses and will hold back on touching certain points preventing their release. The realignment and freeing off process in the advanced stage can be painful. It requires great bravery and facing the unknown. Even without such obstacles, it is a long and tedious process.

For argument' sake, say a diligent and determined cultivator begins at age of 50 and practices five hours daily. This may be able to do away with the natural absorption of energy from the day' functions together with those absorbed from a single day in one's past. If the practitioner continues daily in this way and does not encounter any obstacles to slow down, theoretically it is possible to clear off all detrimental energy forces by one hundred years of age. At that age, the practitioner has perfect peace, harmony, and joy and regenerates as an immortal. Longevity, then comes at a price. No amount of absorbing and creating can enable a person to live beyond a certain limit as this is against nature. To go beyond the limit is to be in complete harmony with nature—a person does nothing, creates nothing, and wants nothing. But that would be existing out of this world.

Overcoming Diseases

CFQ works on a person holistically. The disease burden is unloaded from the physical body, and also from the mental, emotional, psychological and spiritual bodies. Bio-energy flow is purified and enhanced to restore physiological functions. Mental conflicts and disharmony are removed and replaced with peace. This ensures repair and regeneration of the body's systems. Improvements eliminating most types of diseases can be readily seen. Achieving a complete cure differs on a person by person basis depending on the depth and duration of the problem. The physical body of a middle-aged person is typically stiffened by a thick bundle of energy forces accumulated over a long period of time. To completely clear this out is virtually impossible otherwise living immortals would be common place.

However, cure for most disease symptoms can occur even when a small fraction of the troublesome debased energy forces are cleared out. Some disease symptoms can be completely cleared within months. Others, even though initially they may improve quite rapidly, may take years to be completely eliminated. What is very important is that the person, in fact, feels better. A major goal is that he or she be better able to cope with problems and enjoy enhanced physical and psychological well-being.

The most important criterion for overcoming disease is the willingness to do so. The greatest obstacle is reluctance. Unknown to most people, even experts, while disease undoubtedly brings pain and suffering it also sports a kind of grim satisfaction. The patient's psychological state can contain feeling the suffering and wanting to get over it, together with "enjoying"the suffering. The mind can drift into a spaced-out state dominated by painful thrills, sadistic fantasy, ecstatic self-pity, and punitive negative emotions. Moreover, some may feel dependent upon the extra care and attention they get when ill which they might not receive if well. It is surprising how many people, especially among the retired and elderly, fall into this masochistic trap. There are plenty of reasons to enjoy their problems more than suffer from them. Overcoming a disease is much easier for the young, who often tend to be physically busy. The moment they feel better they have things to do and no idle time to further enjoy the disease.

The suffering versus enjoyment feature of being ill alternates in one's psyche and becomes either a help or an obstacle in overcoming disease. Psychotherapy can help people to see the purpose and meaningfulness of being well. When resolved to get well, the person has achieved the pre-requisite needed to be set on the course of healing. CFQ intervention offers a way whereby a person can claim the right to be healthy and in fact live a long, healthy life. It is not a cure-all miracle. For a person who lacks a sincere desire for wellness, little can be done. On the other hand, there are also many people who really want to be well but are misguided by wrong approaches and ineffective remedies. From my perspective, excessive and vigorous exercise burdens an already weakened body. Excessive herbs, supplements, drugs, and chemicals are counterproductive causing further deterioration. For those who have met the pre-requisite of wanting to be well, CFQ provides the way to improvement. At the very least, one moves to a more manageable position. At its best, CFQ promises to be an effective treatment and complete cure.

I will next review several common diseases adults may encounter. Most other problems not specifically discussed here can be satisfactorily addressed with similar strategies. Cancer is given a specific chapter (see Chapter 17).

Alzheimer's Disease (& Dementia). Medically, this problem is associated with a shrinkage in healthy brain cells. The obvious remedy is more varied activity to stimulate mental functioning. Such a strategy, however, has been ineffective in treating AD. The disease affects about four million Americans today. In affluent Japan, the proportion of elderly with AD is projected to double in the next decade or two. Researchers have neither developed an early detection technique, nor a cure.

CFQ involvement can prevent and treat AD. The shrinkage of the brain and the presence of plaque (I call it glue) supports the interpretation of disease I have propose in this book. It is important to remind ourselves that a being exists as a whole. The brain is but one organ, not separate from other organs nor the rest of the functioning body. The whole, energetically, is seamlessly connected. Recall what has been said about the role of tension. It is fabricated by any "doing" whether from the mind or body and surges or suspends upwards. The more the doing, the more the mental activation. In turn the more tension fabricated the faster the deterioration of life. The current idea of stimulating the brain to repair the damaged brain is not only ineffective but is counter-productive.

For those who wish to understand and prevent AD or other forms of dementia, simply follow the downward de-stressing principle of CFQ. A pervasive involvement with CFQ is required here as the AD patient needs to fill up all idle time. Supervision is also needed as even the most sincere patient frequently forgets to practice. The combined times spent in reading, watching television, playing chess and other games must be reduced to no more than three hours daily.

Significant improvements will be seen within three to nine months. Do not bother thinking about the brain, its shrinkage, nor how to repair it. In fact, you best bet is not to bother about anything at all. Just practice CFQ. The de-stressing effect is sufficient to regenerate the still abundant brain cells. Scientists estimate that humans use, on the average, 2 to 5 per cent of the brain. On that basis, we can argue that even if the brain has shrunk by 50 per cent, the person can still have average intelligence (as is the case with hydrocephalic infants who grow up as normal healthy adults). It is neither necessary nor possible to regenerate the brain completely. That only comes about in the rare case of a complete regeneration and in legends about transformation into immortality.

Parkinson's Disease. The shaking and trembling typical of persons with PD is due to excessive blockages, obstructions and deformations originating from accumulated debased energy. These cause a shortening and stiffening of the muscles. As a result of uneven shortening, stiffness, and deformations, trembling and lack of control occur when muscles are excited during movement. When the patient rests and relaxes, trembling is a necessary means for the body to regulate the muscles enabling a better degree of tolerance. Any thought or mental activity that is emotionally or physiologically arousing sends an impulse to the muscles making the trembling more vigorous.

The CFQ remedy is simple and straight forward: Relax, loosen, and be peaceful. This must be done through actual practice. Otherwise a person continues to be deeply entangled in the problem, carrying on stressful activities, or harboring undesirable negative thinking and emotion. Either idling or struggling anxiously to be free from the problem ends up compounding the problem.

Use CFQ to fill up all idle time, to help build up trust in God, and to reduce mental activity, excitement, and emotional disturbance. Be relaxed and peaceful. Claim the right to be well. Curtail reading, watching TV and other dysfunctional mental activity. Strenuous exercising and excessive strengthening of your muscles produces adverse effects. Initial reactions practicing CFQ can include a sense of weakness and numbness. There can be more shaking and trembling all over the body. This is extremely beneficial as the detrimental strengths trapped within the person must be cleared off to achieve a cure. Usually, after every episode of shaking, a noticeable improvement follows. There may be weird sensations of shrinking limbs that feel shortened. The opposite is happening. The muscles have undergone an elongation process. The problem will be greatly reduced in a few months.

What I am offering here is a simple, practical, and effective solution. Simplicity is what works best. Sophisticated methods confuse and deviate from the realm of disease-healing. The simplest evidence that a person is alive is breathing in and out.Deviating from that simple, mindless act kills the person. Neither can a person become more alive by adding oxygen or other gases to the air nor by breathing in some other way. Doing anything other than that makes the person less alive and ends up in death. I hope this observation will help those who admire high technology or sophisticated methods and anxiously await such achievements. The more treatments, more doings, more information, more yearnings and more theories all add more anxiety and disharmony. These reduce our openness to peace—our most potent inner healing resource. Tension building systems are counter-productive and deprive one of the right to well-being.

Osteoporosis. Evidence of osteoporosis occurs not only in old age but is visible in young children and adults. Observe them when they are seated normally to see how it has affected their posture. CFQ healing effectively changes their postures in a few months. The physical deformations, the hunched back, and curvature of the spine will be readily improved. Changes are noticeable from seven to twenty one months. they come with a deeper sense of ease, looseness, and total flexibility.

There is much hype about consuming high dosages of calcium to prevent osteoporosis. Excessive calcium intake can cause harm especially in tropical regions with abundant sunlight. Calcium as a heavy element is not readily absorbed in the bloodstream. It becomes deposited in the muscles forming a heavy load on organs and obstructing physiological functioning. When that happens, the bones become even more fragile and brittle. An elderly person who increases calcium intake might trigger an adverse health effect. The calcium deposits might cause stiffening and blockages.

Strenuous exercise is counter-effective for osteoporosis as it promotes muscular hardness. By learning proper relaxation, the flexibility of the muscles improve and the strain on the bones is reduced. One becomes less prone to fractures.

Arthritis. Normal exercises are of limited effectiveness for arthritis due to their inadequate loosening, relaxation and letting go features. An over-use of pain killers brings on complications and causes major organs to malfunction. CFQ practice enhances whole body looseness and at the same time dissolves and clears out the stiffness and pain from the muscles and joints. Pain and numbness appear with a sensation of flowing-out. Do the meridian and walking exercises naturally and easily. Do not be forceful when loosening the stiffness. In the beginning, an arthritic person may do CFQ movements in an awkward and clumsy manner. Improvement in over-all looseness brings about greater coordination and more harmonious movements. Arthritis is curable so long as the patient takes the initiative in the CFQ way and is motivated to be rid of the problem.

Tinnitis. The problem is not only common among the aging population. It also affects teens and young adults especially those who are tension-prone. Medical remedies have not been satisfactory. Tinnitis, or the constant ringing in the ears, can bring on depression, restlessness, paranoia, and insomnia. Some patients are unable to deal with these symptoms and become suicidal. Some cases may accompany a middle ear infection. The medical speculation is that tinnitis develops when auditory nerves degenerate. From the CFQ point of view, this notion is not true. When the head region is compacted with excessive tension formations, the stiff and glued-together muscles press against the eardrum producing the ringing noise. When this pressure is excessive and the muscles are rigid, deafness may result. If the muscles are less rigid, the body's regulative system causes expansion, making the muscles recoil causing a ringing sensation.

The CFQ remedy is often effective and reliable. It involves whole body relaxation and opening out to flush down the tension. The patient need not be over concerned and cater to the ears as the problem will be greatly reduced with CFQ practice. Some patients will have their problem completely cleared within months while in others, the problem will continue for years. However, most people will soon feel a significant reduction in the degree of anxiety they have with the ringing noise. Even if the noise persists, the patient does not feel depressed, nervous, restless nor suffer from sleeplessness. The problem is as good as solved.

Stroke. Good recovery from semi-paralysis arising from stroke can be reasonably expected provided that the CFQ principles are fully understood and implemented (See Chapter 15). As always, the person is willing to set out to claim his or her right to be well. Stroke normally affects one side of the body leaving the arm and leg on that side paralyzed while the other half remains mobile. Even if one out of four limbs remains mobile, its' use in CFQ practice is sufficient to bring about complete mobility and recovery of all four limbs. With perseverance, there is a greater change of success and with a good understanding of the CFQ approach, improvement is often quite rapid.

Medically speaking, the normal recovery period is two or three months after the stroke. Significant progress after that, however, is difficult to achieve. The medical conclusion is that brain and nerve damage are beyond repair. I categorically maintain that the physical damage is reversible. Please suspend the conventional belief that sets a limit to your full recovery. Good progress and recovery can be made even after a catastrophic stroke. Such a recovery could take about three years of CFQ practice. Brain and nerve damage can be repaired but not by prescription drugs. The healing source is Peace, a source provided by your inner Healer.

A Case Example: *A female patient, in her early fifties, discovered a lump in her left breast. Medical diagnosis showed it was non-malignant. She was given a three month course of medication to dissolve the tumor. This effort was unsuccessful. Subsequently, it was discovered that the tumor was cancerous and a mastectomy was performed to remove her breast. She was hospitalized for two weeks.*

On discharge she was immediately brought to my Center. She was weak and needed help to walk. She appeared disoriented and expressionless. Right after the first energy treatment, she looked refreshed and was able to talk about her problem. She could walk steadily and left the center without assistance. Treatments were arranged daily for the first five sessions. On her second visit, she looked completely different. She walked surefooted and smiled. She told me that her appetite had returned and she slept soundly. By the fifth treatment at the end of the week , she appeared to have completely recovered.

Subsequent sessions were scheduled once a week. She started doing the CFQ meridian exercise. Four weeks later even before she had learned all the movements, her arms had loosened and she could lift them freely and without pain. The surgical breast wound was almost completely healed and free of hardened or lumpy tissue. She experienced some shoulder and lower back stiffness and pain. That disappeared a week later. She said she felt more relaxed than even before she had the disease.

After the fifth healing treatment, I briefed her about CFQ principles and our stance on radiation and chemotherapy. I knew that soon her physician would recommend such treatment. I said it would be up to her to decide. On her check-up with her physician, he made the predicted recommendation. She rejected the treatment. The physician re-examined the healed breast, was apparently satisfied and did not insist.

She returned to my Center for six more energy healing treatments. I asked her practice the CFQ exercises daily. No further direct healing sessions were required.

PART IV

Healing Applications:
Recovery from Life-
Threatening Disease

14

Healing Paralysis and Injuries

Injuries to nerves in the spinal column often result in permanent paralysis. The medical assumption so far is that damage to the spinal cord and nerves cannot be repaired. Several years ago, I heard of a surgical procedure where a certain enzyme extracted from frogs was applied to damaged nerves in the hope of regenerating them. The frog's nerves are known to be self-repairable. Spinal cord research continues to develop new procedures for the treatment of paralysis. But the fact remains that reliable remedies are not yet available.

In this chapter I will discuss the nature of paralysis and spinal cord injuries and propose a viable treatment. The scientific community has certainly not ruled out the possibility of medical miracles since under some circumstances the human body is able to self repair. Life itself is still the greatest mystery and perhaps the greatest miracle of all. If we learn how to meet the conditions of re-generation, the body's self repair response can be triggered to make miracles. Miracles will not be random but will become predictable certainties. I have used CFQ to treat several cases of paralysis and my conclusion is, "It works for certain!" I hope you will continue reading this chapter and test the suggestions presented.

Causes of Paralysis

An obvious fracture or dislocation along the spinal column results in paralysis of the body from the point of injury downward. There are cases where medical investigation does not detect any obvious fracture, dislocation or physical damage but paralysis still occurs. Paralyzed patients will say, "My doctor said that the spinal nerves are severely damaged or severed."

I will share what I believe causes paralysis. The nervous system functions by way of nerve impulses which are bio-electrically transmitted. Should the body receive a powerful physical impact, the shock produces a strong surge of high voltage. If the voltage is excessive, the nerves burn out. This could explain why paralysis occurs even in cases where there is no apparent physical injury. There are also cases where persons do not suffer immediate paralysis from an injury. Gradually, however, they become weak and paralyzed or suffer from other problems such as spondyliasis or muscular dystrophy. Should the nerves be partially burnt out, they could slowly continue to deteriorate. That in turn would cause a breaking down of the physiological functions.

The Medical Setback. Any success in medical intervention either by drugs or surgery depends ultimately on the body's ability to respond and to repair itself. The body is most capable of repairing fleshy tissues such as muscles due to the abundant blood supply bringing in oxygen and nutrients. Blood flow is required for the regeneration of new cells and the removal of dead cells and wastes. The deeper the problem goes the more sophisticated the exchange needed to service the vital organs. As blood vessels and capillaries become finer the exchange becomes increasingly indirect. Drugs are coarse substances that can be effectively transported by blood. They work well where the blood supply is abundant. When quite indirect exchanges are needed for cell regeneration the requirements might well be too fine for the physical body alone. More subtle powers may be required such as one's life force or one's spiritual-energy functions.

The nervous system seems to be completely distinct from the circulatory system. How much (or little) blood supply is required by the nerves is unknown. Therefore making a bold hypothesis that deviates from medical praxis may well be justifiable if the outcome in fact produces solutions for the problem of paralysis.

The Remedy. Nerve fibers are stiff wire-like tissues that are not easily damaged. Even if a vertebra is dislocated or smashed, the nerves may not be completely severed. If the nerves have been completely severed, the damage may include physiological functions such as the blood supply. In such cases the flesh decays, and the person will soon perish. This is often not the case as spinal injury patients usually survive for many years.

What we are discussing here is based on actual cases I have treated. From these experiences I know that repair is possible. Repair is brought about by detraumatizing and opening out from deep inside the spirit to liberate the self repair response. By bringing through radiant healing energy the burnt out nerves can be repaired and the severed nerves removed. Perhaps a direct repair of severed nerve cells is possible. Whatever the facts are, theories and arguments do not matter. What matters is that much can be done. Paralysis is far from hopeless. Certainly, the most practical thing to do is to be realistic. Do the necessary detraumatizing, loosening and letting go and be peaceful. It is unwise to cling to medical theories forecasting doom. It is equally unwise to fantasize about the possibility of an effective medical breakthrough anytime soon.

Spreading of Paralysis. With a proper attitude and perseverance, most paralysis victims do have a fair chance of recovery. Regaining the ability to walk can happen. Other physical abilities can be restored. Other damaged physical abilities can be improved reducing the degree of the victim's dependence. The following phenomenon related to paralysis challenges medical science for a satisfactory explanation and remedy. Paralysis occurs in the lower limbs due to an injury of a lower section of the spinal cord. Yet the paralysis soon spreads to the upper body and arms. The upper limbs become weak and numbed with fingers shriveled and tapered, and the breathing labored. The mind becomes lethargic and easily fatigued. This phenomenon occurs more rapidly in cases of depression, physical neglect, or inadequate rehabilitation.

From the energy point of view, if the energy-consciousness flow is obstructed and unable to complete its path downwards, the energy will accumulate above the obstruction. The energy turns into a compressed, stale bundle which gradually thickens to infect the whole person. This stale energy gradually weakens the muscles and obstructs physiological functions. Injury sets off a high voltage surge along the nervous system and causes gradual damage and the destruction of nerve cells beyond the confines of the original injury. The CFQ energy remedy suggested below has been developed especially to deal with this energetic spread of damage.

CFQ Paralysis Remedy

Peace and Quality of Life. For the patient to be told that paralysis is permanent and nothing can really be done often brings about extreme sorrow and despair. I say, "No, there is hope!" Much can be done to bring about recovery or at least physical improvement. CFQ involvement allows for activities whereby the agonizing thoughts and emotions of despair, pain and a doomed future can be eliminated and replaced by peace. Peace is the healing force that creates physical repair and well-being. It is this state of well-being that effectively replaces psychological agony.

Long Live Energy Butterfly Shakers. A paralyzed person is limited in the use of physical movements that could bring about healing. At the beginning of treatment the butterfly-shake technique described in Chapter 8 might well provide the only way out. Few paralyzed people can move their legs. But if the patient can move even one leg slightly, the prospect of getting both legs moving freely and subsequently getting up to walk is excellent. This can happen within a matter of months. The helper must modify the technique on a case by case basis to ensure that it is "do-able." If the legs cannot move, then move the buttocks, or turn the body, or hands or neck. The whole idea of this technique is to move whatever part of your body you can move. The movements are meant to enhance loosening, flexibility, bioenergy flow, and blood circulation, The exercises clear away dense tension energy, staleness, and numbness. The conventional approach is often counter-productive when it forcefully moves the body in an attempt to gain strength. Therapy should not attempt to exert the paralyzed body or limbs.

Such an approach is doomed to fail since the restoration of physio-logical functions, senses, and control is dependent upon clearing away the staleness. When a person becomes paralyzed, the strength within the muscles become stuck and turns into staleness and numbness. This effect is the basic force that obstructs physiological functions, senses and control. In this crucial state, it can be a helpful attitude to ignore medical information about damaged spinal nerves that are thought impossible to repair. You will soon discover that an open-minded hopeful attitude will bring rewards aplenty. Forceful and strenuous movements work adversely generating stress and the strain of exertion. This further results in deterioration as promoted by obstructed physio-logical functions. If one gets tired and frustrated, despair and dwin-dling peace result.

Nevertheless, external movements while secondary (to a harmonious consciousness) are crucial for enhancing internal peace and calmness. Without any form of physical movement the mind takes flight into negative thoughts and disturbed emotions while the body becomes increasingly stale. The act of moving puts one's entitlement to physical mobility into action. You can honestly say you truly wish to recover, "I do my part. God, I trust you to grant my prayer." Accept your condi-tion calmly but unconditionally determine to change. This removes internal conflict and disharmony which obstruct the healing process. At the same time allow yourself to be aware of your peace (the power of purity and God within). When true peace comes through, the para-lyzed person will vividly feel the revitalization as the staleness and numbness dissolve and leave. This staleness and numbness encompass chunks of debased energy of huge proportions, much more than any-one can imagine.

Patience, perseverance and the willingness to practice long hours daily (three to five hours or more), are necessary. If daily practice is insufficient, it may not be enough to clear past compounded staleness as well as current negative thoughts and emotions. Watching TV, read-ing, and idle thinking are not desirable and should be kept to no more than two to three hours daily. The rest of the day, discounting time for sleep (confined to seven hours nightly), eating and such necessities, should be spent practicing CFQ techniques.

CFQ Procedural Modification. The butterfly-shaking procedure is best performed in a sitting position (with a back-rest) and the feet resting on the ground or a flat surface. Since it is not always possible to move the patient to a seated position, it is acceptable initially to place the patient's legs straight on the bed with the upper portion of the bed raised.

Loosen the whole body and shake at the knees in the sitting position (both knees move inward and outward at the same time). The move-ments should be generous (wide open), gentle, slow (about 60 to times per minute) and loose. As a paralyzed person is unlikely to be able to move initially, someone else must help. Helpers can include loved ones, kin, relatives, friends, and caregivers. When moving, encourage the patient to loosen her or his whole body. At the same time the patient should remain relaxed and attentive to the movements. The patient should attempt to join in the movements. It will be distracting to chit-chat, allow TV, or read while butterfly shaking.

Assisted shaking, of course, is not the same as the patient's own action which is vital to recovery from paralysis. However, for most par-alyzed persons, the legs are the last bodily parts to become mobile. The patient should therefore move whatever else he or she can. If the hands are mobile, turn the hands back and forth in a loose and slow manner. If only the neck is mobile, turn it from side to side. Perseverance is needed. Unlike the hands which are outlets for stale energy, the neck has no clear outlet. The patient should turn the neck with looseness and patience, mentally willing that movement to spread to a wider area through the hands and down the body. Those with mobile hands can practice turning their body from side to side keeping in mind the goal of spreading the movements downward. If done properly, the patient will gradually feel bodily sensations moving down section by section, joint by joint, until they reach the hip and beyond spreading all the way down through the legs. When that happens, the legs become mobile.

These practices must be willingly performed by the paralyzed person many hours each day, filling up all the available time. Irritation and frustrations are inevitable. The patient's willingness to face these problems bravely will ensure that progress occurs rapidly. Within months, legs become mobile as well. All movements should be done as loosely and effortlessly as possible so as to facilitate peace and openness. Watch out for the tendency to want to fabricate strength.

Dedication of CFQ Practice. In addition to helping a paralyzed person by encouragement and shaking the patient's legs, family members and friends can help by practicing CFQ and dedicating the resultant energy to the patient. In this way, they are not only socially supportive but the projected healing power can actually speed up recovery. People with perhaps six months or more of practice are better able to resonate with this dedication method. This, however, should not be a concern. Even if one has only begun practice, dedication helps greatly by showing support and also providing necessary inspiration. The effect of your practice on the paralyzed person is real and over time will become increasingly effective. The dedication practices that help most are the 7-Movement exercises, which are best performed two sets at a time.

The lotus walk, butterfly shake, freedom hands and freedom walk also contribute.

Verbal Persuasion. Anyone afflicted with a disease is literally "held down" by the problem. This holding down is pervasive. The body is stressed by the debased energy. Psychologically, the injured person loses confidence in the body's condition. The patient anticipates pain before it occurs and expects to be unable to move before attempting to do so. If the person has a pain in the leg, he or she holds back when walking instead of stepping down naturally. Mentally, the person's thoughts tend to focus on depression and negativity. Emotionally, she or he becomes restless and irritable. Spiritually, the patient suffers low self esteem. By pacifying the response mode in any or all the physical, mental, emotional, and spiritual domains recovery can be accelerated.

Paralyzed people will not only be mentally, emotionally and spiritually depressed, but also lack confidence in their bodies. They are likely to avoid or fear their paralyzed bodies. To overcome their problems they may limit their efforts to thinking hard or pushing willfully. This increases the tension and worsens the body's condition. Any form of trying to overcome the problem by thinking hard is in fact counterproductive.

To verbally help the patient involves encouraging her or him to be relaxed, let go of anxiety especially as related to a quick recovery, avoid meaningless anger with oneself or one's problem and cheer up. The person needs to open-out, loosen, relax, be peaceful, and breathe easily and deeply from his or her abdomen. A genuine smile, not just on the surface but from one's core is extremely helpful. Smile with every breath, filling every cell in the body. Radiate smiles. To smile involves letting go of every tendency to hold back and avoid dealing with one's paralyzed body. Help the person in healing by moving him or her in the right place to facilitate complete release, loosening, relaxation and smiling.

Manifestations of recovery happen as physical jerks or movements even in the completely paralyzed limbs. The whole idea is to lock nothing in the mind or in the emotions. The more the thinking, the worse the problem becomes. Actualize recovery by taking action instead of thought. A paralyzed person will be powerless to help themselves. Encouragement from another person is the key. Successful encouragement skillfully conducted by an experienced healer can result in tremendous improvement if the patient is inspired to cooperate fully and the conditions are right. Stop, however, if the person shows signs of dissent or boredom.

Energy Healing. By using healing energy generated by meditation, a proficient healer can cut through the stiff glue-like tension energy in a paralyzed person. Such interventions can greatly improve the rate of progress or effect improvements in a stagnant situation. The training of a professional healer, however, requires at least seven years of diligent practice, and much more time is necessary to become a mature and proficient healer.

If a paralyzed person embarks on daily practice, lets go and releases the source of paralysis, cleansing happens within a short time, even in one or two weeks. The staleness and numbness are experienced as glue-like "chunks" in the release process. To effect recovery requires a longer period of training since solidified staleness exists in concentrated forms all over the body and continue to draw in stale energy. The release frees chunk after chunk of staleness and numbness in a succession that seems almost endless. Only through persistent practice does the stale and numb energy dissipate leaving less paralysis. In the process, the patient becomes energetically sensitive to surrounding objects achieving an appreciation of the presence of a large field of oppressive numb energy.

A person who practices CFQ for about six months can reasonably produce some radiant effect in their energy field. When the practitioner gets close to the paralyzed person their radiant energy field can easily trigger a reaction in the patient who can feel the activation and release of numbness. If the practitioner waves his or her hands from a distance of several feet the paralyzed person will feel a release of numbness. This, however, is insufficient to produce significant improvement. Sincerity in helping is what really matters. A practitioner can tune in cooperatively with an experienced healer and help. She or he will have a good sense of what to do and may spontaneously work on the paralyzed person.

Complications, Sensations & Reactions. For a bed-ridden person, bed sores are a problem that can become quite difficult. They can be avoided by turning the body from one side to the other every four hours. When practicing butterfly shaking, take extra care to reduce friction between the buttocks and the chair or bed. It is a good idea to use an air cushion. This exercise can also be performed by shaking the body with the person's back up. For those with extensive healed bed sores the improvement in circulation as a result of practicing CFQ can reactivate the sores. Bed sores for a paralyzed person normally do not heal properly. In the usual superficial process, only a layer of skin grows over the damaged flesh. When the repair process fully activates as a result of CFQ practice, the damaged flesh together with this skin is shed. Gradually it is replaced by healthier tissue. Take extra care with cleaning, dressing and drying.

The numbness and staleness described in this chapter are the most distinctive sensations in the healing process for paralyzed people. The return of sensation to the paralyzed person, includes adverse feelings of heaviness, stiffness, tightness, aches, pains and discomfort. Should these problems become overwhelming, loosen the whole body with a calm and peaceful attitude. Let problems leave in peace rather than fighting or struggling against them. Such battles only result in the reabsorption of the difficulties. Release, in the proper manner, will result in rapid improvement. In cases where CFQ practice began years after the paralysis and extensive muscular wastage has occurred, the repairing process may be extremely painful and uncomfortable.

The release of symptoms such as depression, negative thoughts, and oppressive emotions may be felt intensely together with restlessness, anxiety, and chest congestion. Remain calm and peaceful. At the same time be detached from such thoughts, emotions and discomforts so that they can leave properly. Move the moveable limbs, most likely the hands. Be so occupied that detachment is enhanced. Activate and release the stale energy in thoughts, emotions, and discomforts. Those with lower section paralysis will have more success dealing with this problem than those with higher section paralysis as there is more space to spread the problem.

Stale energy thought forms and experiences released from deep within *mano*-consciousness and *alaya*-consciousness (the subconscious) may manifest in the forms of vivid dreams or nightmares. The outcome can be depression, negative thoughts or disruptive emotions. Ensure continued release as discussed in the above paragraph. Projecting healing energy into the physical body may cause spontaneous movements. Be detached from such movements. At the same time allow the movements to proceed without controlling them until the undesirable forces are fully released. You may use the CFQ mantra to generate healing energy while you remain properly detached.

Training & Rehabilitation. When the patient can shake both legs loosely, this frequently means that she or he is strong enough to stand and walk. The paralyzed person must practice standing and walking with the help of others (e.g. physiotherapists) if necessary. If the patient can sit with little support, it normally means that full physical recovery is near.

In other cases, normal exercises and physiotherapy may be desirable depending upon the possibilities. In all cases, ensure that physical strain and strength exerted are fully released by butterfly shaking with a peaceful attitude as discussed in this chapter. The stale energy pattern of a paralyzed person has a strong resisting and drawing-in tendency that readily absorbs strength being exerted and turns it into more stale energy. Without a full release, strenuous exercise becomes counter effective. When the paralyzed person is able to walk, practice the lotus walk and the 7-Movement exercises to ensure thorough and complete recovery.

A Case Example: *The patient, a construction worker in his early thirties, fell from a height of 15 feet suffering a fracture of the seventh cervical vertebra. He was paralyzed from the neck downwards. After being hospitalized for two weeks a relative requested my help.*

When I first saw him in the hospital, his neck was mobile, but below that he had neither sensation nor control and could not move. As his neck and shoulder pain worsened his limbs became rigid. As soon as I tuned into him to begin treatment, he reported tingling sensations in his hands and feet. He said, "the skin's pores are opening out," and felt a force being cleared out. The muscles of his arms throbbed and jerked to the astonishment of his wife and relatives present. After the half hour treatment, his arms felt lighter. To his consternation and the amazement of on-lookers, he was able to lift the left arm up.

He struggled unsuccessfully to raise his right arm. Yet he felt connected to it for the first time since the accident. Later that day, towards evening, he waved both arms uncontrollably. That night he regained almost full control of them. A week later, after my second visit, he was discharged from hospital.

I followed up with a further eighteen sessions, twice weekly. The spectacular improvement in his arms was not matched by his legs. They remained paralyzed. We mutually agreed to stop the treatment after a total of 30 sessions. He passed away five years later from renal and multiple organ failures.

Comments. It is regrettable, that back in 1992 (before the Night of the Golden Light), I did not have sufficient understanding of healing and energy principles. I was unable then to work deep enough for greater progress as I can today. I believe that he would have regained full physical ability. He did regain full mobility and sensations from the neck down to the solar plexus. He felt a sensation of connectedness from that point down to his feet. He did not deteriorate showing the normal spastic features of paralyzed limbs. He could feel strength in his legs even though unable to move them. He reported a strong release of numbness during each healing session. If he had been taught to do meridian exercises with his hands and body as discussed in this chapter, progress would have continued. That would have worked its way down to his feet reestablishing full mobility.

Pain & Injuries

In any kind of bodily injury, the muscles coil back or draw inward in a gripping-contracting action. This defensive reaction causes stiffness, blocks energy, inhibits blood circulation and obstructs muscular movements. Pressure on the nerves creates pain. Thus the saying in TCM, *"There is pain when there is a blockage."*

The recoil action is initiated from the potential strength latent within the muscles. This muscle reaction is similar to those in normal lifting or body motions except that with an injury the recoil is drawn inward. It goes all the way in from the physical to a mental-emotional pressure on the mind. If the impact is minor as in a pinch, the recoiled strength is released shortly and the pain clears. Otherwise, the pain and stiffness persist until gradually released. More likely, the tension reaction is never completely released and this residual event is trapped in the injured tissues.

When that happens, the nerves gradually adapt, becoming desensitized to the pressure, no longer sending out pain signals. That means neither that the injury is properly repaired nor the pain is over for good. The stiffness remains together with the burden. At some time in the future, when advancing age results in stiffness developing, the additional loading of pressure stimulates pain again. Now it is labeled as rheumatism or arthritic pain. The aging stiffening body of itself also causes pain if the stiffness impinges on nerves.

Stiffness from muscle reactions also shortens the muscles. While the injury mends, the latent tension reaction is only partially released leaving behind muscular stiffness. These muscles are no longer able to withstand normal strain and occasion recurring pain. As the blood flow and energy circulation remain obstructed, the situation can contribute to subsequent health problems. These problems range from simple arthritis to hypertension, strokes, heart disease and cancer.

Broken Bones & Dislocation. The treatment of broken bones and dislocations is well established and will not be discussed here. However, when the limbs are prevented from movement for a prolonged period of time as in cases where they are put in casts or held in slings, the potential energy in the muscles thickens. It adds on to the latent tension caused by the injury. Together they produce extensive muscular hardening or stiffness. This can become a permanent inconvenience restricting physical movements and may lead to other health problems. Normal physiotherapy and an exercise regimen will not be able to completely deal with this basic muscle blockage.

Treating Sprains & Knocks. The contraction of muscles as a result of injuries obstructs blood circulation and traps body fluids thus giving rise to swelling. Some blood capillaries may be ruptured causing internal bleeding which aggravates the swelling.

Helpful suggestions: The appropriate first aid remedy is cold. Apply ice. The muscles around the injured region are normally aroused generating excessive heat. This increased heat together with internal bleeding worsen the swelling. If cold is applied in a timely manner, the heat is neutralized and the bleeding stops. This remedy produces a soothing effect, reduces the swelling and encourages a speedy recovery. Cold application is done by putting a few ice cubes wrapped in a piece of cloth gently on the injured area. Do this for a few seconds repeatedly for a total of five minutes. If swelling persists, repeat two or three times daily at intervals of several hours.

The left-over injury is then remedied by hot applications either by the use of a hot water bottle or a hard-boiled egg (without removing the shell) wrapped in a piece of cloth. Touch the hot application on and around the injured area gently as long as the heat is tolerable. Then gently rub and rotate the application. Repeat for several days two to three times daily until the injury is completely healed. The use of a hot application may commence on the second day for children and young adults. For the elderly, begin only on the fourth day as in this situation it takes a longer time for the ruptured capillaries to heal. Using the hot application too early may cause bleeding from the unhealed capillaries giving rise to swelling.

Far Eastern people love to massage an injury with medicated oil or spirits. This is a bad idea for a fresh injury particularly if done by an amateur. Rubbing and massaging can cause massive injuries and bleeding in addition to the original injury. Most medicated oil or balm has a warming effect that compounds swelling. Also the type used should differ for fresh injuries versus chronic pain. Massage therapy specifies that pressure must be avoided on regions of pain. A skillful therapist will work on the surrounding area to loosen up the muscles and clear the blockages. If improper treatment is applied, the injury will be compounded causing delayed recovery. This may lead to greater residual problems or even severe consequences.

Shortcomings of Exercise: Normal exercise and physiotherapy can be aimed at promoting flexibility and strengthening. However, these approaches suffer several shortcomings. The hardened, stiffened, and shortened muscles may not be able to withstand strain and exertion as required by physical therapy. This results in the problem worsening. The stiffness can only be partially removed when normal physical actions are used to loosen or stretch muscles. Solidified strength remains and conventional remedies are unable to remove it. This prevents repair and the achievement of flexibility. In other words, muscle strength will not return to stiffened muscles.

A second shortcoming of physical exercise is that it cannot remove the mental-emotional stress reaction produced by the drawn-in energy that compacts muscles and continues to affect the person. This relationship is poorly understood in conventional therapy but the adverse effect is genuine. More often then not, an injury is left with some degree of permanent stiffness and recurring pain. In certain cases (for example, severe arthritic or fragile elderly patients) forceful physical manipulation on stiffened muscles can be fatal.

CFQ Remedy for Injuries

CFQ practice is recommended for the treatment of left-over pain and stiffness arising from injuries. It works by dissolving and clearing away the solidified strength, and mentally traumatizing stress arising from the injury. The energy exercises enhance blood and bioenergy flow thus bringing about optimum flexibility and muscle repair. Even old injuries with massive stiffness, ugly scars and keloids have been known to satisfactorily improve with CFQ practice and healing.

The 7-Movement Meridian Exercise. The practice of these meridian exercises promote whole-body looseness to optimize repairs and regenerate healthy tissue. Injuries restrict physical movements especially for those who are bed ridden for a prolonged period. Such immobility causes poor circulation and stiffness in the whole body. Timely and proper practice promises a rebound to good health and prevents health problems resulting from left over stiffness. For the best results, repeat the exercises for at least three sets daily. If the limbs are stiff, do not forcefully stretch them but rather move them easily within the limits of your ability. There is no need to emphasize symmetry of movements, i.e., the left versus right sides of the body. Limb movements need not be even or proportionate.

If the body is stiff, you need not stand straight. If one arm is stiff and is restricted in mobility, you need not lift both arms to the same height. For example, in Movement 3, one hand can be raised overhead while the other can remain at chest level without having to reach up and press on the other raised hand. By working on a whole-body looseness, the loosening effect will be self-sorting and the stiffness will be lubricated quickly. The dissolving of stiffness may give rise to feelings of pain and numbness being released.

Lotus Walk. If one leg is painful and stiff, neither avoid moving nor deliberately holding back while walking. Walk as loosely and naturally as possible. Be aware of the contact of your feet on the ground with each step. Ensure a calm and peaceful mood to facilitate a rejuvenation of physiological functions, enhancement of blood and energy circulation throughout the whole body even to the tips of your hands and feet. You may well feel pain leave the body in a downward and outward flow. Stiffness will be dissolved and leave as numbness. The dissolving and freeing off process can cause muscle throbbing, quivering, and jerks. If an arm is injured and is put in a cast or sling, practice the lotus walk before the injury is healed. This will speed up recovery and ensure that there will be little left-over stiffness.

Butterfly Shake. By shaking the legs, whole body looseness as well as the restoration of proper circulation and physiological functions are promoted. This shaking can be easily done at one's convenience doing away with boredom, idleness and fatigue. The practice can commence while in the hospital or before normal physical activities are recommended. If one leg is in a cast, shaking the other leg promotes whole-body relaxation and facilitates the recovery of the injured leg. It further reduces left-over stiffness.

Note that even an injured leg in a cast can be shaken with modifications thus enabling a good recovery. The criterion is that shaking should not cause excessive pain or stress. Minor pain and discomfort are tolerable and compatible with healing. The healing effect shaking brings makes it a superior way of utilizing time as compared to reading or watching TV. These involvements actually slow down recovery and increase left-over pain and stiffness. The clearing off sensations include flowing pain, muscle throbbing and quivering.

Direct Energy Healing. The healer during the energy session promotes quick recovery from injury and dissolves left-over stiffness and pain. When a new injury is worked on, the patient can normally feel the activation and release of pain, muscle throbbing and jerks. She or he experiences a soothing effect after the session.

A Case Example: *A male patient in his mid twenties was badly injured in an auto accident. A lower lumbar vertebra was fractured leading to a paralysis of his legs. The patient's family consulted a neurosurgeon. Surgery was suggested but the likelihood of restoring mobility to the legs was in doubt. The medical expenses would be extremely high. One year after the accident, a friend recommended that he should come and see me.*

His condition on examination was as follows: His legs were severely wasted and spastic. His feet and toes pointed downwards. His arms were weak and lifting them required a great effort. His fingers were tapered and had little gripping strength. His chest was congested. He had difficulty breathing. His hands and feet were cold. He tired easily and responded to questions slowly. His condition had deteriorated after paralysis.

During the first healing session, his breath became deep and heavy. He perspired profusely from his head and upper back. He felt the numbness leaving his hands. He later said that on the night after the first session, his legs started to jerk and kick uncontrollably. The following day he began to cry aloud uncontrollably. This went on throughout the day but he nevertheless felt good.

On his second visit two days later, he could move his arms easily and he felt stronger. The cold palms were now wet and warm. His chest felt good and breathing was much more comfortable. He reported that a "stone lifted from my chest." He felt connected to his body and experienced sensations to his hip region.

I scheduled another appointment. He called up to cancel and apologize as his brother was unable to drive him that day. He asked for a new appointment. He hinted that many exciting things had happened and he would describe them when he came. Again he did not show up. He called two days later, apologized repeatedly with great emotion and sobbed while he talked. He could not get his family to drive him. I consoled and assured him that I would give him my utmost attention once he returned. I could not interfere in this family controversy as his father preferred surgery for him. I have not heard from him since.

15

Cerebral Stroke: Treatment and Prevention

Stroke, or cerebrovascular disease, is one of the top three causes of death. In cerebral infarction, part of the brain is damaged due to lack of blood from a blocked blood vessel while cerebral hemorrhage means a bleeding into the brain from a rupture of a blood vessel. The overall mortality rate, one week after the acute onset of stroke, is 30 per cent. For survivors (the majority) some 20 per cent recover completely and 10 per cent have a minor disability. In the remaining 70 per cent, disability ranges between moderate to severe. The acute disturbance of the cerebral function can cause disabilities such as paralysis of one half of the body (hemiplegia). As one side of the brain governs the opposite side of the body, an abnormality of the left side of the brain will cause a right-sided paralysis and vice versa. The pattern of disability following a stroke is extremely variable depending on multiple factors.

The Cause: Arteriosclerosis

The development of a glue-like substance called atheroma causing hardening and thickening of the arteries is natural with aging. Such arterial atheroma may be present at an early age (from six months on). Its development is related to the development of high blood pressure. The process, referred to as arteriosclerosis (also atherosclerosis) can lead to an almost complete blockage of blood vessels. Another risk is the formation of plaque or platelets on vessel walls that when released travel in the blood stream and may block a major artery. Such blockages may be temporary in the case of a transient ischemic attack or permanent as in the case of cerebral infarction.

CFQ Therapy. CFQ is recommended as a rehabilitation and prevention tool for stroke and as a supplementary remedy in conjunction with mainstream medicine. CFQ therapy can benefit the 70 per cent of surviving stroke patients that are left with different degrees of disability. Under normal circumstances, if full recovery does not occur within two to six months, the problem is not considered amenable to further improvement.

Stroke is a calamity that affects the victims and their entire families, relatives, friends and co-workers. Care for such patients requires enormous financial and medical resources. The patient may suffer from depression, other psychological problems, loss of employment, restricted social activity, and loss of independence. There can be fear, a constant threat of relapse, a change in the family role, and problems in marital and family relationships. Unless effective measures are being taken, survivors are vulnerable to the risk of more severe subsequent attacks. Complications with heart disease may also develop.

The practice of CFQ along with healing treatments can greatly improve the speed and completeness of recovery. Healing sessions can be utilized or some of the CFQ techniques can be introduced soon after appropriate medical remedies are begun. Treatment can begin even when the patients are still hospitalized. CFQ therapy has been found to greatly benefit patients whose physical prognosis is poor. It has also helped patients up to ten years after an attack. With the practice of CFQ healing, persons with hypertension are able to stabilize their blood pressure and enjoy an improved sense of health. In some cases their blood pressure is reduced without need for further medication. The de-stressing effect of CFQ at this point seems to be able to remove atheroma thus reducing the hardening and thickening of the arteries caused by arteriosclerosis. Such effects are not only important enabling recovery but are also important for preventing strokes or subsequent attacks.

CFQ involvement reduces the time patients might dwell in a depressive mental state. This reduces related psychological problems and at the same time contributes to a sense of well-being.

Healing Principles

People generally believe that normal relaxation is beneficial. Medical experts agree that the ability of patients to relax can greatly enhance recovery from disease. A major problem, however, is that most people (healthy or not) are unable to relax properly. Most freely admit to such an inability. For relaxation to happen, one must proceed in tune with certain principles. Practicing CFQ enhances a deeper than normal relaxation. The principles that bring about such deep relaxation are:

1. Shifting from concerns of the mind to undoing the body's energy blockages

2. Letting go to release downwards

3. Opening out to radiate

4. Melting off the debased energy glue

5. Undoing the binding strength trapped in the muscles

6. Making use of energy channels (meridians)

7. Peace.

Overcoming the Mind-Traps. Anxiety originates in the mind (thoughts). When the mind is allowed to roam freely, it appeals to and attracts the attention of the thinker. As mental activity accelerates it tends to embrace negative ideas, thoughts, imaginations and past events often mixed with fantasy. It becomes deeply entangled with negative emotions resulting in depression, heightened pain, intensified fear and undesirable behaviors. For persons who are physically disabled and suffer limited physical and social activity, such mental wanderings can cause extreme suffering for oneself and also for family members and friends. Relationships degenerate with increased tendencies to be over-demanding, irritable, and interfering in one's dealings with others. These problems deprive stroke victims of chances to improve and recover their health.

The practice of CFQ provides both healing activities to usefully occupy patients and time-out from the mind playing its tricks. The mind is alive and, like breathing and heartbeat, cannot stop for a moment. Any attempts to control it produce adverse effects. It cannot be easily influenced during, for example, counseling as the inputs are far weaker than the thinking habits drawn from internal memories. Understanding this aspect of the mind is crucial to help patients detach from its grip. Meridian activation with the minimum of mental arousal reduces anxiety, pain, and depression. The patient becomes less irritable and demanding so that relationships with family members, friends and relatives improve.

Downward Release. Tension energy is the basis for every kind of disease problem, physical and psychological. Ability to dissolve the tension energy enhances healing. The downward release and letting go process is an important pathway for effective relaxation and de-stressing. As absorbed tension energy is upward suspending, effective relaxation must carry the reverse feature. It must be cleared downward and out. The downward release process dissolves the tension energy according to the TCM premise, "*When the bioenergy flows down, hundreds of diseases vanish.*"

Such a release is especially important in the case of stroke patients. It ensures that blood clots and plaque that leads to strokes are fully dissolved instead of being allowed to travel upward to clog other blood vessels. Such dissolution is necessary to bring about recovery.

This is also the safest way. Drugs dissolve the clots and plaque partially while the remainder can travel up and block major arteries. Without dissolving blockages even patients who have fully recovered may stand the risk of subsequent strokes or face other disease problems.

Opening Out. Together with the downward release process, opening out or radiance ensures true relaxation. Repair of the physical body is enhanced to bring about healing. Opening out dissolves and frees the body of tension energy. At the same time it relaxes the blood vessels, enabling them to expand and improve blood flow. In turn muscles and tissues are loosened. The spaces between the cells become flexibly organized to facilitate physiological functions.

Melting Off The Glue: The cause of stroke is arteriosclerosis resulting from the development of atheroma. This is a glue-like substance which causes hardening and thickening of the arteries. The aging of cells is caused by the formation of another glue-like residue: product of the glycosylation of food, oxidation of free radicals, and cell metabolism. In short, in the aging process, the formation of toxic waste glues cells together, impedes healthy cell functioning, and accelerates deterioration.

The biological explanation of the devastating effects of such glue-like residues helps us understand disease and aging but it has not generated feasible solutions to the problems fabricated. From an energy perspective this glue comes from the basic human "I want" survival instinct. It is because of this instinct to exist that the human life force undergoes rebirth in a physical body with the capacity to absorb energy and store it. These stored packets of energy are located in the energy body in various centers in the form of energy forces with a cris-cross pattern. These net-like energy traps enable a continuous excitation of cells sustaining the instinct of "I want" in life's process. They are like magnets that draw in stimulants, perceptions and experiences by debasing pure cosmic energy. As these packets are absorbed they become energetic components of the body and support thoughts and memories that influence consciousness. Mind, body and spirit thus become burdened.

As far as the mind's normal fabricating tendency goes, such glue exists in a hardened state within the body. Few visible properties can be detected. The letting-go process of CFQ converts the solidified tension energy back into a sticky glue and during the release process it is felt as such. For a stroke patient embarking on CFQ practice the glue effect manifests in different forms and at different stages during the course of healing. The glue-symptoms are experienced simultaneously with improved well-being at each stage of release:

1. Sticky sensations and discomforts of the body and limbs may occur. Body pains and stiffness are felt particularly in the neck and shoulders. Such sensations may also cause depression, chest congestion, indigestion and numbness of the hands and feet.

2. Stickiness in the head and face region may cause tired or watery eyes, fatigue or a temporary speech disturbance.

3. Smelly and sticky perspiration stains and forms into a gel-like or slimy substance. It is visible in clothing when soaked in water.

4. Smelly, sticky and gel-like stools from the bowels.

Remain calm and do not over-react to such sensations or symptoms surfacing. At the same time persist with the practice. It will ensure a proper clearing off to bring about improvements.

Undoing the Binding Strength. Physical actions require muscular strength and generate an equivalent amount of tension-strength that is stored in the muscles. By itself, negative, emotionally involved thinking inputs strength into the muscles. Muscles in action release trapped, pent-up energy. For a person who has become physically injured and immobile, the tensed muscles become stiffened, hardened and produce a degree of muscle wasting. In the elderly the binding muscle strength is compounded so that the muscles are further hardened and gradually waste away. In the stroke victim, with paralysis, the binding muscle strength in damaged limbs solidifies, hardening and shortening the muscles. If the trapped energy is not removed, even if the brain regains full control of the body, it will be unable to move the limbs. Successful removal repairs the brain and restores health.

Proper and persistent CFQ practice will gradually restore sensations in paralyzed limbs. Such recovery is accompanied by sensations from shortened and tensed muscles. This can only be felt with a letting-go, releasing approach. Normal forceful movements do not make the binding strength apparent since these movements continue to fabricate strength. CFQ practice can dissolve away this trapped muscle tension thus freeing the muscles for optimal movements.

Making Use of the Meridians. The 12 major meridians divided into six yin and six yang meridians form a network linking all major organs. This network controls all physiological functions. Meridians are channels for bioenergy flow and according to TCM, the smooth flow of energy enhances blood circulation. This in turn ensures proper physiological functions, heals the body of diseases, and maintains health. The meridians link the body's surface to the muscles and all the internal organs which in turn "open out" externally through the five sense organs. The six yang meridians gather into the head region.

Bioenergy flow and meridian repair can extend full recovery to most stroke cases, including those that are medically considered incapable of improvement. A smooth flow of energy in one or several major meridians in the functioning limbs can stimulate a smooth flow in the other damaged limbs. This smooth flow will gradually restore a healthy flow in the meridians resulting in the repair and restoration of physiological

functions. All internal meridians are connected to the four limbs originating or ending in the hands and feet on both the left and right sides
of the body. As a stroke causes paralysis in one half of the body, I make
use of the other functioning side to restore mobility to the whole body.
TCM calls this *"treating the right side of the body to access disease of the
left side and vice-versa."*

Stroke damages the brain as well. Medical science says that brain
and nerve damage cannot be reversed. Do not be dismayed by this
statement! Brain damage may not be repairable with the available medication. But these are physical substances that react with the physical
body. I contend, however, that energy healing can use what is beyond
the physical body and is more potent than physical phenomena for
healing. The head, in TCM, is also called, *"the merging place of the six
yang meridians."* If the bioenergy flow in all the major meridians is
enhanced, it will repair the yang meridians flowing to the head as well.
In so doing, their energy flow will naturally repair and restore brain
and nervous system structures and functions. To accomplish this is not
to work directly on the head but on the limbs, *"Get to the bottom to
treat diseases at the top."*

Peace: The practice of CFQ should be considered a skillful use of
energy tools to enhance peace. Peace comes about when a person
reduces anxiety and desires (including wanting to be cured) thus doing
away with internal conflicts and disharmony. Without making use of
the right tools, the body will be physically jammed, stiffened to the
point of being slothful, and the mind will revolve around negativity
and conflict. One's emotions get cooped up with harmful and undesirable stress. The spirit becomes so burdened that the life force can be
squeezed out of the person.

If the energy of peace is successfully revealed, it spreads out from our
innermost source to become a light, a vibrant and boundless field of
energy. This can often be vividly felt together with a clear sense of well-
being and bliss. Joy replaces every kind of conflicting thought and

emotion. Such a revealing also clears away diseases from the spirit-emotion-mind-body system and repairs and restores physiological functions. When this peace is found, so is one's spirit. There is a feeling of intimacy, of having drawn close to or connected with God. You have the faith to trust God to heal your problem. Even when the damage seems so hopeless and your faith has reservations, continue to trust this Source. In this way, you better accept your situation and enjoy peace and well being.

Mind as the Key Factor

The single most important factor for successful recovery from a disease is not the realm of medical facts about how life threatening or how acute or chronic the disease is. Nor do we necessarily need to take into account the age factor, or how many disappointing or failed treatments have been endured. It is the person. The enemy is how we use (misuse) our minds. Not to understand how the mind works is to risk having the mind work against you. If a person is willing to get well or at least willing to live, much can be done. The starting point comes from having the right mind-set. Also there must be a right approach to materialize this mind-set. Then the person will never be disappointed since positive energy forces do not disappoint.

No matter how much effort has been expended on unsuccessful treatments, no matter how many frustrations or disappointments these produced, that is now over. The treatments tried may not have been effective enough. The doing, fabricating, wanting therapeutic approach may not be the right approach for you. For those with problems that are deemed incurable, by definition, traditional modalities don't work. To be workable, my experience tells me that treatment must shift to the letting-go, undoing principle. In this way the cause-effect cycle of disease and healing (or karma) can be influenced creating a new destiny in life's course. Some people may be so trapped in the traditional ways that they may not have sufficient spiritual will to live or recover. Their initiative must be revived or it will be impossible for them to heal. Initial attempts in CFQ practice may be frustrated by slow progress, obstacles, old habits and attitudes. Support, encouragement and motivation provided by family members, relatives and friends are necessary. One's community can help by understanding the needs and problems of the disabled patient and inspiring them to overcome their problems.

CFQ Rehabilitation Program

For the Bed-Ridden: The practice of butterfly shaking is recommended for bed ridden patients. For the best effects, the patient should be seated on a reclining chair with a back and head rest. Both feet can be placed flat on the floor about a foot apart. If the patient suffers from bed sores, ensure that proper dressings are applied. Their seat must be properly cushioned so that the sores are not in direct contact with the seat which could cause bruises. It is a good idea to use an air cushion.

Instructions. Rock the legs by drawing both knees inward and outward simultaneously. The patient should try to feel the effect all the way down to the feet. The correct speed is about 60 repetitions per minute. The movements should be done gently, loosely and generously without exerting physical strength. Beginners may find it difficult to follow these requirements. They tend to shake fast and forcefully or are unable to shake at all. That is all right but take care to gradually slow down and reduce the strength used to enhance progress. Family members, friends, and relatives can help by rocking the patient's legs. At the same time encourage the patient to relax and feel the movements. The disease-energy of stroke is dense and sticky. In the release process it can be absorbed by people around the patient. To safeguard themselves helpers and family members should practice CFQ.

If the legs cannot shake readily, check the seating position for obstructions. The paralyzed leg will normally not move in the beginning. When moving, pay equal attention to both legs by neither deliberately avoiding nor emphasizing either side. In time, the movements of the good leg will restore sensations and mobility to the paralyzed one. Throughout the practice, ensure a whole-body looseness so far as possible. The patient should keep the eyes closed.

Comments. The sensations restored can include muscle twitching, pulsations, numbness, stiffness, rigidity, pain, tiredness, a sense of shortened limbs, gripping strength, heat and cold. Such sensations may occur in any part of the body including the normal limbs. Remain calm with a non-rejecting attitude without attempting to avoid, fabricate or do away with the sensations that come. The disease energy is thus allowed to dissolve bringing about physical improvements.

There may be frequent sporadic occurrences of negative thoughts, disturbing emotions, or feelings of impatience. Do not be carried away lest these occurrences lead to depression, tantrums, or a reluctance to practice. Understanding and support from the people present will help to overcome such problems and restore confidence in the practice. Willingness to recover and to enjoy well-being will be manifested by being interested in the practice. These positive experiences will, in turn, help reduce the disturbances.

The patient, between practices, may be distracted by his or her thoughts. Let it be. Return to practice without feeling frustrated. This will help to reduce such distractions. Others present can help remind the patient to practice if they notice that he or she has stopped moving, unless, of course, the patient has fallen asleep. Falling into a deep, sound sleep during the practice often happens. This kind of sleep is restful and very beneficial for recovery. However, the patient must continue to practice no matter how sleepy she or he feels. This is preferable to stopping the moving and waiting for sleep to come. Falling asleep unknowingly is far better than deliberately waiting for sleep to come. The patient should avoid falling into a dreamy and non restful sleep.

Instructions. This practice must be carried out for long hours in order to fill up all available time. This is crucial as unoccupied time fabricates idle thinking accompanied by undesirable emotions. This prevents recovery and causes deterioration. Butterfly shaking brings a healing effect that is much more beneficial than reading, watching TV or unnecessary sleep. Sleep must be reduced to seven hours a day or less. Move the patient out of the chair and turn his or her body every four hours or when the chair gets warm. Allow the patient to rest for 15 minutes every few hours to avoid bed sores. An airy chair is best. Rest briefly (about five minutes) after every hour of practice or when the outflow of disease energy causes excessive discomfort. In that case the patient must stop any movements and remain completely calm and loose to allow the disease energy to leave.

If for some reason (e.g. lack of helpers) it is impossible to move the patient to a reclining chair, practice the shaking exercise in bed. The upper portion of the bed can be raised so that the body is resting in a reclining position, or with a back rest. The exercise can be performed with both legs resting straight on the bed while shaking the feet. However, exercising in this manner is less effective than in the sitting position.

There is no need to exercise the arms. Improvements in the legs as evidenced by the return of sensations and mobility is what is needed. This brings about all-round improvements including in the arms. However, if the patient wishes, she or he may exercise their arms by turning their hands back and forth. Care should be taken not to exercise for the sake of creating strength. If a paralyzed hand cannot be moved, pay equal attention to both hands. Intend moving the bad arm without being bothered by whether the physical movements in fact occur.

Comments. The return of mobility that allows the paralyzed leg to move as freely as the other leg means that complete recovery is in sight. Even well before that, when some mobility occurs in the paralyzed leg, a sense of strength and confidence in the capability of the leg to stand will occur. That is usually the time to practice standing and walking.

The ability of the patient to sit without any form of support can also indicate that it is time to practice standing and walking. Such improvements may occur in a few weeks. When people have been paralyzed for years, recovery may take many months. Persistence and perseverance are necessary.

Learning To Walk. Begin by practicing standing which may commence anytime some degree of strength and connectedness returns to the paralyzed leg. This can be done by holding on to parallel bars or wall supports. In the beginning, this practice must be assisted or monitored by helpers.

Instructions. Stand by putting the full body weight on the normal leg. Gradually shift some of the body weight over to the paralyzed leg to test its strength. Alternate the weight between both legs and gradually increase the load on the paralyzed leg. When this leg is able to take half the body weight, bend the legs to practice squats. Full squats are not encouraged. At the most, go down to the level where the hip reaches knee-height. When the weak leg feels stronger, attempt to shift the full body-weight over. Lift the normal leg slightly for a brief moment. Keep the paralyzed leg rigidly straight at the knee while practicing this. At this stage, control over the weakened leg is limited. A slight bend of the knee might result in a complete lost of control and risk toppling.

Rest generously between standing practices. Do not be over-enthusiastic for a quick recovery. Do not over-exercise. The muscles are still weak and need a long time to recuperate. Exhaustion may result in prolonged weakness and this can be depressive and shatter self confidence. Ensure that the shaking exercise remains the bulk of the practice. The practice of standing should take up only a small fraction of the time. This practice should not be taken as an attempt to strengthen the legs but rather as a balancing and familiarization exercise. Strength is gained through the butterfly-shaking exercise which enhances bioenergy and blood flow. At the same time, shaking melts away the binding strength trapped within the paralysis, thus restoring muscular functions.

When sufficient confidence is restored, the practice of walking may commence. This must begin with assistance from helpers, canes, bars, or stands. It is better to engage the service of a physiotherapist whose expertise, experience and facilities can be helpful. The paralyzed leg must be kept rigidly straight at all times while walking. Move only from the hip.

Walking toward recovery: The return of the ability to walk means that the patient should gradually spend more time walking. Do not be over ambitious at the beginning as that would be exhausting. Gradually increase the time for walking. Walking at this stage is only possible with a lot of concentration and whole body rigidity. It does not facilitate recovery but serves rehabilitation, re-training, familiarization and confidence boosting.

Instructions. Gradually, as walking becomes easier, reduce the degree of concentration. Switch attention towards an awareness of contact of the feet with the ground at each step. Take care also to loosen and reduce the rigidity and strength exerted on every part of the body as possible. The reduction in concentration, strength and rigidity should be replaced by an awareness of contact of the feet on the ground with each step. Whole body looseness is healing. This is doing the lotus walk as taught in Chapter 8. When a satisfactory degree of looseness returns to the body, it also means that the patient has substantially recovered. Improvement in the paralyzed arm will come about naturally without any particular effort when the leg improves. When walking, try to loosen the paralyzed arm instead of holding back. This ensures restoration of bioenergy and blood flow. Keep a calm and peaceful mood for fast progress.

Comments: The most natural idea that occurs is to try and strengthen the legs and body. Deliberate attempts must be made to replace such an idea with an appreciation of looseness. The error of strengthening is one of the greatest obstacles towards progress and full recovery. It accounts for the occurrence of further deterioration common after stroke attacks. With the proper way of walking the whole body loosens and increases flexibility. Such walking makes the body feel light.

Remember to rely on the butterfly-shaking exercise as the most important strategy for recovery from stroke. With improvement evident, it becomes easier to check for whole body looseness. Particularly the paralyzed arm should be dropped and allowed to be loose and relaxed. Any part of the body that is not relaxed will become obvious. The shaking exercise can be practiced at any time and anywhere for long hours, whereas the lotus walk has constraints. Shaking can be used to fill up available time. The lotus walk is best practiced in parks where the feeling of closeness to nature is beneficial. Its practice might thus be constrained by weather and time. But whatever the obstacle do not take it as an excuse for not practicing.

Completing the Recovery Process: After making significant progress, the last bit of recovery (perhaps the last 30 per cent) may be slower. At this stage, most patients feel that only the weak arm requires further improvement as the legs and speech have made a complete recovery. Recovery of speech is natural when the paralyzed leg improves and the degree of anxiety is reduced. Any remaining speech problem will have to wait for further improvement in the arm. The patient should attempt to return to normal work and activity or develop new hobbies and alternative activities. These help to instill confidence and self-worth.

To further enhance a whole body looseness and ensure that no part of the body is neglected, the 7-movement meridian exercises should be practiced. This practice enhances mindfulness of the whole body, relaxes every muscle, restores physiological functions, and facilitates peace. It can commence anytime the patient is able to walk with a reasonable degree of stability. Do not use exertion or the effort of concentration even though there may still be some limping or rigidity. Initially, there may be difficulties. The movements may appear stiff, uncoordinated or there may be problems moving the paralyzed limbs.

Instructions: 1. Practice the first three movements together with the affirmations and conclusion. Repeat until the movements become freer, more coordinated and the effort of memorizing is no longer required. Then gradually learn the subsequent movements.

2. When performing the *song kua* (relaxing the hamstring), the paralyzed leg may appear more rigid than the stable leg. There is no need to forcefully balance both legs physically. Put equal and impartial attention on both. Bend the knees slightly to drop the body weight from the normal standing position. There is no need to make an effort to bend the knees. Loosen sufficiently to drop the weight from the body.

3. The paralyzed hand may not be able to move to the same height as the other. Move naturally without any attempt to equalize the hands. For instance, in Movement 1 the paralyzed hand may go up to a lower point than the other hand. In Movement 3 the paralyzed hand can be moved to the front of one's face while the other moves as required above the head without the hands touching.

4. There should not be deliberate attempts to make the movements symmetrical or elegant. Practice effortlessly to ensure that the movements become loose, relaxing and peaceful. The proper movements of the normal side will stimulate repair and gradually loosen the paralyzed side. Both then become symmetrical.

5. Initially spend about 15 minutes in practice. Gradually increase to about one hour, preferably twice daily, depending on available time. Follow the patterns discussed in Chapter 6. A complete set takes about 15 minutes.

6. Continue to practice the butterfly shake and lotus walk, filling up all available time, to enhance continuous improvement.

Comments: With patience and perseverance, every bit of damage can be repaired. There is no excuse remaining to prevent healing. Where there is a will there is a way. The physical body is still the shallowest problem. Beyond that is the mind (including emotions), then the spirit. There may be limits to the scope of one's recovery if one attempts to heal only the physical body. My method ensures healing from the spirit out through the mind and the body. Every damaged physiological function is repaired. Take care not to be impatient, not to be angry with the problem, yourself or other people. Do not demand or even hope for recovery. In some cases, the last bit of damage may take years to eliminate, sometimes without your even noticing it go. That really does not matter. Be relaxed, be peaceful, enjoy your wellness and trust God.

Common Mistakes

1. *Strengthening.* A stroke leaves behind paralysis and a limited ability to move. This suggests body weakness. The first inclination is to figure out how to strengthen the body to overcome the obvious weakness. CFQ dares to question this paradigm. Thoughts of strengthening and/or actions to strengthen the body and paralyzed limbs are as dangerous as pouring gas on fire. According to TCM a person is *"weakened by inappropriate strength."* Stroke is due to the formation of a binding strength that has a vice-like grip on the body. This also causes hardening and narrowing of the arteries, and fabricates atheroma. This process need not lead to a stroke. For a stroke to occur one's limit of tolerance must be surpassed. Binding strength is fabricated by muscular actions (output) which at the same time leave behind a residual tension energy coiled in the muscles. The residual glue will continue to be accumulated and eventually cause old age and death.

Binding strength is also created by thoughts, memories and emotions (particularly negative emotions). Mental and physical work leave behind large amounts of binding strength in the muscles and organs. The person may continue to enjoy strong muscular movements or develop muscle bulk. If the strength becomes excessive and obstructs its release, the person then feels weak. Such binding strength continues to damage the body and causes the muscles to shrink and eventually be replaced by fat and body fluids.

In the unfortunate onset of a stroke, the resultant paralysis causes movement disability for at least several days. This is enough to solidify and coagulate a large part of the binding strength into stiffness. When the person attempts to exercise the paralyzed limbs after partial mobility returns, the stiffened muscles further obstruct the output of strength but readily absorb unused strength. This further burdens the body and is highly detrimental, resulting in further deterioration and the possibility of another attack.

For those who show progress in recovery, the output of strength is not obstructed. That does not mean that exercise should stop. In fact, it is important that the person remains optimistic and resilient as shown by his or her interest in continuing to exercise to overcome the problem. But exercises must be done in a non-strenuous manner to facilitate rapid recovery. Also remember that negative thoughts and emotions resulting from the disease fabricate anxiety, fear, worry, and depression. These contribute to the build up of hazardous binding strength. Just the thought of strengthening creates binding strength.

2. *Inappropriate Stretching.* One residual effect of stroke is stiffened, hardened and shortened limbs and muscles. The common sense remedy is to stretch to loosen the stiffness. This is also the normal practice in physiotherapy. Most stretching is in fact beneficial. The exception is stretching the arms and hands above the shoulder level. It is a common habit when exercising to swing ones hands up

and down briskly to relax the shoulders. Stroke patients often enjoy swinging their hands up to feel relaxed and are advised to continue to increase stretching. In physiotherapy work, weights and pulleys are attached to lift the patient's hands.

However, from the CFQ perspective, lifting the arms and unnecessarily pushing the hands above shoulder level fabricates more harm than good. The following experiment can demonstrate this:

1. Stand with a whole body looseness and drop the hands at both sides of the body.

2. With the arm straight, raise one hand forward to shoulder level while maintaining the whole body looseness. Observe the pressure within the head.

3. Raise the hand further up and observe the increase in pressure within the head.

4. Drop the hand slowly and observe the decrease in pressure which becomes normal as the hand descends to shoulder level.

5. Repeat this action for a few times to verify the tension formed by the increased pressure in the head.

6. For those who are curious, maintain the hand in a lifted manner for a prolonged period of time (say ten minutes) and note the discomfort ensuing over the day.

Unnecessary raising of the hands even for normal exercises can be harmful to anyone, and more so for stroke patients. It is does not even help with relaxing. For people with frozen shoulders, stretching (sometimes with weights and pulleys) does not loosen the shoulder. On the contrary in time it makes the shoulder stiffen more. To fix the problem, drop the hands, loosen and undo the binding strength. Similarly, for a stroke victim, the paralyzed arm is only open to improvement by dropping and loosening. Raising the hands up over the head will produce a compensating action and increase the pressure within the head.

After-care. Persons who recover completely from stroke through the practice of CFQ are different from those who recover in other more usual ways. At least 70 per cent of stroke survivors are potentially capable of making full or close to full recovery without much remaining disability. The lack of initiative and unwillingness to practice are popular obstacles. Those who recover in the CFQ manner enjoy a whole-body looseness, flexible muscles, suffer little pain or other disease problems. They also enjoy much calmness and peace. Such people have little risk of a subsequent stroke or other disease problems related to the stroke.

On the other hand, only about 20 per cent of stroke survivors recover completely in the normal way. Why should the rest have to suffer some disability? The normal treatment approach is confined to working on the physical body. But what is beyond in the mind and life force (spirit) is deeper and much more important. Compare the body to a box which contains a cake. When you buy a cake, do you want the cake or the box? Treating the body amounts to regulating, managing and controlling the box. It does not have a real effect on making a significant improvement in the cake. That level of healing must come from working on the spirit and mind by way of unloading, letting go and subtracting instead of inputting. To do so is equivalent to unveiling peace and trusting God to heal. There is truth in the old wives saying, *"For ordinary problems, let people fix them. For severe problems, trust God."* Those who recover by normal treatments succeed because the attack has not damaged their capacity to recover. Those who do not recover having received improper treatment add to their troubles with an incorrect understanding of healing.

Typical survivors of stroke, whether recovered fully or with lasting disabilities, continue to have stiff bodies with blocked channels, hardened and narrowed arteries, and hampered physiological functions.

These risk factors are conducive to subsequent strokes or other diseases such as heart attack. The victims may try to forcefully regain strength and suffer fear, anxiety, and conflict. This puts them at greater risk of renewed illness.

Those who practice CFQ should not be complacent even with full recovery and little risk. Become meaningfully active increasing your sense of purpose and contentment. That enhances peace and well-being. Moreover, recovery time is time to show gratitude to God. We live in and consume resources from the world. To be fair we must show respect for our privileged state by contributing service to humanity and society. Do not forget to relax daily no matter how busy you are with work and activities. You know by now idle time is wasteful and harmful. Long sleep time is hazardous. If you sleep less than 7 hours do not attempt to catch up. You cannot! With this attitude you can reclaim that hour extra to relax. Relaxation is truly possible if the tension forces fabricated during the day are properly melted and released. Muscles should be loosened, bioenergy and blood circulation enhanced, thoughts and emotions cleared of all conflicts. Disharmony is dismissed, peace fills your body completely, extends to infinity and helps you discover just how close God is.

I know that CFQ can do this for you. Practice it for any length of time, in whatever manner you prefer. Perhaps you would profit most from the 7-Movements exercises (repeated 3 sets in a row), followed by the lotus walk, butterfly shaking, freedom hands and freedom walk. Perhaps you want to do meditation. Perhaps one set of the 7-Movements is all that is possible. So be it.

A Case Example: *A female patient, in her fifties, suffered a stroke leaving her paralyzed on the left side. On the fourth day after the attack, she requested my treatment while she was still hospitalized. My initial examination indicated that her limbs were completely limp, she had normal speech ability but drooled, and suffered numbness on one side of her face. Within the first half hour of meditative treatment, she was able to exert some strength and push her paralyzed leg. Her doctor happened to come by* *on his rounds and witnessed this feat. Half in jest, he exclaimed,"You should join our physiotherapy team!"*

A brain scan taken that afternoon, however, could not detect any cerebral infarction nor hemorrhage. The patient was quite unhappy that the medical diagnosis did not pin-point her problem. She arranged to be transferred to another hospital where she stayed for a week. Again the scanning drew a blank. I visited her for the second time. After my treatment, I asked her daughter to hold the patient while she tried to stand up. The patient stood up but was unable to move her paralyzed leg forward.

Upon discharge from the hospital, she went in search of other traditional treatments, apparently dissatisfied with my approach. She soon gave up and came to my Center three weeks later. By then, she could walk with some assistance. Her right hand, however, was still completely limp. I gave her another six bi-weekly healing sessions. I noticed that her leg was much stronger and she could walk without assistance. Her hand, however, remained completely limp.

She did not progress according to my expectations. I taught her the butterfly shake. I reminded her to do it on each of her visits. I suspected that she did not and confronted her. She finally admitted that she did not even attempt to do so and each time I reminded her she would lie. I told her off and said that at least she should be personally interested in recovery. She was displeased and skipped three weeks obviously looking for someone else who could fix her problem. When she returned, I told her that I would stop treatment unless she showed some commitment and effort to help herself. In addition, she should stop her habit of constantly rubbing and moving her paralyzed hand with the other. I suggested that she should, instead, divert her energy to the job of butterfly-shaking.

A week later she was able to move her fingers and elbow. She could almost walk normally. Despite her reluctance, she had practiced for a total of an hour daily for the past few days. After two further treatment sessions her hand showed good progress. If, however, she had been more cooperative, she could have regained full physical recovery. She was still unable to lift her arm above her shoulder and her hand had no gripping strength. She reluctantly kept to her 1 to 2 hours of daily shaking her legs.

Afterward. Another obstacle was getting her attention away from her paralysis. She persisted thinking that she should continuously rub and massage her hand. She also had the notion that she should strengthen her weak limbs. These are common erroneous ideas that prevent recovery. She had previously practiced a kind of Qigong for several years. Her idea was to strengthen, absorb more qi power, and move forcefully. I told her that if such beliefs were right, she would not have had the stroke problem in the first place.

Her paralyzed leg felt heavy and did not move freely. That was expected. A paralyzed leg will take a long time (even years) to be able to move loosely and freely. It requires every physical defect to have been repaired. That normally is beyond conventional treatment. The barrier is that if any part of the body is suffering stiffness and restricted mobility, no matter how minor, the leg will not move well. Improvement in this means a breakthrough with regard to the residual problem.

16

Reviving Comatose Patients

Any of the following incidents may result in a coma: Accidental injuries, extreme emotional arousal (as in the case of shock or in severe trauma), chemical ingestion (drugs or alcohol), infections or diseases (such as stroke or heart attack). There may be physical damage evident in the form of a swelling, injury, blood clot, hemorrhage, burst vessel or pressure build-up in the brain. However, these are not what prevent a person from waking up. The very fact that a person can be kept alive with life support systems means that she or he stands a good chance of waking up. The inability to awaken is caused by excessive energetic tension and the squeezing and surging effects of trauma which prevent the return of normal consciousness.

The Energy-Consciousness Factor

Any event, occurrence or experience registers within the body in the form of an inward-drawing and upward-suspending energy pattern. For a person in a coma this occurs not only from the input of shock or trauma but also from the person's internal bodily resistance. Excessive tension forms into a thick and elastic shield of drawn-in and upsurging energy forces. The tension shield pushes away and blocks communication between external activity and one's consciousness. Comatose patients often do not suffer a complete loss of consciousness. If that happens it usually occurs within the first few hours of the onset of the problem. After that their physiological functioning compels them to struggle to wake up. However, unless the tension shield gives way the patient will struggle in vain and be unable to wake up.

The strong tension shield in a comatose patient does not break loose easily. Eventually the patient wakes up when the body's system manages to reduce the obstructing influence of this tension shield. However, unless treatment is done from the spirit-consciousness energy level, the victim might suffer permanent disorientation, physical damage or amnesia. The tension shield and the squeezing effect that obstructs physiological functions threatens to shut down the body's systems. At the spiritual-consciousness level, the drawing-in effect attracts energy forces from the first seven levels of consciousness (the five senses, the mind and mano-consciousness) to be sorted and condensed into the eighth consciousness (the milky white light-body of the *alaya*-consciousness). These become the seeds of karma that will survive death.

The deterioration of physiological functions together with the sorting out process of energy-consciousness is natural and automatic. It can lead to death within hours, days or weeks. The longer a person is in a coma, the more critical the situation. There are some patients who hold on much longer than others. Events leading to a coma and the damage inflicted differ from case to case. In some people, after the necessary medical remedies are administered, or after the person calms down from the initial shock, the recovery process occurs naturally though gradually. Medical remedies, of course, work on the physical level. What lies deeper is beyond the scope of medical science. The life and consciousness of the patient are critical in a potential death situation like this. In these circumstances CFQ shows its true worth.

Some patients are able to hold on for months. There is more to such perseverance than the nature of the damage inflicted. Psychological and emotional factors are protective and include the will to live and reasons for living. Such factors exist prior to the onset of the problem since a comatose patient is unable to exercise any control. Attempts to influence or encourage a patient during the crisis, though helpful, may be inadequate. Discouragement or a wrong approach can have a tremendous adverse impact on the patient's ability to survive. The ability of a comatose patient to hold on depends heavily on the psychological and emotional support of loved ones and relatives. Loving care helps to hold back deterioration. It can stabilize or reverse the process of tension energy moving inward into the *alaya*-consciousness. Otherwise, the energy forces surge upward shutting down physiological functions and squeezing life out of the body.

Medical Constraints. First aid, emergency measures, and medical remedies are necessary. Bleeding must be stopped. Broken bones must be set, and damaged tissues repaired. A blood transfusion might be required to replace lost of blood through injury. Bleeding in the skull must be drained. Oxygen must be given in case of breathing difficulties. An incision in the throat (a tracheotomy) might be required to facilitate breathing and to extract phlegm. The heart beat needs to be monitored, food and medicine must be given intravenously and so on. These are some of the necessary processes required to keep a comatose person alive. For some patients, after such measures are taken, recovery gradually occurs. Our discussion and suggestions here apply to those patients who are not able to come out of their coma spontaneously.

Medicines and drugs work only on the physical body. Even in the mental realm, medical science is confined to the physical brain. Attitudes and thinking belong to the field of psychology and are thought unable to control a coma. The vast reality of the spirit lies beyond the mind and is medically unknown. In my view, memories of troubling past experiences are energetically stored in the sub-conscious or unconscious mind. These memories burden the basic life force and jeopardize the birth right of every human being. Memories and experiences are necessary to stimulate ongoing vitality and existence. But every such function draws in more memory in the form of tension and this diminishes the basic life-force. When the tension burden reaches a point of saturation, physiological functioning stops and death draws near.

Limits of tolerance are not necessarily distributed evenly within the life force. As in the case of heart failure, the heart may be quite damaged but the other organs may still be functioning well. In a comatose person, the life force and consciousness are very close to their limit of tolerance and have reached a point of saturation blocking proper communication between external activity and internal consciousness. The basic life force needs to be replenished to dispel the tension burden that caused the saturation. Treatment is such cases can only be effective by harnessing the energy of transparent *alaya*-consciousness which radiates the purity of God. When effectively done, consciousness returns bringing with it a hive of activities that restore all the physiological functions. When the person wakes up from the coma, there may still be some physiological damage that needs further repair. Complete repair may not always be possible and in any case can be time consuming. The earlier the energy treatment after the onset of a coma, the less the damage build up.

I am aware that many of my observations and understandings are considered nonsense by people in the scientific world. The present scientific assessment is that brain or nerve damage is non-repairable. It rules out the possibility that the whole person, with cosmic help, can do such repairs on her or his own. Why the scientific hopelessness? I think because drugs cannot stimulate a regeneration of brain and nerve cells. In my experience, the organism's rejuvenating ability lies deep within, beyond blood vessels, in energy systems that are too fine for the blood to enter. In my view, the bottom line is that the body itself does the physiological repair. Even surgical interventions depend on the body to do the repairing.

Healing energy goes deeper than the body's five senses and works from the eighth consciousness outwards. It is a deeper way of stimulating the body to carry out the necessary functions. It also includes mental and spiritual realities not dealt with by science. In energy healing, we believe that it is Nature that does the healing. The healer only provides the connection. Cosmic healing can repair and regenerate brain cells. God is ever willing, even anxious to help, but we must take up our privilege to help. Our work is necessary to ensure that the patient recovers. The rules of healing must be understood. Otherwise one might interfere with the healing and the recovery process, which is often the case.

A Case Example: *A sixty year old male suffered a heart attack. He was a businessman, martial arts expert, and fitness enthusiast. While out jogging in a hilly area he collapsed. Hours later he was found unconscious by passers-by and taken to a hospital. His face was badly bruised as a result of the fall and a brain scan showed his brain to be blackened except for the core. The doctors estimated over 75 per cent brain damage. They speculated that after suffering the heart attack, he had a massive stroke, and his breathing stopped, cutting off oxygen for a critical period.*

During the first three days in hospital, his fingers appeared rigid and were held in a tight grip. Tears flowed and he displayed some facial emotions. All these stopped on the fourth day. He was placed in intensive care and on oxygen. After five days he was transferred to the ICU of another hospital. The family also tried to revive him using Qigong methods but none of the healer's attempts were effective. More signs of deterioration became evident. On the eighth day a member of his family managed to convince the others to engage me to help.

Initially, I observed that his eyes were slightly opened and blinking sluggishly. His breathing was shallow and high in the chest. His body and limbs were immobile without any involuntary or twitching movements. He was connected with the oxygen unit and his heartbeat was being monitored. He was in critical condition. He could die at anytime.

On my first meditation healing, his legs jerked a few times as he gasped deeply and drew in air. He discharged a huge amount of sticky yellow phlegm from the tracheotomy opening in his throat. His abdomen began to heave with deep breathing and eye movements increased rapidly. I followed up with two more sessions in the week. His breathing was now normal and the crisis was over. After that he was transferred out of the ICU.

Other family members intervened to replace my treatment as I was considered to be an outsider in their healing circle. Eventually I was asked to resume. I continued with twice weekly sessions for a total of twelve sessions. On the fifth session, he bled from his nose due to a latent injury sustained from the fall. His limbs gradually stiffened and regained slight mobility. After twelve sessions (over four weeks) he was fit enough to be discharged. He stayed in a nursing home for two months and was taken home after that.

I resumed weekly treatments. His tracheotomy was removed and his improvement continued. The limbs had progressively loosened and his hand grip was stronger. He showed limited movements of all his limbs while his knees could not be straightened completely. By now he could be fed by hand, vocalize intelligible sounds and showed expressions of comprehension.

Afterward: After eighteen sessions, I asked his family to bring him to my Center for weekly sessions. I was confident of a complete mental and physical recovery as the patient was showing good signs. Together with weekly treatments and butterfly shaking, I expected he would be able to walk within six months to a year. However, the family, still controlled by internal conflict, declined further treatment.

Waking Those in Coma

Signs of Struggle. A person in a coma does not appear the same as an unconscious person. Normally, after an initial period, perhaps hours, the comatose person shows signs of struggling or expresses discomfort. The body or limbs may appear rigid or cramped. The fists are clenched, the fingers stiff, the toes pointed downward and the eyes rolled up. This is clear evidence of the upsurge of suspended tension energy discussed previously. The remedy is to reverse the tension energy, de-stressing it and bringing it down. This is my constant recommendation for every kind of disease. The worldly wise mentality that relies on "doing"to treat illness, involves a belief in the value of sophisticated technology, complex procedures, and an emphasis on the more-is-better value system. This approach is too powerful in comparison to what does work—a simple, letting go-undoing approach. "Doing" may fulfill one's needs for stimulation and excitement fired by the "I want" attitude. "Undoing" downloads the burden enabling the person to be more alive. The former can be fine for dealing with less life endangering health problems but not for the comatose. They are so weak that they should not be imposed upon with any attitude other than cooperation with their need to hang on to life.

For the comatose to be able to hold on, the body and limbs (at least one) must be firm or turgid. This means that some tension remains in the body instead of being rapidly and completely drawn deep within the *alaya* consciousness. If that happens, there is no physical anchor to keep the life force intact. Complete limpness without some degree of rigidity returning means that the patient will be gone within hours or days. When CFQ treatment is applied, rigidity gradually returns first. It then takes a lot of effort to complete healing by working further on the rigidity and releasing it.

The patient must personally struggle to wake up. This can be aided by activating the body's self-regulatory ability. Evidence of this struggle is often shown in involuntary movements. The observer can be unaware that the patient is often mentally and emotionally in a turmoil which prompts uncontrolled movements. The patient incarnates tension compelling the body to release by jerking, stretching, or struggling. He or she may also cough or yawn. Eye movements and rotations, blinking, facial expressions and changes in breathing patterns are also symptoms of the patient's underlying emotional and mental activities.

A person in a coma does have some degree of consciousness including mental and emotional activity. She or he is not completely unaware of external surroundings and can still feel, hear, see and understand in varying degrees. The patient can be in a continuous state of panic, struggling to get up. Care should be taken to help the patient feel reassured and peaceful. Refrain from doing anything that excites, increases exertion, or inputs more tension. That only worsens the patient's situation. The comatose person, trapped in tension, finds waking up immensely difficult. In less severe cases right actions initiated at the start reduce panic, relax the person and help him or her stop fighting or struggling. This reduces tension and can quickly reverse the condition, setting the person on the path of recovery. When such actions are delayed or unhelpful the comatose person's life becomes threatened. New attempts to revive the patient become complicated, tedious and time-consuming.

Normal Mistakes. Learning that a loved one has fallen into a coma is news that is often difficult for anyone to take calmly. After the necessary emergency actions, life-saving interventions and intensive care are being provided, the patient's condition may stabilize. You can be sure that at this time, the patient is actively but vainly struggling to wake up. The frantic, unsuccessful struggle exhausts, frustrates, and fills the person with fear and anxiety.

This is the time when the patient's loved ones most need to do the right things to help. However, loved ones, relatives, and friends visiting often do not know what is best. They are usually anxious, panic-stricken, and in tears. In their interaction with the comatose patient they display their desperation and distress. They may frantically say anything they feel. They might encourage the patient to be strong. They might express how important he or she is. Some may literally shake the person to wake her or him up. The visitor may make a lot of noise, turn on the radio, sing, or act as if waking up a sleeping child.

The problem with a comatose person is that she or he is already in a state of anxiety and panic. In that state, he or she struggles in vain and becomes caught up with tension. The types of "helpful" actions mentioned above evoke greater panic and fear and the outcome is deeper tension. The experience is much like being pulled into quicksand. The more one struggles, the faster one sinks. Tension from inappropriate attempts to save a comatose person only result in further deterioration. The noise and hullabaloo can irritate. Even someone who has the flu prefers to rest in a quiet environment as noises sicken the patient more.

A comatose person vacillates between states of unconsciousness and an awareness of the surroundings temporarily conscious of feelings with some comprehension of what is being said. The person may shift, becoming engrossed in his or her own thoughts, emotions and dream-like events. Awareness of external perceptions becomes sharply reduced and appears to come from a distance or through thick walls. At other times she or he becomes alert and quite aware.

Instructions. What is helpful for the comatose patient is to be comforted and assured that he or she will be all right. Encourage the patient to relax, breathe deeply and calmly. Doing this is the equivalent of throwing a life-saving rope to the person trapped in quicksand. If she or he grasps the rope, pulling the person out will be easy.

When stretching and massaging a comatose person, make sure not to use much force. He or she won't be able to protest if the experience is painful. Excess pain is a trauma that may terminate life. I know of cases where forceful stretching and massaging on post-stroke patients and arthritic children threw them into a sudden coma and death.

For comatose patients, attempts to stimulate brain activity are undesirable. For example, the use of drugs to boost brain functioning or to nourish the brain can be detrimental. Such an effort increases the patient's brain activity. It encourages energy from the entire body to surge upward increasing tension and quickening deterioration. The reverse (the downward release) is what is needed to help recovery. You can help by attending to the patient with encouragement and confidence building assurances.

A Case Example: *A male patient, in his early twenties, had a motor-cycle accident resulting in a broken left thigh bone. He was hospitalized and the surgery was apparently successful. Unknown to his parents, he was addicted to drugs and friends who visited him brought some for him to use. After taking them he slipped into a deep coma. The doctors, after medical tests, announced that he was in critical condition. He could be kept alive with a life support system but full recovery was unlikely.*

A month later, I was called in to help. On first sight, I observed him moving his limbs involuntarily and uttering incomprehensible sounds. I spent a minute touching and patting his lower abdomen. Then I went into meditation. Ten minutes later, he was in a delirium and screamed. He woke up, complained of pain and hunger, and asked to see his girlfriend. I calmed him down. Five minutes later he sat up asking for food and for his friend. He was fully awake but was still in a daze. Gradually, he recognized his brother and noticed my presence.

Later his doctor was amazed with his recovery and asked him to explain what happened. He did not disclose my visit. After three days he was discharged. Subsequently his father brought him to my Center to have his broken leg treated. His mental and physical functions were fully restored. One month later, after four sessions, his leg was completely healed and he stopped using crutches. His legs were straight without any shortening or limp.

The CFQ Remedy

In *"Energy Meditation: Healing the Body, Freeing the Spirit,"* I wrote a chapter about how to revive a comatose patient. Some readers may react to suggestions in this book in a manner similar to some of the reactions to that chapter, "Sounds too simple and unbelievable. It won't work." Many people are controlled by the prevailing admiration for highly specialized medical knowledge and technology. The insight that healing is linked to simplicity is something few people really appreciate.

Here simplicity is analogous to Nature's simplicity. Survival comes from natural, simple acts such as breathing in and out to sustain life and the ability to walk by extending one foot forward after the other. Perhaps the prevalence of some illnesses today springs from forgetting to simply breathe in-and-out. "Fanciful breathing" hardly does the job. Replacing walking with fanciful vehicles and technology hardly helps our bodily well-being. Indeed, getting back to plain, healthy living requires a lot of time and physical work. Fortunately, all I am advocating is openness to what is relevant (the power of simplicity). Without an acceptance of the place of simplicity in creation, I hardly expect anyone to try my suggestions. I am convinced that if the method suggested here is properly followed, at least 50 per cent of the comatose patients so treated will benefit and recover rapidly from their coma. For severe cases, a healing ability backed by long years of CFQ practice is probably necessary.

The Human Factor: A comatose patient is usually in a state of anxiety and panic that he or she is unable to control. If the patient is your loved one, you will of course be equally anxious and distraught. In that state you will not be able to help. Try to let go, cool off and calm down with deep diaphragmatic breathing. This is difficult but a pre-requisite. Use CFQ if you can. Your ability to realize peace is obviously much better than that of the patient.

Instructions. Calming yourself and having a sincere desire to help will reduce the patient's anxiety and panic and pave the way for recovery. Clear your thoughts and emotions to replace tension with peace. This is not the time to become erudite by studying medical facts. Nor does it help to worry about what the doctors say regarding the patient's poor condition and prognosis. If you hold on to negative ideas, you only help materialize the patient's doom. Your actions matter. Remain in a calm and optimistic state (even if cynics consider you silly) so that God's healing power can flow through you.

Tune into CFQ energy through the technique suggested under "dependent healers." Those who have practiced CFQ for at least six months will have sufficient ability to do a good job. If you have just picked up this book and want to try this method, I encourage you to trust it and wish you the best. Reading through this entire book will help you to understand the principles and improve your healing power.

The Revival Procedure: The first thing to do is to talk calmly and lovingly to the patient, asking him or her to loosen the body. Keep assuring the patient that she or he will be fine and that you have learned how to help. Touch the patient's lower abdomen in the area just below the navel with your palm and tap gently. Encourage the patient to breathe easily and deeply all the way down to the abdomen. This area is traditionally called the *"Palace of Life,"* and is crucial for bringing life back or keeping a person alive. It is also crucial for de-stressing and bringing down the upsurged tension-forces and releasing all the way down through the lower limbs. Guide the patient, *"Continue to breathe deeply. Inhale. Let your abdomen expand. Exhale. Let your abdomen contract. Breathe calmly."* Place the palm of your hand on the patient's lower abdomen. Encourage the patient to breathe easily and loosely.

If done properly, some patients may display an obvious change in breathing pattern within minutes. You may observe rapid eye movements or blinking, and an increase in involuntary movements. These are indications of positive changes. Continue with this procedure for ten minutes.

Touch and pat the person's body in a downward direction from the head all the way down through the limbs. This tapping helps to dispel the numbness and lack of sensations, thus restoring physiological functions. The patient's sense of feeling is likely to be strongest in the upper torso including the face, head and chest region. These are the areas where physiological functions still likely remain intact. Touching and tapping further down the torso is to encourage and expand normal physiological functions here. Touching in this manner flushes the sensations down to restore life activity. Doing anything that provokes an upsurge of energy means abandoning the whole body. This would include a focus on the head such as medication does trying to nourish and activate the brain. Such interventions could end the patient's life even for patients with only moderate problems. If the patient survives, it is because, fortunately, the patient's survival instinct is able to overcome the adverse interventions.

Repeat these energy releasing actions as often as possible. Take care to do so gently in order to avoid causing pain. The final touch is achieved by patting the bed moving away from the hands and leg regions to complete flushing the tension down and out through the limbs. Encourage the patient to loosen and relax. Assure the person that she or he will be all right at the same time as you do this procedure.

Move, shake, stretch and loosen his or her limbs gently. Take care not to forcefully stretch stiff joints. When stretching the fingers, stronger force can be applied as this tends not to be painful. Encourage the patient to relax any way she or he can. Peace, attend to peace.

A bedridden person is susceptible to poor circulation and bed sores. Turn his or her body to alternate the pressure on each side every two to four hours. Pat gently downward several times each day for five to ten minutes. This disperses numbness and enhances blood circulation. Talk to the patient often in a normal conversational style on pleasant issues and light topics. Avoid words and issues that can cause any worry, pressure or concern for the patient. Sound as calm and confident as possible and tactfully assure the person that he or she will recover completely.

Bringing Through CFQ Healing Energy. When the above procedures are properly followed, about half of all comatose patients will show daily improvement after one to two days and even wake up within one or two weeks. However, progress may not be readily obvious so it is important to repeat the procedures daily. Continue beyond two weeks if necessary with full faith and sincerity.

Some patients may improve rapidly until a certain point and then level off. Some show little response to the described procedures alone. These are the cases where bringing through direct CFQ healing energy might make the difference. The most powerful healing process is the use of CFQ meditation to radiate Metta. Meditative healing dissolves the sticky glue-like dark cloud of tension, opening it out and flushing it down. Only a proficient practitioner backed by long years of practice will be able to do this.

Those who are able to successfully tune in as "dependent healers" will have a sense of rapport and an energy connection with the patient. They will have clear ideas of what to do. They may spontaneously tap, move, and massage and also do some sweeping, cleansing, and flipping actions. Take care not to be carried away by vanity, excitement and ego. In healing it is important to remain calm and detached at all times. Avoid using excessive strength to stretch or massage. This is unlikely to happen if the healer remains calm and is not carried way. When the process is completed, the healer will spontaneously conclude, ending the session's rapport with the patient.

In addition, the helper can dedicate CFQ exercises to the benefit of the patient. They need not do these exercises in the patient's presence. They can also be done at a remote distance, say at home, while the patient is in the hospital. Neither does the patient need to be informed. Full faith and sincerity will provide the connection and rapport. When performed with calmness and a loving, selfless attitude, the practitioner will often feel a vivid sense of benevolence, connection, and purposefulness.

Prayers. In the presence of a person in a coma, loved ones and relatives will normally turn to prayer in an attempt to resolve their predicament. No matter what faith one believes in, there is a great truth: the Divine helps through the one who prays. The helper is used as a channel. Therefore, the helper must allow time to achieve deep relaxation in order for the Divine's healing power to come through. During prayer, the helper must calm down, relax and loosen up and should vividly feel the Divine power. The most common obstacles are the helper's disturbed thoughts, emotions and inability to remain calm and peaceful. Leave out your intentions, wishes and desires. Be sure to remain calm and detached from any disturbances. Allow whatever happens to happen without fighting to change it.

The Waking Up: In many cases, the waking up process is abrupt and observable. The patient may fight and struggle to wake up. Some may cry in pain while twisting and turning their limbs. If you witness this, encourage the patient to let go, to remain calm and easy, not to hold back, and allow the pain and cramps to move out. Some patients may dream-talk their way out. In that case, remind them who they are and tell them to wake up from their dreams. Patients who wake up in this manner often do not retain any serious damage.

Other patients may wake up gradually. These people are often left with serious problems or defects such as paralysis, a stiffened or immobile body or limbs, memory loss, and deficits in mental and physiological functions. What is most important is that the patient wake up. The sooner the right procedures are applied, the faster the probability of succeeding with the least damage. Given time and perseverance, most damage can be remedied (refer to other chapters on how to use CFQ).

A Case Example: *A female patient, in her early twenties, was returning home from lunch when two men jumped out of a car and tried to abduct her. She put up a struggle and screamed for help. Passers-by joined in to shout for help and the would-be abductors fled. The patient was in a state of shock after returning home and was strangely quiet. She did not tell anyone about the incident. Suddenly she attempted to jump off the first floor of the house. Her fiancé and sister, both CFQ students, were present and* *stopped her in time. Still in shock, she struggled and lost consciousness. Despite trying for two hours they were unable to wake her up. They took her to see a doctor who was unable to do anything. Finally, she was driven to my Center.*

The young woman, when brought in, was completely limp except for her tight jaws. She had no eye movements, the pupils were dilated, and her lips black. Her breathing was shallow with slight chest movements and her faint heartbeat was rapid. Her condition had become critical. It had been two and half hours since she became unconscious.

I normally do not work on emergency cases and only after normal medical treatment. However, I knew this family well and was sure that I could do this job. I began my own procedure for coma cases. Touching her lower abdomen, I spoke aloud to her encouraging her to breathe deeply. She did not respond. Her body and limbs remained completely limp when touched and shaken. I repeated the procedure three times without success. I held on to my composure while resuming touching her abdomen at the same time breathing deeply and visualizing that she follow me. All of a sudden she drew in a strong gasp of air and her abdomen began to heave with her breathing.

I went into meditation. After 15 minutes she screamed as if in pain. She was struggling, raising and twisting her arms. She waved them uncontrollably in the air with her hands and fingers wringing and strangely twisted. Her legs seemed to be cramped and her toes were twisted. I spoke to her softly to encourage her to calm down, be relaxed and allow the pain and cramping to move out. I encouraged her to remain detached. Finally it was over, she sat up and was fully conscious. She drank a glass of warm water and calmly narrated her traumatic encounter. Since then she has returned to normal with no remaining stress reactions.

17

Resilience To Overcome Cancer

○ ○

Energy flow is the basic premise of health in TCM. If qi (energy) and blood flow smoothly, the body's immunity to hundreds of diseases is strengthened. Poor energy flow gives rise to diseases and diseases in turn hinder energy flow. Blockages give rise to lethargy, weaknesses, depression, and hamper physiological functions. The restoration of health is basically achieved by restoring smooth energy flow and clearing away blockages.

CFQ practice is equipped with the necessary processes to enable a person to recover: It dissolves and unloads the energy burden of disease facilitating all-round repair and rejuvenation in the physical body, mind and spirit. It harnesses the bioenergy flow of all the major meridians to revitalize all the organs and restore overall well-being. The key is to loosen, undo and move out tension forces in the body parts, even if the body has become weakened by disease.

The Nature of Cancer

Our prevailing understanding of cancer describes mutated, malignant cells as the cause of cancer. This chapter attempts to go beyond this line of thinking and proceed to suggestions focused on how cancer can be overcome. Throughout this book, I have been asserting that the primary agent of disease is debased energy fabricated by trauma-provoking thoughts, actions, emotions or physical inactivity. These problem making aspects of life can be authored by ourselves or others. The absorption of debased energy is a natural time-involved process and is increasingly evident in aging. Drawn-in energy accumulates as enormous forces that become condensed and solidified within and around a physically unbalanced body. This accumulation forms deformations, folds, lines, and wrinkles. The physical appearance of a person will not usually show these features until old age. However, when excessive debased energy is fabricated, a person feels stiffness and discomfort often described as tension, stress or trauma. With adequate rest, an individual is able to absorb these forces and might feel refreshed, but in actual fact, the problem is not released. Prolonged and continual exposure to such accumulative and destructive forces is extremely harmful.

The radiating, dissolving and releasing features of CFQ healing energy are in sharp contrast to the absorbing feature of the tension-accumulating process. The opening-out process of CFQ reveals the true nature of the absorbed debased energy, solidified as a "glue-like" force that renders cells and organs dysfunctional. This energy-glue consolidates in the body, causing the formation of physical folds and stiffness as well as energy blockages. Eventually, physiological functions of the body such as blood circulation and essential supply and waste removal operations are obstructed. Gerontology studies have revealed a deteriorating pattern with every successive generation of replacement cells. The reason is obvious from the tension-related energy perspective.

The Decay Factor in Cancer

The elimination of waste products related to metabolic and cellular activity is a critical biological function necessary for the maintenance of life. Obstruction of the waste-and-dead-cell removal process gives rise to the accumulation of toxic substances. Corrosive residues are trapped and contaminate the body. When this decaying contamination sets in, healthy cells become corrupted. But healthy cells are resilient by nature and resist dying without a fight. They "mutate" to adapt to the adverse conditions fabricated by decay, and they feed on the toxins. Eventually, they coalesce and may form a tumor or lump in their common effort to prevent the decay from spreading. These are the cells called cancerous.

Cancer cells in this view are victims of a deplorable condition. CFQ understands cancer as a defensive system developed to protect the body by holding the decay in check. The emphatic message is that the cancerous cells are not the perpetrators of the disease, as is commonly believed. From this perspective, a systematic approach that attempts to destroy cancer cells does nothing to eliminate the cause of the cancer. The situation might be compared to the ancient king who killed the bearers of bad news or to a nation that banned its artists because they were expressing the political failures of the nation's leaders. Sooner rather than later, the consequence to the country, as to the body, is nothing short of disastrous.

If the body's defensive system succeeded and the decay process was properly neutralized, the resulting condition might be diagnosed as a non-malignant tumor. In my view, if the body's defenses do not allow an escalation of rapid decay, the resultant growth may well be controllable. This condition may persist for years. This benign "cancerous" growth may contain the decay for 20 or 30 years or until the person achieves old age, without showing further undesirable symptoms. On the other hand, when conditions are conducive to escalating decay, by reason of the body's defenses being excessively provoked, cancer cells proliferate, spread rapidly and ultimately die with their host trying to protect life.

It is not uncommon for people to have non-malignant tumors. Treatment approaches, the patient's knowledge and beliefs play an extremely important role in determining the outcome. Sometimes the body's defense system is allowed to function in the best possible way and contain the decay (develop undetected tumors). Sometimes the body's health protective function may be undermined in a way that inadvertently enhances rapid decay.

Cancer is, of course, not a privilege of the elderly but may be suffered by people of all ages. Its cause, in my view, remains the same:the decay factor provoked by energy blockages to the waste-and-dead-cell removal process. The risk factors for this lethal obstruction include the following:

1. Genetic factors constitute a major risk. In these cases genes can be viewed as, providing from birth, an extremely strong, inherent energy trap. When activated, this trap becomes a lethal obstruction where decay can set in.

2. Another significant possibility is the role of infections that destroy cells. These infections may lead to cancer where physiological functions are unable to repair the destruction. One example in this category is uterine cancer. However, any form of infection can be suspect, as even common ones such as colds, flu, and infected cuts and bruises can contribute to a cumulative weakening effect. When the body's system overcomes an infection, some of the viruses or bacteria may be more resistant and may form into "pockets" that hide within the body. Such residual, infectious pockets may be hidden in areas where normal blood flow is not abundant. They may continue to destroy cells, causing decay. Often such symptoms are not apparent until the decay becomes massive.

    Other decay related risk factors include:

3. Injuries and forceful physical impacts or blows that do not completely heal. Injuries often result in the stiffening or hardening of muscle fibers that may then obstruct physiological functions. Existing physiotherapeutic methods do not adequately clear away this stiffness or hardening. Dead cells thus trapped may eventually decay giving rise to cancer. Improper massage of an injury may cause destruction and decay.

4. Exposure to pollutants or environmental hazards including the absorption of electro-magnetic waves or radioactive exposure can cause extensive cell death.

5. A high tension lifestyle can cause an excessive "gripping effect" which derails the body's normal postural alignment and hinders physiological functions.

6. Unhealthy habits such as drinking, smoking and overeating, burden the body with toxins. Intake of undesirable or contaminated food and water also burdens the body with excessive wastes that urgently require removal. Finally, there is the iatrogenic risk factor—the situation in which treatment itself causes complications that exacerbate the course of a disease. Conventional medical, pharmacological, or behavioral treatment based on the absorbing-fabricating approach to managing, controlling or boosting the immune system can increase the risk of spreading infection and decay. The alternative holistic treatment with the letting-go and undoing process proposed here, can efficaciously drain off the decay factor and ultimately counter the problem.

The Psychological-Emotional Factor

The patient's psychological make-up has been substantially ignored in Western medicine. The biomedical model commands great authority with regard to treating life-threatening diseases. This approach to cancer treatment allows for drastic and intrusive interference using cell-destroying chemicals and painful hi-tech and sophisticated methods.

Medical experts detail the genetic and biochemical causes of cancer. For the public, the threat of cancer, knowing the victim's experience with its painful suffering, deforming physical scarring, and the belief that survival and cures are uncertain, have left a deep, fearful impression. Medical information has been very successful in driving home this negative message. It has taken on a mass propaganda-like tone to declare war on cancer. The public is advised to be constantly vigilant about the threat of cancer and patients are to combat the disease with a "fighting spirit" and to accept the necessity of conventional (slash-burn-poison) treatment.

Yet it is well known that a person's mind-set directly influences his or her physical problems and disease. There is a good deal of physiological evidence of the mind's role in determining a person's state of health, physical problems, and the course of recovery from a disease. Negative personality traits can contribute to cancer proneness. Social-emotional support can also extend survival and potentially reverse life-threatening disease. Few cancer researchers, however, highlight the significance of personality or cognitive-behavioral-emotional links between mind and the physiological pathways of the diseased body. This omission has unfortunate consequences for the search for a cancer cure. I, however, believe that the stress of living, particularly in modern society with its emphasis on mental activity is the primary root of cancer. Other factors such as pollutants, and on, as listed above, though important, play only secondary roles.

A person exists as a holistic being with body, mind and spirit. Each dimension is mutually dependent and no part can be separated. If the study of the body and treatment methods in medicine are complex, the mind can be many more times complex. The mind assimilates knowledge instantly. It thinks and responds to experiences freely without the rigid limitations of the body. The spirit is yet more complex as it is the basis of mental and physical existence. It is the mysterious life force that encompasses every existence from past to future.

The psychological state of a cancer patient (or of anyone suffering from a life threatening disease), all too frequently holds negative thoughts, anxiety, restlessness, depression, irritability and fear. This is not intended as an observed finding or implying personal fault on the part of the victim. I rather seek to join others in a compassionate understanding of the difficulty faced. The cancer victim can in no way be blamed for feeling helpless. The fact that the biomedical approach has not been spectacularly successful (in contrast to overcoming heart disease) and the expectation that cancer treatments are often immensely painful and dangerous have powerfully contributed to pervasive negative psychological expectations. The cancer survivor can find him or herself drifting into a state of self pity, faced with a compelling reminder that time is running short. Mental activity, in many cases, may overwhelmingly dwell on past events rather than face what lies ahead. Life can easily come to revolve around what has been done and what else should be done, how to fight the disease, and what other remedies are required or available.

Such an undesirable and counterproductive psychological state is often the response to a cancer diagnosis. The physician's exhortation to fight the disease further strengthens the patient's stress response. Facing an "incurable" disease may fabricate further obstructions to the patient's physiological functions leading to rapid deterioration. The victim becomes exhausted from this state of mind which offers no feasible solution but rather awakens more psychological, emotional and physical pain.

Truly, over-awareness combined with the mind's heightened imagination stimulated by frequent media coverage certainly puts the fear of cancer in everyone. From the very young to the very old, when an individual feels discomfort or fatigue, understandably an idea that may flash across the mind is their vulnerability to cancer. Some patients may experience undesirable psychological states such as compulsive negative thoughts, anxiety and irritability long before a diagnosis is given. These often prompt them to go for check-ups. Some who are especially vulnerable take the idea as real and insist on medical tests to determine the possibilities. Even if the outcome is negative some people may insist on further tests to confirm the fact that they do not have cancer. Some, vulnerable to the fear of cancer, may assume they are ill even in the absence of corroborative medical evidence.

The psychological impact on a person diagnosed with cancer can be extremely severe. In fact many, even now, take such a diagnosis as a death sentence. Consider the person hearing the diagnosis of cancer. Many instantly go into shock. Consciousness rockets sky high or blanks out. Visions of calamity may appear like nightmares and their ears may buzz strangely. The over-stressed mind can come to a dead halt and leave one feeling dry and depleted. Some patients may physically collapse or become disoriented as they leave the physician's office. The days that follow feel like an unending nightmare, life in a world apart from ones surroundings. Each of these sensations is non-erasable and really exists at the consciousness-memory-spirit level. No amount of counseling and positive thinking may be good enough. Often such efforts hardly scratch the surface of the mountain of trauma formed. How many people (even when healthy) can survive this kind of punishment? Few do!

The problem is further compounded if the cancer patient deviates from the normal routine of work and activities. Absorbing the news of the disease is shocking enough. A person so weakened and depressed may no longer feel confident enough to work or, for that matter, do anything. The usual treatment of surgery, radiation and chemotherapy make it almost impossible for a person to continue with a normal routine. Recuperation can quite absorb weeks and months. With all these changes, a most natural outcome involves being swept away by a whirl of depressive thoughts and undesirable emotions. This is also unfortunate as the cancer patient frequently has too much idle time. Few people can actually emerge triumphant, resuming normal work and activities. Many people are so caught up in the cancer relationship that they remain obsessed with it until their last breath.

Those who are able to avoid this psychological trap stand a much better chance of recovery, suffer less, and are better able to deal with the problem. These people can best be described as resilient. Resilience comes from being determined to carry on normal life and activities, and to avoid the web of doom too frequently spawned by the mind. Resilience is not about telling oneself to be "strong", or to "fight the cancer" in the way proposed by many theorists, clinicians and specialists who base their recommendations on logic.

My experience suggests that it is best to follow the guideline: "Do not fight, just carry on living!" That means, as much as possible, to carry on with the normal activities expected of a person who is alive. "Fighting" cancer leads to the arousal of an unending stress response depriving the patient of a state of relaxation. That prevents the possibility of switching on one's self-regulatory ability to "walk out" of the disease problem. Once the patient resorts to fighting in a seemingly incurable situation, he or she is quickly drawn into a psychological pit of doom. Negative thoughts inevitably arise. Thinking positive thoughts at such a time is a herculean task.

The basis of many psychological problems stems from an energy matrix encompassing the spiritual, mental, and physical levels. This can be fabricated by debased tension-laden energy. It cannot be changed by positive thought re-programming. Rather, it is necessary to dissolve the tension-laden energy and unload the burden it places on the body and the mind. But even with effective energy unloading, it takes time to produce a significant positive change. Meanwhile, one must keep meaningfully busy and avoid being drawn into undesirable states of mind.

A Case Example: *A male patient in his late fifties complained about indigestion. Hospital tests diagnosed advanced liver cancer. No treatment was recommended. The physician told him he would not live more than three months. He came to see me with his brother at the suggestion of a relative. The initial healing session relaxed him and he soon regained his appetite. A second session together with a weekly meditation practice was scheduled. During initiation he manifested varied spontaneous movements. However, his wife and daughter objected strongly to his coming for CFQ treatment. They wanted him to adhere to a herbal remedy (which he did) and to join another meditation group which claimed astounding healing. He refused the latter and was encouraged by his brother to continue CFQ. Treatment went on for three weeks. On the fourth week, however, he wanted to quit* *and complained that he found the meditation depressing. His brother continued to attend the meditation classes regularly.*

He joined the other meditation group and was an immediate hit. Whenever he meditated, he manifested dramatic and impressive movements which were interpreted by that group as divine guidance. This involuntary movement effect probably occurred as a result of his CFQ meditation initiation. When he joined the other group, self-suggestion capitalized on his releasing ability. That moved him into a trance, a feature that other members had not developed. They failed to understand the patient's movements but held them in awe.

I did not hear further about him for eight months. His brother came and asked me to see him. He had felt unwell two weeks earlier and was admitted to a cancer hospital in grave condition. One week later his family convinced the hospital to give him a chemotherapy drip. This was a last resort as his condition was terminal. He became paralyzed, semi-blind, and could no longer eat nor have bowel movements. He spoke to his brother about wishing to see me.

He was delighted when I visited him and expressed regret for discontinuing the CFQ sessions and meditation. His complexion had darkened and it showed slight jaundice. He complained of a pent-up, indescribable discomfort yet suffered no physical pain. I proposed a healing session so as to help him in whatever manner possible. He gladly accepted. After the session, he said he felt much better and thanked me repeatedly.

I suggested another visit the following day. On the second visit, he was obviously anticipating my arrival. He narrated how much more comfortable he felt since my first visit. His dark complexion had become lighter. I performed another healing session on him. At midnight he passed away without any obvious suffering.

Comments: The reason for the decision to discontinue his CFQ involvement was probably his experiencing a release from emotional burdens. These had become unbearable as a result of the strong objections from his wife and daughter. Personally, he felt that CFQ helped him. That was why he wanted to see me again during his last moments. Despite the fact that he had only received healing three times and practiced CFQ meditation for three weeks, he was helped to the extent of surviving nine months instead of the three predicted by his doctor.

The Energy-Consciousness-Karmic Factor

For practitioners of CFQ, the body-mind is understood to be a cosmic created system that is faultless and can survive throughout a lifespan. Every activity, however, leaves an imprint. Certain activities, experiences, traits or environmental influences fabricate heavier than normal loading. This overload can disrupt physiological functions, giving rise to life threatening conditions. In the case of a cancer patient, not only is the physical body diseased, the mind is more affected and the spirit even more. As the body-mind-spirit holistically and mutually influence and contribute to the problem, the ability of life to carry on becomes increasingly limited.

Reflect on our understanding of human consciousness in terms of the depth of the various levels of consciousness. All obstructions, burdens or debased energy forces are drawn deep within one's mind and spirit. Such energy forces not only degrade and impede physiological functions but give rise to atrophy. They also burden the mind with negative thoughts and depression. A depressed person's mood is felt to be shadowy and gray. The dark forces of *mano*-consciousness (beyond the body and mind's consciousness deep into the unconscious) are too strong and bloated to be ignored. When a person is facing a life-threatening situation, if the right corrections are not adopted in time, the natural process itself can give rise to rapid disintegration. Diseased and depressed states arouse and excite the rapid absorption of debased energy. Normal interventions aimed at resolving the problem unwittingly quicken the rapid absorption.

With the intensification of debased energy forces activated, the tension within the individual strengthens. The body is further seized up causing more physiological malfunction, while consciousness-energy continues to be pushed upwards. The possible consequences are further depression and even hallucinations if the person becomes "spaced out." The drawn-in and compacting effect registered in the first seven levels of consciousness also entangles the *alaya*-consciousness. The energy force takes the form of "karmic seeds" that are sorted out and summarized in the milky white body, which survives death.

Again, karma is the rule of cause and effect. The process of suffering in the course of a disease is due to personal and/or non-personal past actions. The causes are often too complex to be explained by a right or wrong analysis. Whatever happened, who is right and who is wrong, is no longer an important issue especially when the disease is life threatening. Some people are obviously not personally in the wrong, yet they suffer. For instance, a victim of violence who suffers the trauma might eventually fall victim to cancer. The victim is certainly not personally responsible but has been unable, through no fault of their own, to satisfactorily deal with the trauma.

Karma is certainly not unfair if completely understood. Attempting to analyze rights and wrongs often results in hatred and vengeance. It is better to focus loving and compassionate energy on changing the karma by melting away the debased energy at the core of the cancer. Whatever happened in the past, it is still incidental to the fact that one is alive. Accept the facts as they occur and "walk away" from the ones you do not like. No analysis, no right or wrong and no why. Let the infinite Wisdom guide.

The past cannot be recreated. Once you have learned what the past has to teach you, thinking about the past is futile. Worst of all by doing so you shield off your entitlement to a better future. But neither can the future be created by idle thinking. Living out of love, peace and compassion is needed. Such living naturally expresses itself in a smile.

When you truly smile from your depths your radiance extends to the whole eternal reality. You find that God is within you and you are within God. Ultimate intimacy is real. Nothing else can be more real than the peace that dwells within your consciousness. Even if the mountains tremble, not a ripple need be stirred up in the tranquil lake of your heart. What disease? What problem is there? What pain? What karma? Good or bad, embodied things are minute indeed. If you touch the spiritual reality even for a second, you will see the miracle for yourself!

Western & Alternative Medicine

Western medicine considers cancerous cells as perpetrators of more and more renegade cells that have multiplied out of control and so must be destroyed at all cost. While the treatment approach is the outcome of years of clinical hard work and research, the side effects are obvious. Research into new treatment procedures as well as alternative approaches go on relentlessly. However, despite all medical and scientific findings, the human body together with it's physiological functions remains very much a mystery. This is due in large part to the constraint effected by a basic assumption that the physical body is all that matters for human life to go on.

Most people view with horror the common slash-burn-poison treatment approach to cancer. But they uphold the trust that the medical profession is the recognized authority and no other perspective can do a better job. The idea of dispensing with conventional treatment is unimaginable and unforgivable. Cancer, however, despite some medical successes, remains a killer disease that annually claims millions of lives world wide.

No healer should confuse a patient by proposing alternative treatment to begin with. Patients should be encouraged to choose the treatment they believe in with full faith and without regret. To be fair, conventional cancer treatments are the fruit of an immense amount of good hearted work by highly trained clinicians dedicated to saving lives. However, we need to be reminded that despite differences in paradigm and approaches, the well-being and cure of cancer patients is the priority.

Our discussion of an alternative decay causation theory of cancer, seeing cancer cells as victims rather than as perpetrators, has the following treatment implications:

1. The formation of lumps or tumors is where the decay products are being "dumped." Their roots, however, may be widely distributed. If the tumors are surgically removed, the decay may find new dumping grounds. After surgery, the surrounding tissue becomes hardened and deformed. This combined with the surgical shock is highly conducive to further decay.

2. Radiation therapy burns off large sections of body tissue resulting in massive hardening. Not only are the side-effects of such treatment bad for overall health but the hardening obstructs various physiological functions. The body is forced to dispose of or deal with the destroyed cells. But if the body had been able to efficiently carry out this process in the first place, there probably would not be any disease. And now with treatment extensively destroying cancerous as well as healthy cells, can we hope that the body will be able to satisfactorily eliminate the waste? If not, a delay in the removal of dead cells can cause further massive decay.

3. Chemotherapy kills off cells in the whole body by poisoning. As a result, the patient becomes drastically weakened. How many of the already weakened and depressed patients can survive further weakening to return to reasonable strength? Moreover, can the body satisfactorily and rapidly dispose of the poison and the dead cells left in the body after treatment? In terminal cases, cancer has spread to the whole body. Might it be that the spreading of the cancer is in fact due to the poison and the massive decay of dead cells?

Alternative Medicine. According to a recent estimate by the American Association of Alternative Medicine, one out of two cancer patients have tried out some remedy classified as an alternative medicine. With the prevailing attitudes, it is hard to expect that the public will sit back and rely on one form of treatment. More often than not, they resort to multiple remedies simultaneously, including religion, faith healing and shamans.

There are genuine alternative medical practitioners who rely upon secret skills passed down for generations, or on personal knowledge, practice and research. Some of them can be so skillful that they bring about amazing results considered impossible by Western medicine. However, due to the varied methods and quality, and the difficulty distinguishing true healers from quacks, the pursuit and discovery of good alternative possibilities depends largely on luck.

Herbs. There are herbs that may give positive effects in the short run but have adverse effects in the long term. There are a few hundred herbs (mainly those that produce a cooling cleansing effect) that give a sense of improvement within a few days. But after several months the adverse effects become obvious. There are also herbs that give a mood boosting effect to make the patients feel cheerful and strong. But some of them also boost the spread of cancer. As far as I have been able to discover there is to date no reliable herb of any kind that can provide lasting benefits for a cancer patient.

There are hundreds of herbs derived from plants that grow abundantly in the wild. Many are derived from exotic species. Many herbs are promoted by direct selling companies. Some give an almost immediate sense of improvement but produce adverse reactions after prolonged usage. For those patients who want to increase their chances of a good recovery, careful evaluation of hearsay and the recommendations of well-wishes is necessary. Their intentions may be good but they may not know the full implications of what they tell you. For example, the popular herbal root for overcoming fatigue, ginseng, should be avoided. Ginseng has a boosting and refreshing effect which makes a patient feel strong and cheery but may also bring on effects undesirable for a cancer victim.

A popularly used herbal plant that grows wild locally is rodent tuber (*typhonium divaricatum*). This herb might prove, with much more testing, to be beneficial in the long run. Some studies show that it can control the spread of cancer and some anecdotal evidence suggests that the juice extract has extended the life of terminal cancer patients by over ten years. I suspect that it has an anti-decay property which stops the decay from spreading.

Preparation: Use the entire plant, about 50 grams from three plants, for each daily dose. Clean by washing the plants and crush them by pounding. Wear rubber gloves in the preparation as the root causes skin irritation on contact. Squeeze out the juice using a piece of thin cloth. Mix with some honey to consume one to three times daily. Ingest the juice on an empty stomach and wait thirty minutes before taking any food. For those with gastric problems, do not take the juice on an empty stomach.

Traditional Chinese Medicine. I have discussed the issue of cancer with several Chinese physician friends. Their general tendency is a reluctance to be involved in any manner with cancer treatment. Some are confident that they are able to help relieve and manage the pain and side effects of mainstream medical treatment. TCM, however, does not enjoy much recognition here and local practitioners are content to play a supportive role.

Food. The popular belief is that since cancer patients are generally weak, they need to be stronger and thus need more nutrition. I disagree with this thinking. Cancer patients generally suffer a lack of appetite. The lack of appetite many be interpreted as the body's natural response trying to slow down deterioration by cutting down food intake. Plain, simple cereal based food with vegetables supply an abundance of fiber readily digested and absorbed. Highly nutritious food not only sabotages the body's natural response but adds another burden to it. The poorly digested food is likely to be stuck in the cancerous region and becomes a toxicant with rapid decay effects. Observing the rule of plain simple food (try not to go without regular meals) is to respect the message given by the body. The practice of CFQ will enhance physiological functions and at the same time minimize undesirable thoughts and emotions. It will restore a good appetite rapidly. Take care not to be overly concerned with nutrition even when your appetite returns. Trust the ability of your body to process and convert plain food to satisfy your nutritional needs.

The idea of cancer patients observing a total vegetarian diet is fast gaining popularity. I have a reservation: Over tens of thousands of years of human evolution, human beings have developed a habit of omnivorous eating. A complete change may be problem free if done systematically over a few generations. Healthy people, however, who willingly switch to a vegetarian diet may experience adverse consequences. For a cancer patient, the risk of severe consequences is too high. An abrupt change of diet may be interpreted by the body's system as a deprivation and provoke a stress response.

However, meat with its acidic and decay-provoking properties is not good for cancer patients. They should therefore switch to a cereal based diet with abundant vegetables and little meat. For those who go on a complete vegetarian diet, a generous supplement of milk to reduce the stress response to the drastic diet switch is advisable. As always, do not be overly concerned about the issue.

The consumption of large quantities of fruits and vegetables is widely advised. I know of people who daily consume a half dozen assorted fruits and vegetables blended together—an amount that should last a week. The amounts I've seen are sufficient to make a healthy person quite ill if taken repeatedly for several days. Here the rule is to take fruit and vegetables daily in reasonable amounts and in a natural way (avoid blending) to ensure that you do not consume too much. Suitable commonly available fruits and vegetables include: apples, pears, cucumbers, carrots, guavas, star fruits, bananas and oranges. Consume them on a rotation basis and exclude those that disrupt digestion.

Exercise. Patients concerned with recovery will often exercise vigorously in an attempt to regain muscle strength and overcome weakness. This might include strenuous jogging, a heavy work-out in the gym, and even weight training. I do not encourage strenuous or vigorous exercises. The weakened muscles of a cancer victim lack endurance, are easily injured, and take a long time to rest and recover from tiredness. The reduced food intake common among cancer patients also does not encourage strain. Furthermore, the exertion from exercise fabricates tension which compounds the disease. Those who exercise vigorously will experience deteriorating abilities leading to frustration. This shatters an already thin sense of confidence, compounds anxiety and depression, and aggravates the disease problem. CFQ exercises do not give rise to the above problems and enhance rapid progress. It is therefore recommended that you replace normal exercises with a CFQ practice. Note, however, that exercising for the sake of socializing and adding a variety of activities is encouraged.

The Nuisance: In many instances, recommendations and suggestions from well-wishers are not lacking. Some victims, aided by such "helpers," will end up receiving hundreds of names, places, addresses, secret herbal formulae and recipes and suggestions. The intention and heart of well-wishers may be good but they can become a troubling burden. While proper and appropriate responses are crucial, the rule here is that the patient should not be allowed to get confused by too many suggestions. When they all sound convincing, which one should the patient try? Assuming that most of the suggestions are helpful, following one may be good but following a few concurrently can be disastrous. With so many options to select from, the cancer patient may hop from one to another without the patience to wait for lasting effects. It is better to ignore the suggestions than allow them to make life harder.

The true remedy for any serious problem arises from within the patient. The person needs to calm down and relax, reduce emotional anxiety and mental disturbance, and set about doing the right actions for recovery. Trust God to help. If the person is disturbed and frustrated by multiple treatments she or he may no longer have peace. If the patient is impressed with one or two suggestions but refrains from trying them out, the yearning itself is harmful. If carried away in a relentless search for a cure, the patient can get exhausted and easily deviate from the true remedy. The right help is: Respect the given treatment, respect peace within, respect your God.

Extreme caution must be exercised in dealing with claims touted that are clouded with exaggeration or mystery. Such features appear impressive to vulnerable patients suffering great anxiety but appear ridiculous to a normal person. For example, a so-called secret recipe for cancer turned out to be a common herb used for minor aches and pains. There was a claim about a rare fruit extract that blooms every seven years and found only in the deep jungle. It turned out to be part of a plant used for arthritic pain. People who make fantastic claims are not necessarily ill-intentioned. Perhaps they assume that cancer patients are so helpless, without any real cure, that giving them some hope can boost the placebo effect. The fact remains that every cancer case is different but the common need for all is to be alive. And to be alive depends upon understanding one's claim to be alive! It is our birthright.

Qigong and Meditation. There are reputed Qigong masters and meditators genuinely able to restore the health of cancer patients either by teaching or direct healing. They have the skills and experience to heal but patients must seek them out carefully, being aware of their true healing records and not influenced by rumors or claims. All too often, Qigong practitioners claim that they are able to heal cancer in a few days to a few months of training. They have been taught that once they start to feel some warmth or tingling sensations in their hands, they are equipped with the precious Qi needed to heal other people. But cancer is among the most difficult of problems to heal. Some cancer patients yearn for help and have strong faith and immediately feel better. Genuine healing of cancer, however, is not that simple and does not depend on "precious qi." Cancer is a challenge even for a healer with decades of experience. With a life-threatening disease like cancer, the karmic load is as heavy as a mountain and as wide as an ocean. Precious energy stored in the body is, at best, equivalent to a bucket of water used to wash away the mountain or fill up the ocean. Of course, a kind and compassionate heart matters but that is not enough to eradicate cancer.

A Case Example: *A male patient, in his fifties, was diagnosed with lung cancer. The tumor measured eight cm. in diameter. Radiation therapy was recommended. Chemotherapy, however, was not proposed probably due to his weak and depressed state. His children privately made extensive inquiries. They concluded that even radiation therapy was offered mostly for the sake of a placebo effect. However, their father was looking forward to the treatment.*

My first healing session with him preceded the start of the radiation. His children asked whether they should advise their father against keeping to the course of radiation. I told them I was not optimistic about his situation. Since he was so keen about it he might feel that the treatment was his only hope. So they should encourage him to go. I scheduled healing sessions for once a week because of the long distance they had to travel. My healing visits went on together with the radiation.

Interestingly, he did not suffer any side-effects from the radiation—no discomforts, not even hair loss. On the other hand, in my healing sessions, he often felt extreme discomfort: "My body feels like its being torn apart. My thoughts and emotions feel like exploding." However, his appetite and sleep returned after two energy healing sessions.

A month after completion of radiation (and two months since he began energy treatments—a total of 10 sessions), his x-rays showed that the cancer lump was halved in size. After 12 more sessions over a three month period he returned for the hospital check-up. The x-ray revealed that the lung cancer spot was completely gone leaving a scar. I advised that he learn CFQ meditation so that in future he could rely on his own practice without further need for direct treatment. Together with a few family members, he was initiated into meditation.

Meanwhile he continued to receive his weekly healing sessions. However he stopped meditation practice at home after a couple of sessions. Neither did he join in the group practice. He explained that he did not enjoy meditation as it lacked challenge. He preferred to do his rigorous daily walking. Knowing that it would be difficult to change his attitude, I taught him the "lotus walk" in the hope that he would use it rather than his normal strenuous walking. But he declined saying that the lotus walk also lacked challenge and excitement.

Three months later, on his routine check-up another lump measuring two cm. in diameter was discovered on the other lung. He was immediately sent for another 20 sessions of radiation therapy. At the end his X-ray showed that the cancer was arrested. But what amazed his doctor most was that the scar from his first tumor had completely vanished, a situation that was difficult to explain. About a year had passed since he was diagnosed with lung cancer.

Since he had received a total of 50 energy treatments and was now completely cleared of cancer, I felt he did not require further sessions. I again advised him to return to practicing CFQ regularly. He, however, expressed more enthusiasm about going to the next three-month checkup. I had to question him about the wisdom of such an attitude. I explained extensively the importance of living without a mental state of worry about cancer. Worries are not worthwhile, I said, as they can actualize the disease. He retorted that to ensure that no cancer is left, the "microbes" must be relent-

lessly searched out and destroyed (many local people have the idea that cancer is caused by some "germ"). He would continue on with the regular checkups.

His children complained to me that their father did not practice CFQ at all. I told them to bring their father in for a monthly energy treatment as doing something was better than nothing. He was a retiree with few social and no physical activity except his half-hour morning walk. His daily routine involved spending his time reading newspapers, and long hours sleeping in the late morning and afternoon. I was concerned that that amount of sleep was not only bad for health but could trigger the cancer again. With long hours of idle time, he could dwell on the fear of his cancer returning, and be obsessed with thinking and improperly fighting his cancer.

He still thought the energy treatment was worthwhile because of the positive mood it helped him achieve. He recommended me to a number of friends. However, he did not agree with my principles of healing. He stuck to his belief that hi-tech medical treatment would cure him while my treatment could merely play a supportive role. Over the year (1999) he came for a total of only a half dozen healing sessions.

Follow-up. In February, 2000, his regular check-up revealed that some fluid had accumulated at the bottom tip of his right lung. To his great disappointment, his physician did not propose pursuing any treatment. His children came and discussed the problem with me. I recommended that the father be brought back for weekly sessions. I reminded him to resume his CFQ practice and lotus walk. He responded with a silent protest. Three months later the x-rays showed that the fluid had accumulated further filling up half of his right lung. On his insistence, the doctor agreed to conduct a whole-body bone scan. He consumed a few glasses of a mild radioactive solution for the scan which upset his stomach. After this test, he asked about further treatment and the prognosis.

His physician gave him a pessimistic response which greatly upset him. He vowed not to return again, not even to for the results of the scan.

He came back to see me. He had lost his appetite (since the test). I told him that his condition was not hopeless. He needed, however, to help himself and act by practicing CFQ. I taught him the 7-Movement meridian/organ cleansing exercises together with the butterfly-shaking technique. He was also to resume the weekly healing session.

I found out that he did not attempt to practice on his own. He complained that when he did, he felt throbbing pain and numbness oozing all over. He claimed that he did the butterfly shaking but that was only for a few minutes. I tried to persuade him to take greater interest, explaining that clearly the practice had been effective in clearing out his problem. I assured him that if he would be more committed in the practice, he would surely recover. He kept silent. I persisted in explaining further. He finally admitted that he was unable to overcome his negative thoughts which had been disturbing him since he was first diagnosed with cancer.

To my disappointment, he did not willingly do the meridian and other exercises. No amount of encouragement from his wife or children could change his behavior. His condition continued to deteriorate. His weight loss was apparent. I spoke to his son saying that without helping himself with CFQ practice and with his unchanging attitude, the healing sessions with me were only to relieve his discomfort. This would not be sufficient to cure him. The family should not, however, force him to come unless he wished to. Indeed the father commented that after each energy treatment, he felt comfortable for two or three days. He also looked forward to the next session. Some months later he complained of dizziness when traveling by car. The dizziness was unbearable and he chose to discontinue coming to the Center for treatment.

The CFQ Remedy

I have used the CFQ energy healing method on several hundred cancer patients and conclude that at least 80 per cent show positive responses. That does not imply that 80 per cent of my patients survived. Cancer is one disease that brings extreme fear and panic. A panic-stricken person will often resort to frantically searching for a cure. Until now, CFQ has been virtually unknown except when recommended by word of mouth. Those who do not have an open-mind tend to react with disbelief and ridicule when they hear of it. In many cases, those who came to me were in the final critical stages of their illness. These victims were in a state of physical and mental desperation making a last try after everything else had failed. And yet some of them managed to recover completely. Even among those who did not survive, most of them experienced some relief from pain and discomfort where previously even morphine could not help.

A Case Example: *Three years ago, a young adult, in his late thirties, was diagnosed as having nose cancer. He was treated with a complete course of radiation therapy and chemotherapy. Two years later, however, cancer was again detected in his nose and he received a second full course of the routine treatment. Since his first course of treatment, he had suffered a side-effect that his doctors pronounced had no known remedy. He had a smelly pus discharge which dripped continuously from within his ear flowing down his cheek.*

He lived a long distance from my Center so treatments were scheduled on a weekly basis. After three sessions, the discharge was reduced. By the fifth session it had completely dried up. His dark complexion had lightened, he was no longer over-sensitive to sunlight (over-sensitivity and reaction to sunlight is common among cancer patients after having conventional medical treatment), and his stomach upset was reduced. By the eighth session, he told me he felt strong enough to resume work. He had put a new work project on hold since he had come down with the cancer.

After 12 healing sessions, he looked and felt good. His dizzy spells and other problems had vanished and he had fully recovered. I told him to start the CFQ exercises. When he could do that regularly he would not need any further direct treatment.

Incomplete CFQ Cures

There are certain trends influencing the possibilities of successful treatment which have sometimes overridden the cancer's nature and the state of the patient on first seeking CFQ treatment. Retirees and those who had been deprived of employment and normal activities did not fare as well as others. The capacity to continue to work and keep busy is important. The clinically depressed are most likely to be the ones who become trapped in negative thinking that shatters their self confidence to bring about fatigue. They may also feel hopeless and have little confidence in recovery. They feel helpless to do anything for themselves. They are less likely to survive as no amount of treatment is adequate to overcome the long hours they spend in self-sabotage, fabricating huge amounts of disease energy. The well-educated and knowledgeable also do not do as well. They tend to cling to conventional knowledge about the disease to such an extent that any alternative disease paradigm and treatment appear nonsensical. They might initially feel good about alternative healing but at the same time distrust alternative healers. Their minds tend to be fixed on the conventional wisdom: "Fight! Fight! Fight!"

Self Help. The most powerful strategy for the treatment of life-threatening diseases like cancer is to make good use of a person's survival instinct. Self help techniques may turn out to be more effective than direct energy healing. When the help of a healer is available, the patient may adopt a dependent attitude and will not do anything to help themselves. This is the single most important cause of deterioration. The patient has all the time in the world for the self-sabotage that strengthens the disease process.

Reversing the Disease Process. Problems in life (including diseases) arise from a loading at the energy level which affects the physical, mental and spiritual aspects of a person. The physical body's consciousness is superficial as well as rigid and difficult to change rapidly. The spiritual component is too deep, beyond normal understanding and very hard to alter directly. The most flexible component and the one that changes most rapidly is the mind (sixth consciousness). In turn, the mind affects the physical body and the spirit for good or bad.

The most viable way of overcoming a life-threatening disease is to start off with the mind. That does not mean just thinking positively. Positive thoughts are too weak against the overwhelming negative thoughts which become aroused the moment a positive thought is introduced. The tendency of the mind to fabricate negative thoughts must be sidestepped. The person must set about acting in ways that are conducive to recovery. These actions must override the negativity of the mind. Deterioration is slowed down or stabilized at the point of calming down enough to feel safe in the conviction that the disease is curable. Taking concrete action avoids the mind catastrophizing. Actions speak for themselves and gradually unload the energy burden blocking all levels of recovery.

The CFQ Strategy. The methods recommended here can be reasonably practiced by a self-helper for long periods of time without causing exhaustion. No matter how weak the person is, he or she should not take excessive rest as this opens the way for the person to unknowingly drift into negative thoughts. The patient should take seven hours of sleep. In some cases even less is fine. The rest of the time, after deducting for daily chores or normal work and activities, should be spent in the practice of CFQ exercises. So I am suggesting about 15 hours of daily practice for the convalescing patient. For those who are meaningfully occupied with work, however, two to four hours daily will suffice.

Strictly speaking, CFQ is not a treatment regimen but is a systematic way of living enabling the victim to claim his or her rights to survive and recover. Actions rather than mental activity speak for this claim to life. If a person is genuinely interested, she or he can realize that God has already given the birthright to life. Interest and commitment enable a claim to what you already have.

In most cases, mental deterioration occurs more rapidly than physical deterioration. A person who willingly follows the recommendations I'm offering will be able to avoid the mind's pitfalls thus bringing about an overall improvement. Even near the time of dying, few people's physical body are so worn down that life can no longer exist. More often than not, the person has already mentally given up to such an extent that their negativity can be interpreted as the mind being dead months before the body's final demise. Whatever the situation, to predict a person's doom is inhumane. That is God's decision. Human empowerment is present to be able to do away with mental interference so as to leave life's ultimate determination completely to God.

If the CFQ practice is followed, it can generate true well-being, free from agony, pain and suffering, with a genuine prospect of recovering. For those who do not make it, there is a place in the after-life. There will be few who will not make it. If they cannot, they are not likely to be able to practice either. Therefore, I hope that people put their willingness and strength into the practice.

Indeed reversing the disease process is working against the odds. To overcome the odds, begin with a willingness to succeed and put into action what has been proposed. The mind will find doubts and every excuse not to move the body, "You are too weak. That is too tiring." Such helplessness means wallowing in sorrow and despair.

Hope and healing come with freedom from the gripping force of tension and lethargy enabling one to arrive at a loosening, relaxing, and opening out pattern. The combined effect of hope and healing clear away and drain off the decay of dead cells and which is the basis of cancer. Decay remains if it is confined in its stagnated state. But once drained into capillaries and blood vessels, it is disposed of through normal secretion and excretion. When that happens, the cancer cells are freed from the decay and without their "food" they die off to be replaced by a new generation of healthy cells.

One point to note is the importance of paying no attention to the disease problem or area. This is in total contrast to many treatment methods including most Qigong. By concentrating on the disease, the victim becomes mentally entangled which undermines any prospect for a true cure. By over-emphasizing the disease, the mind and emotions become attracted to it which leads to a drawn-up, coiled-in, fabrication process. This strengthens the disease instead of clearing it out. It also likely gives rise to a vindictive, violent attitude which commonly occurs with most life-threatening events. The victim wants to destroy the perpetrator (in this case the cancer), while the perpetrator is trying to destroy the victim. In the end karma prevails. Both sides get their wishes as both are destroyed. But sorrow remains for your spirit and your loved ones.

CFQ reiterates the importance of a holistic approach. The physical health status of a person is dependent on the overall well-being of the person. By working for the well-being of the whole, the unwellness of any specific problem has no refuge. Given the extreme despair and anxiety caused by cancer, it takes a powerful strategy to avoid concentrating on the disease. The effort to switch attention away from the disease is an important feature in CFQ practice. Thoughts and emotions frequently focus on the disease. Each time you become aware of that happening, go back to the practice. It may seem like a frustrating effort, but with every try, you become more alive.

There is never a shortage of treatment approaches to cancer. What is lacking are methods with a high success rate. In CFQ, I propose a systematic, holistic set of actions to claim the human right to be alive. In a frantic search for treatment, a patient may become so driven as to fabricate further fear, panic and pain. The victim loses track of the fact that trust in peace or purity within is very powerful. For those for whom my experience and approach makes sense, I am very pleased and sincerely believe that their trust is well founded.

A Case Example: *A female patient in her early fifties had multiple tumors in her head. She was diagnosed with brain cancer. Radiation therapy was scheduled for 20 sessions. While waiting to begin, she sought my treatment. When she first came to my Center, she was so weak that her son had to help her walk in. She was severely depressed, disorientated and in pain. Twice weekly healing sessions were scheduled for 20 sessions. After the first two sessions, her appetite improved and she regained strength in her legs. By the fourth session her insomnia ended and she could walk without assistance. She then commenced radiation treatment. She completed it without suffering any uncomfortable side effects (except for losing her hair).*

Her son was surprised to notice that the radiation therapy was directed at a section of her forehead whereas the multiple tumors were throughout her head. He checked with the nurse. She revealed that the cancer was terminal and so widespread that treatment was offered merely to discharge a duty.

The patient continued with CFQ healing sessions. After completing the full course of medical radiation at the cancer center, she returned to see her family physician. He was amazed to see her alive. He told her son that he had expected that she would not survive the treatment.

She continued the healing with me. After completing a total of 30 sessions her body pains, discomfort and the lumps on her head had vanished. Her hair had grown back. I ended direct treatment and I asked her to learn CFQ meditation. I encouraged her to practice for at least three years to be completely safe. She agreed and together with her son received initiation for meditation. They attended regular classes at the Center and her son ensured that she practiced at home daily.

Afterward: For two years things went on smoothly, and she remained healthy. Then one day a neighbor told her that she too suffered from cancer and received "two injections" which promptly cured her. The neighbor teased the patient for having to practice CFQ daily. The patient asked her son and me on several occasions where to obtain the "two injections." She demanded to know why she was forced to meditate. As the days went by, her resentment built up and her practice had a punitive effect on her. She started to feel some pain in her legs and gradually develop weakness spells during which her body became limp for several minutes.

Her son brought her for several healing sessions but these did not appear effective. She was obviously depressed alternating between anxiety and revulsion. Her condition rapidly deteriorated until she was hospitalized. Soon she lost her appetite and became semi-paralyzed. Two weeks later she was in a coma and passed away.

In the last few days, however, she did not suffer the normal pains or discomforts nor did her body emit any odor typical of terminal cancer victims. She died peacefully. Despite the terminal prognosis, she had survived 30 months from the first healing session.

CFQ Cancer Interventions

For The Severely Sick. For the cancer victim who is mentally and physically weakened there are few activities that they can reasonably be expected to perform or take interest in performing. Within the CFQ system, the energy butterfly shaking exercise is recommended. However, the cancer victim may not want such an opportunity even though it is a simple exercise that seemingly anyone is capable of performing for long periods. The patient may prefer to do nothing and find excuses for not doing the CFQ exercises. Counseling may provide the motivation to claim his or her right to recovery. Otherwise, an unwilling client will think of excuses: "The exercise is boring. I'm too tired. I need to rest."

1. Butterfly shaking is best performed with eyes closed in a seated position as recommended in Chapter 8. However, in the begin-

ning the very weak patient may not be able to perform in the optimal loose and slow manner. They either shake rigidly and rapidly or not at all. That is acceptable so long as they continue to move. Ensure that they gradually loosen and slow down which implies that their overall condition is improving.

2. The bed-ridden and mentally "spaced out" patients may not be able to move at all. If they still display a will to survive, someone can help by manually moving their legs. Encourage them to be aware and to attempt doing the exercise on their own. By the time they can do it, their condition will also be improved. For those sunk in deep despair and who display little will to live, efforts to help are most likely in vain.

3. Helpers must also, after each healing effort, cleanse themselves by practicing the CFQ meridian exercises.

4. As the disease energy is released, the legs will feel heavy, numb or painful. Stretch and loosen, then remain completely motionless allowing the disease energy to leave. Resume the shaking after that. There may be periods of restlessness or anxiety due to the excitation of negative mental and emotional energy in the dissolve and release process. Do not follow the mind but remain detached from it. Do something else to distract your attention if the mental attacks are too strong.

5. For those with insomnia, they need not force themselves to sleep. Insomniacs often try to catch up by sleeping during the day time. That is extremely bad as it leads to lethargy, compounds the weakness present, and fabricates a vicious cycle including not being able to sleep at night. Just continue butterfly shaking even if tired. If one cannot sleep at night they should get up to energy shake. More often than not, during the shaking, even healthy people with no sleep problem, drift into deep, sound sleep.

6. Insomnia is only a problem if a person wants to sleep and cannot fall asleep. If the person spends the time butterfly shaking instead of attempting to sleep, she or he finds that sleeplessness ceases to be a problem. In all cases, energy leg shaking is best performed with a whole body looseness and eyes closed. No matter how sleepy the person, continue to shake instead of stopping and waiting for sleep to come.

For The Not-As-Sick. The main CFQ activity, the 7-Movements meridian exercises and the lotus walk should be practiced to enhance all-round improvement and recovery. Those who have time should occupy every minute possible with CFQ, rotating between the meridian movements, the lotus walk, energy shaking, freedom hands and freedom walk. The severely sick should try these techniques to speed recovery as soon as they feel well enough.

The meridian/organ cleansing exercises may take some time to learn. Even moderately weak patients may not be able to stand and practice for even five minutes at the beginning due to the strong downward release of stale energy which makes the legs numb and sensationless. This is evidence of a strong clearing-out and cleansing effect that adds reason to persist in the practice. Rest in between in a loose and motionless manner allowing the stale energy to leave and the numbness to pass. After that, resume the exercises.

Clinically depressed people will find it extremely difficult to remember the movements, in which case a helper must practice together with them until they do remember. In case of resistance (numbness and failure to remember), practice only Movements 1 to 3, complete with the affirmations and conclusion and repeat for a second set. If the patient can repeatedly practice for a half hour, this indicates that his or her condition is greatly improved.

Dealing with Disease Energy

The various CFQ motion activities unload and release disease energy. For cancer patients, experiencing sensations and various unusual phenomena are to be expected. These include numbness, staleness, lethargy, pain, electro-magnetic pulsations, muscle twitches, throbbing, heat and cold. These are often felt as sensations moving away or as a field that spreads beyond the physical boundary of the body. There are also the static sensations that cause much discomfort. Do not be concerned or bothered with them but give them time to dissipate.

The unloading of mental and emotional energies can give rise to anxiety, restlessness, breathlessness, anger, fear, and hatred. Excessive fear is a distinctive feature of cancer associated with common assumptions about the disease. Cancer also evokes violent or vengeful feelings that are readily manifested during the release process. Curtail living in "the head" by being fully occupied with your CFQ practice or other routine physical activities. Do not give yourself time for negative mental and emotional distractions. By regular and willing practice, these distractions become unreal and non-compulsive. For strong distractions, do something else to relax and watch them like an onlooker. Be detached and ignore negative thoughts and emotions without attempting to avoid them. There may be other symptomatic release experiences in the form of excessive or odorous perspiration and excretion. When deep-seated cancer tumor lumps become freed and surface in the release process, the appearance of sudden multiple lumps under the skin can be frightening.

The release of the disease may manifest in many more ways. Whatever happens, remain calm in the face of it so that the debased energy can be cleared off without willful interference. Once you have chosen CFQ, trust your choice with full faith. Otherwise your effort will be wasted and your chance for full recovery sabotaged.

In fact cancer patients who encounter pains, discomforts, depression and other phenomenon typically seek relief and remedies for such symptoms. While such treatments may or may not help, they can give a sense of actively doing something. The idea of doing nothing and feeling helpless is unacceptable. During CFQ work, in the clearing out process, many of these same symptoms are experienced but are much milder. However, the "demonic" character of the disease manifested in thoughts tends to make the cancer patient feel that their symptoms are overwhelmingly serious. They can use medication to calm down as there is no healing accomplished by attending to such thoughts. Be cautioned against over-doing. The proper attitude is a peaceful consciousness. "My situation is already pretty bad. What else can be worse? So whatever needs to happen let it be. Trust God who knows best." Let yourself absorb the gift of life available to you and smile. Smile your way to full recovery.

Final Message: The Miracle Factor

Life threatening diseases like cancer normally awaken despair. Yet, a person in despair is likely to experience miracles. I will examine why and how miracles occur in an attempt to know better how to make them happen.

Every disease problem is the consequence of a combination of physical and psychological factors that give rise to bodily symptoms and discomforts. From the energy viewpoint, the psychological factor is equal in importance to the physical or biological factors. A variation in one factor will gradually influence a variation in the other. Assume a scale of 0—100 distress units and think of these examples: if medication is taken to reduce the pain by say 40 distress units, the psychological pain factor will also be reduced by a similar quantity (40). Similarly, if a patient is having an anxiety attack so that the psychological pain factor rises to 70 units, the physical factor will be affected and gradually catches up to 70 units of distress.

Assume now that a person's normal consciousness state has a 50:50 (physical: psychological) ratio. When the patient learns that she or he is suffering from a life threatening disease, the intense fear and anxiety drives the psychological factor from neutral (50) to 80 and continues to increase rapidly. The physical dimension will also increase rapidly to catch up with the psychological stress level. The bad news is that a diagnosis itself can therefore greatly speed up the body's weakness and drive some people to a state of pessimistic doom. A person in such despair is similar to a person drowning and grasping at anything that can help to stay afloat.

Assume that a male patient's physical/psychological ratio is 65:90. In this situation the sick man may be so weak that he feels almost paralyzed, barely able to stand upright, and his eyes are blurred to the point of being blind. At this point, with no reliable option, if the man learns of something that promises a miracle, his mind wants to become absorbed into this belief with full faith. Putting this faith in action drastically reduces the psychological distress that had been evoked by the cancer diagnosis. The miracle factor reduces the psychological: physical ratio to 45:55. It would be almost the state of normal consciousness prior to the bad news. That means the victim can get up and walk and his vision becomes clear.

To awaken a miracle, the person must often do something requiring much effort and perseverance. For instance, a miracle-seeker may make a pilgrimage traveling a long way, climbing a holy mountain, or getting to a sacred place, or contacting a saint. All these actions will automatically influence the person's psyche without conscious effort, "I've worked for it, so I deserve it." When fulfilled, the achievement materializes as a cure. However, the cure may not last.

Genuine cures require physical, psychological and spiritual transformations grounded in energy changes. Miracles achieved through the reduction of psychological distress, while often instantaneous, may not produce a dramatic change in the physical realm. The physical body needs more time to change and requires a systematic and effective intervention. Without that, the problem condition will soon recur and the miracle factor dissipates. Without clearing the disease-causing energy, a miraculous impact may not result in a lasting cure. That is why, for instance, a cancer patient who has experienced "tumors the size of oranges melting like snowballs on a hot stove" may be disappointed on returning to the hospital for a medical check-up to find that the malignancy is still there.

The patient needs to follow up the initial dramatic improvement with a beneficial treatment that can eliminate the cause of the disease. The miracle factor provides the motivation and momentum for recovery. There are also instances in which a person who experiences the miracle factor changing his or her lifestyle and attitudes, then resumes healthier activities and is able to recover fully without any follow-up intervention.

For the miracle factor to occur, the actions must involve such objects or persons as normally are believed to create miracles. These include holy places or persons such as a basilica or temple, statutes, shrines or saints. The credibility of a physician or an alternative health provider or healer does not give rise to miracles, no matter how impressive the immediate response. They are merely human.

Miracles are more likely to happen to good, salt of the earth people. Sophisticated people are normally too cautious and less trusting in anything or anyone to enable a miracle. They are also more loyal to the prevailing knowledge and attitudes of the well educated. They are less likely to expand their beliefs to include anything occurring outside the scientific rules and prevailing, so called, facts of life. Holding rigidly to their acquired belief system, they will aggressively defend their way of looking at things. Such a patient may imagine that God's willingness to help is irrelevant or that she or he knows better than to believe in God. Of course, God will then not contradict the purpose of creation by overriding the opportunities a person has been given to take responsibility by choosing his or her own way. The miracle factor is not available for purposes in conflict with life or unconditional love.

I write this book with a sincere wish that it will bring about extensive miracle-making and lasting cures. I pray that you will help me to materialize my wish. To do so, you must willingly leave behind your notions about disease and read the book with an open mind. Hard nosed scientific studies based on and restricted to the reality of the physical body often conclude that metastatic or terminal cancers are incurable and at best merely manageable medically.

From my extensive clinical experience treating and healing this major killer disease I have a different view: Expand beyond physical and biological limits into the mind and spiritual domains with an energy-consciousness-spirit perspective and no disease is really untreatable. Complete cure and lasting recovery is probable. A mind that denies such a possibility obstructs its own reality.

CFQ healing energy is radiant and is not confined to space and time. The reader with an open mind can sense this energy awakening as is displayed in each chapter. The principles I offer open a new approach to therapy and knowledge that can lift the restrictions on conventional conclusions about which disease problems are curable. Your willingness to practice the methods and therapies I suggest will ensure that miracles become normal physical realities. For those who do not experience instant cures, the gradual disappearance of disease problems constitutes another possible outcome—a gradual do-it-yourself miracle.

18

Path of Healing & Recovery

A fundamental pattern in all creation is impermanence. As a consequence of the natural process of being alive, pain arises. How much suffering they cause is controlled not only by their nature but most importantly by how the individual responds to them. Thus a person crying out in pain, though appearing to have great suffering may not really feel that their suffering is so bad. The moment the pain is felt the screaming out for this person reduces it to a minimum. If prevented from expressing pain vocally the person might experience their pain as excruciating while onlookers might think the person is better. Another person seemingly struggling in a semi-conscious state may not be in pain at all but rather be absorbed and trapped in a dream experience.

In a profound sense, the degree of suffering is greatly determined by how a person takes and accepts the illness. Pains and discomforts can be greatly compounded by the fear and uncertainty they bring and the struggle that results from a refusal to accept them. The common practice of using pain-killers to suppress a physical pain can shift the pain to internal emotional and spiritual levels. This is often reflected as anxiety, restlessness, depression or manifested as referred pain. More often than not, a person in pain will continue strenuously to search for relief or a cure. With the pain suppressed the victim may have trouble knowing exactly what the problem is. The experience becomes one of feeling disturbed and restless. A great deal depends on how you want to deal with illness. Whatever approach you take, however, you cannot overrule the law of impermanence. The process of clearing out deep seated and excruciating pain often involves spreading it out to a wider and shallower area thus reducing its intensity. If the cultivator does not understand the principles of such a clearing approach, confusion is possible.

The first step toward a cure is to face things as they are. Since one is living with the problems as they are, a realistic starting point from which to work toward a cure is to accept them as they are. Accept your ability to respond and deal properly with them. Blame only misdirects and wastes your energy. To blame yourself or think yourself guilty in some way greatly increases your problem.

Need for a Reliable System

Accepting your self together with all your problems and faults and wanting to become as responsible as possible, however, is not good enough. You need, as we all do, to have a proper system to deal with problems. You need to do something to concretize your acceptance of life and desire to respond well to it. You need to switch your attention so that you continue neither to struggle nor fight with your problems, actions which only create more pain and conflict. You need to harmonize physically, mentally and spiritually so that your problems will find no home in you. Without such a system you waste your energy. To heal you need an outlet, a way to let go of all sources of trouble. CFQ is designed to be such a liberating system. By practicing CFQ you shift your attention away from your problems and activate what is necessary to flush them out of your system. You need a process of your own. You need a shelter from turbulence and troubles. You need a trustworthy friend whom you can count on to help solve every problem you might face. CFQ can fulfill such needs. It asks *no-thing* of you, only the focus of your spirit. Put your heart into it and the best of life can become yours.

Spending Time to Let Go. How do you put your heart into something? Simply spend time with it. How one spends the time is a matter of choice. Most people have time enough beyond working, eating and sleeping. There is time to rest, to relax, to recreate and practice hobbies. If you have time to read this book, you surely have time to enjoy CFQ. Resting as the world advocates often results in anxiety, tension or life in a fantasy of dreams. Spending time in "recreation" may even create problems. Try CFQ. Make it your hobby, your source of relaxation and restoration. Many find that an hour given to CFQ that used to disappear in sleep makes them feel more rested than ever before.

Spending a hour daily on CFQ will reasonably enable you to deal with most of your problems. Some people may need up to two hours, depending on the types of problems, how life-threatening they are, or how much time is available. If you have a lot of time it is better to put some of it into CFQ rather than run the risk of using it to create more problems.

In a true sense, when you practice CFQ, you are doing practically nothing. Normally, when you are not actively doing anything, your mind will be busily doing everything! It is an automatic process of thinking, but it forms into an energy cloud that can make you dreamy. People normally enjoy that and call it relaxing. But that it is not. When you practice CFQ you do not participate in thinking. If thinking happens, let it be. CFQ provides a time for peace, a time to let-go of any disharmony. Whether problems exist or not, considering them is irrelevant. Your acceptance and responsibility shift you to another attitude; "My business transcends the physical world."

Letting-go means to eliminate the burden from deep within. It is the freeing of the spiritual aspect of a person. But the spiritual aspect is intimately united with the physical aspect. Any spiritual burden one might have is deposited on the physical body causing deformations and stiffness. The physiological body, through the nervous system, is equipped with the ability to feel. This ability is mainly located below the skin and in the muscles. Therefore shallow deformations in the muscles result in discomfort that is interpreted by the senses as pain, numbness, stiffness, heat, cold and on. Deeper deformations do not normally give rise to clear sensations of discomfort. One can experience them as a sense that something has gone wrong but there is no clarity as to what it is. These experiences can be felt as restlessness, fatigue, depression or emotional and spiritual discomfort. These sensations block and prevent proper physiological functioning and are real life-threats. Even in the case of a fatal heart attack, the excruciating pains and cramps are merely superficial manifestations (the tip of the ice-berg) of an immense and deep force that grips and squeezes life out of a person. This force is beyond our abilities to measure. What remains of a person's life is inversely proportional to the burden of debased energy a person is carrying.

Emerging a Victor

> *If someone were to scold me, I reply, "Good! Good! Good!"*
> *If someone hits and beats me I allow myself to fall and lie down*
> *If spat on, I allow it to dry without mopping*
> *In that way I save my strength and he saves his trouble.*
>
> —*Song of a Cultivator of Tao*

Becoming well is the natural outcome of CFQ action. Thinking without action is not only futile but is a source of further problems and suffering. Actions speak louder than words and the effects of action thunder. In time you actually participate in your own transformation. Not only do problems disappear but nothing can provoke a problem for you. You begin to recognize that no matter what the world does to you, no one nor anything can take away your heart's purity and peace. You begin to realize that though you can give away your purity and peace you never have to do so nor is there ever a good reason for doing so.

Jesus Christ was getting at this same achievement when he said "If anyone strikes you on the right cheek, turn to him the other also; and if any one would take your coat, let him have your cloak as well," (Matthew 5: 39,40). This also is the true wisdom or treasure within the

Tao. If any worldly person understood how to do this she or he would have fulfilled the Tao and would soon be liberated.

A true cultivator's song is so carefree, boundless and sung with a heart so unmoved that worldly values cease to be. He or she is truly an enlightened being who chooses to remain and play on in the "hostile world of filth and red dust." I cannot yet do so, nor do I expect you to be able to do so. If someone were to scold me, I would be hurt. If someone punched me, I would kick back. But there is also someone inside who continues to smile no matter what happens.

CFQ Reactions

Throughout this book we characterize diseases as loads and burdens which have unfortunately been created in one's life, perhaps even in lives prior to the present one. They are now part of our experience. Compare this situation to a major home renovation. Digging and repairing will certainly cause a lot of clutter, inconvenience, and disturbance. You might have to sleep among the construction debris. If you are reluctant to bear with that, it might be wise to avoid renovating. If things in your home are damaged, simply patch and paint. This tactic, of course, incurs the risk that one day your home might manifest much worse damage. Compare your body with your home. Sometimes I observe people being much kinder to their homes than to their bodies. They investigate and repair damages and leaks, check for ants and termites, look for cracks in the roof or basement. They vacuum and sweep the rubbish out daily and regularly make sure that even the hidden corners are cleaned. As for their bodies, they daily stuff them with rubbish. If there are problems, they take medication or try to cover their difficulties in some way. If something goes painfully wrong, one of the first ideas is to cut and discard. Little does it occur to people that if their bodies were their homes the act of digging and discarding a vital part might cause complete collapse.

The choice is yours. To continue with the usual keep-everything-inside and cover-up way or let-go and start clearing-the-rubbish way.

Once you start clearing, I know from experience, you will discover more rubbish than you ever thought possible. Such a personal clearing requires enough bravery to face the complete truth. The exercises are carefully designed so that the problems revealed by them are reduced to the minimum. This is equivalent to having a group of skilful and responsible workmen hired for your renovation job. It is thus easier to practice the exercises than to meditate. You will still see rubbish and suffer some discomfort and inconvenience with the exercises, but you need not be faced with the whole mess.

The healing process involves a thorough tuning, stretching, elongating and realigning of the physical body's every structure and organ. Also, every burden and disharmony within the spiritual body is converted and cleared within the physical clearing. Such events are felt. This is the way to total healing, otherwise you get relief but not recovery. So with CFQ exercising, the pain and discomfort flow out. Not only the existing pain but also those past pains that might have seemed cured, but in fact were hidden and trapped at a deeper level. Furthermore, spiritual and emotional pains that, until now, have never been felt as pain or discomfort might surface.

The unfolding of hardened muscles causes pain and discomfort. The release and elongation of shortened tendons cause pain and discomfort. The same is true when realigning misplaced bone joints. Correcting the position of the organs causes pain and discomfort. So does the surrender of mindfulness when making way for the body's wisdom. The melting off, diluting, and dispersal of debased energy-glue which is energy rubbish causes pain and discomfort. How could it be otherwise? Those things have been stored and compounded over 30, 50 or perhaps 70 years of living and have roots traceable into the very distant past. During the clearing process you might recall some past experiences up to now hidden. For example, you might remember the time when your doctor advised you to have bed rest to quicken your recovery and now that appears as counter productive. The furious display of your physical prowess or mental abilities in the past now shows up as tiredness and lethargy. The sore that seems to have been healed now bursts out with a discharge. The frequent past bouts of flu become a runny nose lasting for several weeks. The revelations go on.

Reactions during the CFQ healing process can be quite varied. They involve physical sensations, thoughts, struggles and emotional outbursts. But since CFQ is a releasing process, in actual fact it limits pain to outgoing symptoms and does not pose any danger. If, however, a person is not doing the practice voluntarily or actively denigrates the practice, s/he might well experience fear, anger or panic. Such a reaction can cause much harm. With proper understanding and a willingness to face revelations about one's past, the experience becomes quite mild, even interesting. Moderate or severe pain and discomfort rarely occur, and given time (say a few days) fades away.

You must allow time for the clearing and reversal process to happen. As with eating and sleeping, you should make it a point to unload at least the burdens of the day. The CFQ experience is relaxing and enjoyable if you take it with the right attitude. Do it unconditionally. You need not worry about the clearing or reversal of symptoms. Such events come gradually, unfolding one after another. The unstable periods with strong reactions normally occur within the first three months. One hundred days is the usual foundation period. After this period, your overall well-being greatly improves. Some recurring problems, as for example, migraine headaches, body pains, insomnia, and indigestion may seem to clear off within the first week. They may occasionally recur with less frequency within the first year. They may persist with less intensity and far shorter durations over the next few years until you finally forget about them. All problems take time to clear off and become undone layer by layer.

With consistent practice over one to two years (for some even six months) most symptoms tend to disappear. Some perhaps may be reduced drastically and become more tolerable. Medical diagnosis often verifies this. For example, your physician may advise you to reduce or do away completely with medications for diabetes or high blood pressure. Many people may stop further practice feeling that there is no longer any need to take care of their health. This is a great waste. I advise caution: It is better to go on and completely clear oneself, eliminating any karma that might re-instigate problems. People, of course, have the freedom to stop. But should they develop problems again they may not be so lucky as to experience the ease of curing experienced this time. Karma strives to stay in charge and prevents a person, if possible, from doing the right things to totally eliminate problems. The change in the course of life that comes with the removal of disease is a great blessing. It is an opportunity that rarely occurs over again, no matter how lucky a person is.

A Case Example: *The female patient, a CFQ practitioner aged 41, was riding a motor-bike when she was rammed from behind with extreme force. She landed hard and felt great pain on her lower hip. By the time she was taken to the hospital she was no longer able to move her legs. She was also losing sensations in her legs that became tight, numb, and cold. That night, she phoned me as her back pain became unbearable.*

I remained at my Center and performed a remote healing on her. Half an hour later, her husband phoned from the hospital to say that her legs felt loosened and the pain on her lower back had diminished. The next day, her entire body felt stiff and rigid and she could barely move her legs. X-rays found a fracture on the sacrum. Her doctor immediately recommended that she should be confined to a complete immobile position with her body in a cast. They phoned me up in a panic. I did another remote healing. I also asked her husband to help by using CFQ to sweep down to loosen her legs. She should herself use the CFQ mantra as often as possible (both have been practicing for four years).

The following morning the doctor on his rounds checked in on the patient who surprisedly could raise her hip by pushing her legs on the bed. Visibly puzzled, he told her she need not be moved for traction or restrained. She should simply carry on doing whatever she had done to help herself. Her progress continued steadily and by the fifth day she could sit up. After a week's stay she was discharged. She drove directly to my Center and walked in on her own accord. Subsequently I gave her five treatments. It took four weeks by which time she had recovered completely from her injury.

Comment. An interesting caveat was that despite her previous consistent CFQ meditation practice, she was unable to recite the mantra when she was in intense pain from the injury. She repeatedly could not remember the three simple words that she had been reciting several hundred thousand times. The energy forces that caused the injuries also prevented her recovery. Her training was insufficient to overcome the karmic obstruction. The serious injury could have paralyzed her from the hip down had it not been for my timely healing.

Freedom from Pain. In time you will notice that your body and mind become loose, relaxed, and comfortable. You will feel calmness, peace, and joyousness more and more consistently. Few things will be able to cause agitation. The time that becomes least comfortable might well be during your practice when you move in to deal with your imperfections. After that you will have every reason to enjoy the fruits of having done the right thing for your body and spirit.

You will do well to continue with CFQ practice throughout life. This will insure that you be able to depart this world with a broad grin. Further, in old age, when you are no longer needed at your work place, you can have a real friend, a true companion in CFQ. You will not feel betrayed, lonely, or discarded by society, your friends or children no matter how they treated you. You will be pleased with yourself and able to keep the faith that God is also pleased with you. You will be free to enjoy entering the wonderful place God has prepared for you.

The following guidelines are derived from years of experience in energy medicine:

1. Fighting the disease aggravates fear and speeds up deterioration. There should be no fighting, just letting-go. It is enough to do

what is necessary to claim your right to be alive. Face the reality and just let-go. Neither courage nor cowardice makes a significant difference.

2. Wanting to be strong brings exhaustion that weakens you further. Wanting only to let-go and let God take care of you helps eliminate the problems that come from self-centered wanting.

3. Holding back and holding on facilitates the inward-absorption and energy surging process that brings death. Loosen and let-go so that destructive forces will be unable to influence you.

4. More unbalanced treatment and more doing bring more damage. Select a clear direction for a better chance. Too much rest brings conflict and unrest. Be meaningfully busy and active and give yourself, at the most, five to seven hours of sleep a day. Thinking positive thoughts makes you discover that you have plenty of negative thoughts left. Don't think, just do the unconditionally loving thing for yourself.

5. You actually need no humanly fabricated things. If you want to live on and be much better off, go into action to claim your birthright. Very importantly, you need to trust God. It is all right if you did not trust God in the past. You are long since forgiven. Trust God now. This is a crucial time. Let cosmic wisdom decide for you. Do not tell God what to do. That only messes up the job. The source of boundless love cares for you and gives you peace that will replenish your life.

Epilogue

o o o o o o o o o o o o o o o o o o o o o o o o o o o o

Perfect Peace equals
Truth-Purity-Good-Beauty
Perfect Boundlessness equals
Compassion-Relaxation-Joy equals
Complete freedom and harmony equals
Emptiness of all that conflicts with your Perfection.
Equals the Ultimate Destiny

Ushering in CFQ

The need for treatment of diseases is obvious. Large numbers of people with health problems are busily seeking remedies. There maybe an equally large group suffering pain passively. These people are resigned to the idea that nothing can help them. They have not benefited either from mainstream medicine or the methods of alternative medicine tried, or ready-to-use remedies and food supplements. For their sakes it is very important to discern what went wrong.

The reality is that healing originates from a person's own system. Any external help, remedies, or medication can at best only enhance a person's bodily functions enabling them to overcome problems from within. When a person develops an attitude of dependency on other people or some remedy, that person limits the power of their body's natural wisdom. While all problems are real and need genuine attention, many are intensified by the mind's fabrications. Looking for people to fix a problem seems natural. It is apparently justified in the sufferer's hard work making money to spend on their cure. They often can not forgive themselves for failing to get even the most expensive

397

treatment. However, treatment itself sometimes gives rise to side-effects that can become life threatening.

For a person's bodily system to function well and thus clear problems or prevent problems the body must relax and settle down. This initiates the stilling of the heart, which reduces emotional conflicts and disturbances, slows down mental anxiety, and loosens the body. All this activates the self-repair response. This is the self reliant procedure needed. We simply cannot depend solely upon experts to bring about desired changes. People must spend time each day to make the right things happen. Without that their efforts are not good enough.

The development of medical science and health care services approaches can be seen as natural efforts arising from our need to deal with the problems of life. They are part of the *"methods-of-the-world,"* health-seeking creations inspired by the "fix it" mentality. Disease remedies range from conventional, recognized medical approaches to alternative medical approaches to less reputable approaches. Whatever your choice, if it solves your problem and if you are not worried about any future problems, there may be no need to introduce any new possibilities into your life. If, however, you are interested in *out-of-the-world* methods, CFQ training promises a true cure for a variety of diseases including the eradication of the suffering brought by pain and discomfort. Nature has given you a body that is energetically functional, ordered to keeping you alive without any problems for your entire lifespan. It is hardly in your best interests to tamper with this order by being negative. A simple willingness to accept your problems will reduce your pain and suffering by undermining the anxiety and anger that often arise from negative thoughts and attitudes. Let go, let your body relax, let your muscles loosen. Disease symptoms will dissipate and healing can begin its course.

What about CFQ training? Sincerity, justice and honesty are required. If anyone is not willing to examine the effects of their practice honestly they waste their time trying the process. Benefits will only be temporary as they convince themselves that the practice is not effective. The "undoing" feature of CFQ is the direct opposite of normal "doing." Undoing can lack excitement and may even seem boring for beginners. Such boredom, if observed without judgment and allowed to persist over a period of time, reveals the deeper experiences of peace and joy. Excitement arouses the body's systems making a person feel happy and satisfied but it also fabricates a craving and leaves behind a residue which eventually leads to ill-health (a high price to pay).The person becomes compelled by the craving to constantly look for excitement. The absence of further excitement makes the person feel lost and depressed. Peace and joy arise from stillness or not-doing. They are profound, lasting and healing.

During practice, the letting-go of negative traits and tendencies from deep within arouses the mind. Attempts to fight the thoughts will make them stronger and entangle you deeper. The right way, the way that is in your best interest, is to detach yourself from the thoughts and allow them to say whatever they like. In this way, destructive thoughts cannot pick a fight with you. You loosen their power and grip on you, dissolving and clearing them out. Proceed with your practice unconditionally. It is not worth giving anything distracting power, not even your diseases, health problems, or whether you get well or not. Getting well is natural. Don't think of it as impossible. Detach, let go. Just do your practice, everyday, the same as you eat, work, bathe, sleep, read papers, or watch TV.

With an appreciation of letting-go and freedom from any intention to fabricate or retain sensations, CFQ practice eventually leads to a state of the "*sensation of no sensations.*" During such practice, you feel freedom, boundlessness, looseness, weightlessness, peace, joyousness and a smooth energy flow over and above the still yet-to-be loosened stiffness of the body. The pleasant sensations continue throughout the rest of the day. Normal physical activities become effortless. The mind becomes clear, quiet and alert, and thinking becomes sharp. The spirit becomes peaceful and centered so that hardly any incident can provoke an emotional disturbance. In this way the body's systems are brought to optimum functioning. Where is pain and suffering then? The question is irrelevant as diseases do not arise in this state. Transformation and transcendence are set on course. One's final destiny approaches.

References

❖

Books on CFQ

Hiew, C. C. (2001). *A Guidebook on Meridian Healing: Resilience and the Energy-Consciousness Connection.* CFQ Healing Workshop. New Brunswick: Author.

Hiew, C. C. (2000). *The Tao of Healing: The Incredible Golden Light.* Lincoln, NE: Writer's Showcase , an imprint of iUniverse.com. Inc

Hiew, C. C. (1999). *Energy Meditation: Healing the Body, Freeing the Spirit. In Conversation with Master Yap Soon-Yeong.* Lincoln, NE: toExcel an imprint of iUnivers.com. Inc

0-595-21939-X